RAFFAELE MATTIOLI LECTURES

In honour of the memory of Raffaele Mattioli, who was for many years its manager and chairman, Banca Commerciale Italiana has established the Mattioli Fund as a testimony to the continuing survival and influence of his deep interest in economics, the humanities and sciences.

As its first enterprise the Fund has established a series of annual lectures on the history of economic thought, to be called the Raffaele Mattioli Lectures.

In view of the long association between the Bocconi University and Raffaele Mattioli, who was an active scholar, adviser and member of the governing body of the University, it was decided that the lectures in honour of his memory should be delivered at the University, which together with Banca Commerciale Italiana, has undertaken the task of organising them.

Distinguished academics of all nationalities, researchers and others concerned with economic problems will be invited to take part in this enterprise, in the hope of linking pure historical research with a debate on economic theory and practical policy.

In creating a memorial to the cultural legacy left by Raffaele Mattioli, it is hoped above all that these lectures and the debates to which they give rise will prove a fruitful inspiration and starting point for the development of a tradition of research and academic studies like that already long established in other countries, and that this tradition will flourish thanks to the new partnership between the Bocconi University and Banca Commerciale Italiana.

THE MAKING OF KEYNES'
GENERAL THEORY

RAFFAELE MATTIOLI FOUNDATION

Richard F. Kahn

THE MAKING OF KEYNES'
GENERAL THEORY

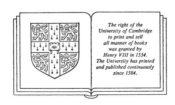

The right of the
University of Cambridge
to print and sell
all manner of books
was granted by
Henry VIII in 1534.
The University has printed
and published continuously
since 1584.

CAMBRIDGE UNIVERSITY PRESS

CAMBRIDGE
LONDON NEW YORK NEW ROCHELLE
MELBOURNE SYDNEY

Published by the Press Syndicate of the University of Cambridge
The Pitt Building, Trumpington Street, Cambridge CB2 1RP
32 East 57th Street, New York, NY 10022, USA
296 Beaconsfield Parade, Middle Park, Melbourne 3206, Australia

Edited by Angelo Porta

First published 1984

Printed in Italy

Library of Congress Catalogue Card Number: 82–19761

British Library Cataloguing in Publication Data
Kahn, Richard
The Making of Keynes' General Theory
(Raffaele Mattioli Lectures)
1. Keynes, John Maynard. General Theory
of Employment, Interest and Money
1. Title   11. Series
330.15'6   HB99.7
ISBN 0 521 25373 X

CONTENTS

Foreword   IX

Editorial Foreword   XV

Preface   XVII

Chronology   XXIII

FIRST LECTURE

Some comments on the earlier economists up to early Keynes   3
1. Say's Law: Adam Smith to John Stuart Mill, pp. 1-10.
2. Say's Law: Alfred Marshall, pp. 11-14.   3. Dennis H. Robertson
in his *A Study of Industrial Fluctuation*, pp. 15-20.   4. Dennis
H. Robertson in his *Money*, pp. 21-2.   5. The impact of the
young Piero Sraffa on the Cambridge of the Twenties, pp. 23-6.

SECOND LECTURE

The Quantity Theory of Money   27
1. Introduction, pp. 27-9.   2. The basic logic, pp. 30-6.
3. Quantity Theory: Locke and Hume, pp. 37-8.   4. Quantity
Theory: John Stuart Mill, pp. 39-40.   5. Quantity Theory:
Alfred Marshall, pp. 41-3.   6. Quantity Theory: Cambridge
versus Yale. Arthur C. Pigou and Irving Fisher, pp. 44-6.
7. Quantity Theory: Dennis H. Robertson in his *Money*,
pp. 47-9.   8. Quantity Theory: Keynes in his *Tract*, pp. 50-5.
9. Quantity Theory: Keynes in his *Treatise*, pp. 56-7.
10. Quantity Theory: Keynes in his *General Theory*, pp. 58-9.

THIRD LECTURE

The *Treatise* and economic policy issues, 1928-1931   61
1. Keynes' *Treatise on Money*, pp. 61-76.   2. Economic
policy issues, 1928-1931, pp. 77-90.

FOURTH LECTURE

From the 'multiplier' to the *General Theory*   91
1. The 'multiplier', pp. 91-104.   2. The Cambridge 'Circus',
pp. 105-111.   3. From the *Treatise* to the *General Theory*, pp. 112-18.

FIFTH LECTURE

The General Theory of Employment, Interest and Money   119

1. Introduction, p. 119.   2. The word 'general', pp. 120-1.
3. The character of the achievement, pp. 122-5.   4. The money-wage, pp. 126-33.   5. The propensity to consume, pp. 134-6.
6. Liquidity preference, pp. 137-41.   7. The inducement to invest: foreword, pp. 142-4.   8. The inducement to invest: Keynes' basic chapter, pp. 145-9.   9. Keynes' chapter on investment in real life, pp. 150-7.   10. Limitations of the *General Theory*, pp. 158-61.
11. The post *General Theory* Keynes on 'finance', pp. 162-8.

SIXTH LECTURE

Personal relations with Keynes   169

1. Introduction, p. 169.   2. My own first contact, pp. 170-2.
3. Keynes' impression on the Fellows of his College, p. 173.
4. Working with Keynes, pp. 174-6.   5. My part in the *General Theory*, pp. 177-8.   6. Keynes' relations with Lionel Robbins, pp. 179-84.   7. Keynes' relations with Dennis H. Robertson, pp. 185-8.   8. Keynes' relations with Arthur C. Pigou, pp. 189-99.

DISCUSSION   201

Joan Robinson, pp. 203-5;   Giacomo Becattini, pp. 205-10;
Giangiacomo Nardozzi, pp. 210-12;   Franco Bruni, pp. 212-16;
Paolo Savona, pp. 216-18;   Fabio Ranchetti, pp. 218-21;
Pietro Manes, pp. 221-2;   Luigi Pasinetti, pp. 222-5;
Ferdinando Targetti, pp. 225-7;   Alberto Di Pierro, pp. 227-8;
Angelo Marcello Cardani, pp. 228-9; Piercarlo Grandi, pp. 229-30; Orlando D'Alauro, pp. 230-2.

Comments by Richard Kahn   233

Biography of Richard Kahn   259

The Collected Writings of John Maynard Keynes   269

Bibliography   277

Index   295

FOREWORD

The problems that confronted the economic systems during the Seventies' and the difficulties encountered by so-called Keynesian policies have not dimmed interest in the figure of Keynes. On the contrary, they have helped to keep the work of the great economist firmly at the centre of the economic discussion.

The analytical frame of reference of Keynesian policies lay in the macroeconomic model that emerged from the traditional interpretation of Keynes' thought. But when the first symptoms of crisis appeared, Keynes' ideas were not ousted by those of other economists. What happened was a process of reinterpretation of his theories, which became the focus of renewed and closer meditation.

This process brought out once again the depth and range of Keynes' theoretical contribution, many aspects of which, overlooked in the overschematisation of the IS-LM model, were pursued with great interest.

One example is the theme of uncertainty, which played such an important part in the formation of the *General Theory* and on the consideration of which Keynes had explicity based the line of demarcation between his theory and that of the classical economists.

Another is the theme of effective demand which, despite the fact that it was the pillar on which the Keynesian theory rested, had been relegated to a secondary role in the more fashionable macroeconomic models.

In the past few years the debate on the reinterpretation of Keynes' ideas, which reached its height in the Seventies, seems to have been less intensive.

But one has to admit that Keynes is still at the centre of the most important theoretical developments which in recent years have devoted increasing attention to the analysis of expectations, a point which is at the heart of Keynes' theoretical approach.

And so the celebration this year of the centenary of his birth has not just been a passing rediscovery of Keynes but rather the occasion for a deeply felt tribute to an economist whose ideas are as fresh and original as ever.

In inviting Lord Kahn to give the second course of lectures in memory of Raffaele Mattioli the Scientific Committee of the Mattioli Lectures wanted his testimony to take us through an extremely interesting chapter in the history of economic thought and to reconsider the roots of Keynes' theory, too often forgotten in the cut-and-thrust of the debate that has raged during these years on macroeconomic theory and policy.

Lord Richard Kahn needs no introduction and it would be out of place as well as presumptuous to outline his claims to our attention. We were all more or less brought up on his celebrated article of 1931, 'The Relation of Home Investment to Unemployment'[1] and his important contributions to various fields of economic theory are well known.

However, it gives me great pleasure to endorse a sentiment and a memory of Lord Kahn's common to all the sponsors of the Raffaele Mattioli Lectures: the long-standing and deeply-felt links with Piero Sraffa and, through him, with the Bocconi University, Cambridge and Milan.

I do wish to express my warmest thanks to Lord Kahn for accepting the invitation to give these Lectures and for devoting so much time and energy to preparing them both in the spoken version and in the final form in which they appear in this volume.

The original title of the course of lectures was 'The Development of Theories of Employment and Prices'.[1] In rewriting them for this volume Lord Kahn has chosen to concentrate on the evolution of Keynes' thought up to the publication of the *General Theory* and not to go into its subsequent developments, on which

1. *Economic Journal*, June 1931, pp. 173-98; reprinted in RICHARD KAHN, *Selected Essays on Employment and Growth*. Cambridge: Cambridge University Press, 1972, pp. 1-27 (Italian version edited by Gabriele Pastrello with the advice of Michele Salvati: RICHARD KAHN, *L'occupazione e la crescita*. Torino: Giulio Einaudi Editore, 1976, pp. 3-28).

he had made many most interesting comments in the course of his oral exposition.

A happy choice, in my view, not only because it enabled him to throw more light on the roots of Keynes' thinking and its links with the Cambridge tradition but also, and more importantly, because it takes the reader back to the climate of the Thirties in which Keynes' ideas took shape. We all, and I think especially the younger among us, need to be reminded of that Thirties' atmosphere, of the sense of anguish and despair at a situation with which economic policy was utterly unable to cope as solutions could be found only in a courageous quest for new theoretical approaches.

In that crucial moment what was written in Cambridge was without doubt a seminal page and Lord Kahn has performed a valuable service in conjuring up the Cambridge atmosphere of those days by calling to mind not only its great men but also that indefinable tissue of circumstances that goes to make a great centre of culture.

Since the quarter century 1948-1973, when the world experienced economic growth at hitherto unheard-of rates, many past problems have resurfaced: the extinction or blunting of the forces of economic growth, the triggering of inflationary spirals, the grievous problems of unemployment, the reappearance on the international scene of severe signs of financial instability, especially in exchange rates and debt structures.

The context is undoubtedly different from what it was then. One need only consider the fact that present international debt problems are largely attributable to extensive borrowing by developing countries on international markets in a general context of international trade flows that have a momentum unthinkable in the Thierties. However, despite the differences in general pattern, there is no lack of likenesses: the recent resurgence of protectionist tendencies should be enough to warn us that the shades of the past are still with us.

The dip into the climate of the Thirties and the re-evocation of the courageous response that theory brought to bear on the

---

1. See also Lord Kahn's Preface in this volume, p. XVII.

problems of those tormented years are fraught with meaning for us today.

Theory, as the great masters have taught us, must continually be refashioned by historical research. Lord Kahn's Lectures are a wonderful example of how the history of ideas can be made to yield the roots of theory by tracing the connections between the course of events and the appearance of ideas and simultaneously by applying theories to events in order to explain them.

The content and pervading spirit of this volume are certainly worthy of the man in whose memory these Lectures have been instituted. Raffaele Mattioli, as a banker – and he was a banker in the true sense of the term at a time when banking was not fettered by all the constraints that hamper it in our country today – was always alert to the problems of his time but he combined the gifts of a great entrepreneur with an awareness of culture and above all of history.

This volume will be followed shortly by two others that are in press: one by Professor Franco Modigliani on 'The Evolution of Monetary Theory and the Debates on Stabilisation Policies' and the other by Professor Charles P. Kindleberger, who deals with 'Economic Laws and Economic History'. The series is intended to include the following volumes currently in preparation: the lectures of Professor Peter Mathias on 'The Industrial Revolution in England' and those of Professor Erik F. Lundberg on 'The Development of Swedish and Keynesian Macroeconomic Theory and its Impact on Economic Policy'.

The range of interests spanned by the Lectures listed above reminds me of Raffaele Mattioli's library. A stupendous library whose riches included books on the history of economic thought – many of which are first editions, a real joy for a bibliophile –, works on the latest economic theories, works of literature, and where the leaven of history was ever present. In a sense, while saying little about him, because of the discretion and reserve with which we surround our inmost feelings, with these Lectures we enter the library of the man whose memory we cherish. And this is the finest way of getting to know him.

I would end by expressing the profound gratitude of the Bocconi University to Banca Commerciale Italiana, the sponsor of these Lectures, and to all members of the Scientific Committee for their valued contributions to the organization of this venture.

It is a venture in which numerous leading men of learning have taken part, witness the wide-ranging discussion reported in this volume. We are committed to continuing on the course on which we have embarked and shall gradually add further note-worthy volumes to this series.

INNOCENZO GASPARINI
Rettore
Università Luigi Bocconi

EDITORIAL FOREWORD

In this volume we have supplied footnotes as and when needed, to help the reader follow through the various topics dealt with in these Lectures.

The organisation of some parts of the book call, however, for a few general explanations, which we give hereunder:

CHRONOLOGY. This is the briefest factual record of some salient events, circumstances, authors and studies connected with the formation of Keynes' ideas that recur in the course of the Lectures.

LECTURES. As Lord Kahn recalls in his Preface, the final text of the Lectures that appears here differs in several respects from the spoken version. Most importantly, allusions to the developments of Keynes' ideas after the publication of the *General Theory* and to current problems of economic policy, which had stimulated many contributions to the discussion after the Lectures, have been dropped.

BIBLIOGRAPHIC REFERENCES. The volume contains numerous references, which for works of authors other than Keynes often mention several editions of the same book. It has therefore been decided to include in the footnotes as well as in the general bibliography (pp. 277-94) the full bibliographic information on the works quoted, using abbreviations only in the body of each Lecture. In the references, unless otherwise stated, we have quoted the first edition.

DISCUSSION. The text of the discussion that appears in this volume does not include the contributions referring solely to topics subsequently dropped from the final version of the Lectures. In the published contributions there remain a few references, which we saw no reason to cut, to the parts that have been dropped or to comments Lord Kahn made in the course of his Lectures that do not appear in this final version.

COLLECTED WRITINGS OF JOHN MAYNARD KEYNES. For the works of Keynes, references are given in abbreviated form with the indication KEYNES, followed by the number of the volume of the *Collected Writings of John Maynard Keynes*, published for the Royal Economic Society. The complete list, updated to the publication date of this book, is given on pp. 269-75.

BIBLIOGRAPHY. Includes all the works quoted in the volume. In addition, it gives the specific studies of John Maynard Keynes referred to and indicates the edition and the corresponding volume of the *Collected Writings*.

ANGELO PORTA

PREFACE

The six *Raffaele Mattioli Lectures* which I delivered in June 1978 at the Luigi Bocconi University are presented in this book in a completely rewritten form. I am most grateful for being allowed to make this transformation. Even the title has been changed from *The Development of Theories of Employment and Prices* to *The Making of Keynes' General Theory*.

In accordance with the wishes of the Trustees of the Raffaele Mattioli Foundation, the book is an exercise in the development of thought, culminating in the completion of Keynes' *General Theory*.

By stopping at that point I have been able, within reasonable compass, to deal more intensively than I did in my Lectures with the process of development.

In my Lectures I devoted a considerable amount of time to controversies provoked by the publication of the *General Theory* – right up to 1978 – and to the behaviour of an economy under conditions which Keynes, in the *General Theory*, had not envisaged, although when the occasion arose, he readily applied his fundamental concepts to the problems of an economy operating under the stress of the War. I also in my Lectures devoted some attention to the tragic mismanagement of the world's economies at the present time, partly attributable to disastrous misinterpretations of Keynes' teaching. All of this calls – if presented – for a quite separate book. And indeed many books, and many articles – usually highly controversial – have been written.

In the first two Lectures of this book I begin – in so far as relevant to my theme – with a few words about Locke, Hume, and Adam Smith, and somewhat more extensively about Malthus, Ricardo, and John Stuart Mill. Even Marshall takes up little space – and my treatment of him is based partly on Keynes' Obituary.

A young Keynes already makes his appearance in Sections 3 and 4 of the first Lecture as the adviser in 1912 and 1913 of

Dennis Robertson in the writing of his pre-War (published 1915) book and of his first post-War book (1922).

After the first and second Lectures I deal exclusively with Keynes, and am thus able to treat in detail some aspects of the development of his thought. Between 1912 and 1935 it was completely transformed. A study of the transformation is truly an exercise in the development of thought.

In accordance with the wishes of the Trustees my Lectures delivered in Milan included a number of passages about personal relations, in which I myself figured prominently but by no means exclusively. I have in this book collected them all in the final Lecture.

Professor Joan Robinson and I were close collaborators in the discussion with Keynes. She helped me tremendously both in the preparation of the Lectures and in their transformation into this book.

To Donald Moggridge (Professor of Economics at the University of Toronto) I am indebted in a number of ways. Under the guidance of Professor Sir Austin Robinson, he has produced *inter alia* those magnificent Volumes XIII, XIV and XXIX in the Royal Economic Society edition of the *Collected Writings of John Maynard Keynes* (the series is set out on pages 269-75). The publication of these Volumes has led, and will continue to lead, to a vast output of books and articles on Keynes' thinking.

An article by Donald Moggridge in *History of Political Economy*[1] I have found especially helpful.

Moggridge's work on the Royal Economic Society edition means he has been devoting most of his spare time to Cambridge, England. I have benefited from the advice and encouragement of one who, for many years, has been immersing himself in Keynes' unpublished papers and correspondence.

He is now starting to work on a second official *Life of Keynes*.

---

1. DONALD E. MOGGRIDGE, 'From the *Treatise* to *The General Theory*: An Exercise in Chronology', *History of Political Economy*, Spring 1973, pp. 72-88.

This book, like Keynes' books, is insular, and centred on Cambridge. The two most significant independent developments of thought parallel with Keynes took place in Stockholm, where they still continue, and on the part of Michal Kalecki, the great Polish economist.

In Section 1 of the third Lecture I quote from an article published by Professor Ohlin, the Swedish economist, and refer to the articles published by Ohlin in 1937. Recently Ohlin has stated that

it seems quite clear that apart from the very considerable influence of Wicksell on Keynes, any other influence of the Swedish work on Keynes's development from 1930 to 1936 is very uncertain.[1]

Wicksell, the great Swedish economist of the turn of the century, plays a considerable part in Keynes' *Treatise* with his 'natural rate of interest', only to be discarded in the *General Theory*.[2]

Had I mentioned Kalecki at all I should have felt obliged to devote to him a considerable amount of space. Here again, as with the Swedes, but far closer to Keynes' thinking, was an independent development – by one isolated and remarkable individual. Remarkable in many respects, Joan Robinson describes how

he had taken a year's leave from the institute where he was working in Warsaw to write the *General Theory*. In Stockholm someone gave him Keynes' book. He began to read it – it was the book that he intended to write. He thought that perhaps further on there would be something different. No, all the way it was his book. He said: 'I confess, I was ill. Three days I lay in bed. Then I thought – Keynes is more known than I am. These ideas will get across much quicker with him and then we can get on to the interesting question, which is their application. Then I got up.' [. . .]

At the end of his life, Michal told me he felt he had done right

1. BERTIL OHLIN, 'Some Comments on Keynesianism and The Swedish Theory of Expansion before 1935', in DON PATINKIN and J. CLARK LEITH (eds.), *Keynes, Cambridge and 'The General Theory'*, Appendix III, Proceedings of a conference held at the University of Western Ontario. London: Macmillan, 1977, p. 163.
2. KEYNES, vol. VII, p. 242.

not to make any claim to rivalry with Keynes. It would only have led to a tiresome kind of argument. Perhaps scepticism about my [Joan Robinson's] claim for him was due to the difficulty of believing that anyone was capable of taking this high line in our degenerate age.[1]

I have enjoyed much help and encouragement from the Rector of the Bocconi University, Professor Innocenzo Gasparini. I owe an immense debt of gratitude to the Editor, Professor Angelo Porta. I have given him immense trouble. In addition to correcting numerous misprints in my text, he has made a large number of valuable suggestions for amendment. I owe to his scholarship and pertinacity great improvement in the bibliographical footnotes, and the bibliography itself.

The Bank's printer, Signor Martino Mardersteig (of the Verona firm Stamperia Valdonega), has played a most important part in simplifying the footnotes and providing such a beautiful text.

Dr Bernardo Crippa of the Bank, who was in charge of organising and publishing the 'Raffaele Mattioli Lectures', in addition to giving me encouragement, has also played a valuable part in the editing of the book. After the text of the book reached the Cambridge University Press there still remained a great deal of editing to be done – involving close co-operation with Dr Crippa, Professor Angelo Porta and Signor Mardersteig. My Cambridge editor, Mr Francis Brooke, has carried out a task of considerable difficulty with masterly skill; his patience has been inexhaustible. His scholarly suggestions for amendment have been most acceptable. Miss Lynn Chatterton, Production Controller of the Cambridge University Press, has also played an important part. I would also like to thank Mrs Alison Rowlatt, the indexer. In the background have stood the Raffaele Mattioli Foundation and the Banca Commerciale Italiana, represented by the Chairman, Dr Innocenzo Monti, and by Dr Bernardo Crippa.

---

1. Contribution by JOAN ROBINSON ('Michal Kalecki on the Economics of Capitalism') to ÉPRIME ESHAG (ed.), 'Michal Kalecki Memorial Lectures', *Oxford Bulletin of Economics and Statistics*. Special Issue, February 1977, pp. 7-18 (the quotation on pp. 8-9). Reprinted in JOAN ROBINSON, *Collected Economic Papers*, vol. v, Oxford: Basil Blackwell, 1979, pp. 184-96. The quotation will be found on p. 186.

If we had been obliged to rely on the Anglo-Italian Postal Service, in its present sad state, operations would have been quite impossible. The Bank undertook the conveyance of letters, telex messages and typescript. In the London Branch I am indebted to the Management, and for the readily provided services of members of his staff.

I owe much to my Secretary, Mrs Verna Cole, and to Mrs Marlene Gillson, who have, patiently and uncomplainingly, coped with my dreadful handwriting. Finally I am indebted to the Bursars of my College for the use of our xerox machine and to those in our College Office who have so skilfully handled it.

I am proudly grateful to the Raffaele Mattioli Foundation, the Banca Commerciale Italiana, the Luigi Bocconi University, the Stamperia Valdonega and the Cambridge University Press for the publication of this book.

RICHARD F. KAHN
King's College, Cambridge

CHRONOLOGY

1842   Alfred Marshall's birth at Clapham, London, on 26 July.

1877   Alfred Marshall's marriage with Mary Paley in July.
Arthur C. Pigou's birth at Ryde, Isle of Wight, England on 18 November.
Publication, for private circulation, of *The Pure Theory of Foreign Trade, The Pure Theory of Domestic Values* by Alfred Marshall.

1879   First edition of *The Economics of Industry* by Alfred Marshall and his wife Mary (London: Macmillan).

1883   John Maynard Keynes' birth at Harvey Road, Cambridge on 5 June.

1884   Second edition of *The Economics of Industry* by Alfred Marshall and his wife Mary (London: Macmillan).

1890   First edition of *Principles of Economics* by Alfred Marshall (London: Macmillan).
Dennis H. Robertson's birth at Lowestoft, East Anglia, on 23 May.

1907   Fifth edition of *Principles of Economics* by Alfred Marshall (London: Macmillan).

1909   Keynes' election to a Fellowship at King's College, Cambridge (his dissertation was published, in a revised form, as *A Treatise on Probability* in 1921).

1912   Publication of *Wealth and Welfare* by Arthur C. Pigou (London: Macmillan).
Dennis H. Robertson started his *A Study of Industrial Fluctuation* (published 1915, London: P. S. King & Son).

1913   Publication of Keynes' first book: *Indian Currency and Finance* (London: Macmillan).

1920   Eighth (last) edition (few changes) of *Principles of Economics* by Alfred Marshall (London: Macmillan).
First edition of *The Economics of Welfare* by Arthur C. Pigou (London: Macmillan).

1921   Publication of *A Treatise on Probability* by John Maynard Keynes (London: Macmillan).

1922   Publication of *Money* by Dennis H. Robertson, with an Introduction by John Maynard Keynes (London: Nisbet & Co).

1923   Publication of *A Tract on Monetary Reform* by John Maynard Keynes (London: Macmillan).
Publication of *Money, Credit and Commerce* by Alfred Marshall (London: Macmillan).

1924   Death of Alfred Marshall at Cambridge on 13 July.
Second edition of *The Economics of Welfare* by Arthur C. Pigou (London: Macmillan).
John Maynard Keynes started his *Treatise on Money* (finished in September 1930 and published at the end of the same year).

1925   Dennis H. Robertson finished his *Banking Policy and the Price Level*.
John Maynard Keynes' marriage with Lydia Lopokova on 4 August.

1926   Publication of *Banking Policy and the Price Level* by Dennis H. Robertson at the beginning of the year (London: P. S. King & Son).

1928   Reprint of *Money* by Dennis H. Robertson (London: P. S. King & Son).

1929   Publication of *We Can Conquer Unemployment*, Liberal Party Manifesto, in March (London: Cassell), soon named the 'Orange Book'.
Publication of *Can Lloyd George Do It?*, by John Maynard Keynes and Hubert D. Henderson, in May.
Publication of the 'Government White Paper' on *Certain Proposals Relating to Unemployment* (*Memoranda*) in May (Cmd. 3331. London: His Majesty's Stationery Office).
General Election on 30 May.
Macmillan Committee on Finance and Industry appointed on 5 November.

1930   John Maynard Keynes finished his *Treatise on Money* on 14 September.

Publication of *Treatise on Money* by John Maynard Keynes at the end of the year (London: Macmillan).

Economic Advisory Council set up on 15 February (first meeting on 17 February).

Committee of Economists of Economic Advisory Council appointed 24 July and reported on 24 October.

1931   Macmillan Committee reported in June.

Cambridge 'Circus' from January to May.

United Kingdom pushed off Gold Standard on 21 September.

1932   John Maynard Keynes started his *General Theory*.

1933   Publication of *The Theory of Unemployment* by Arthur C. Pigou (London: Macmillan).

1935   John Maynard Keynes finished his *General Theory*.

1936   Publication of *The General Theory* by John Maynard Keynes at the beginning of the year (London: Macmillan).

1946   Death of John Maynard Keynes at Firle, Sussex, on 21 April.

1948   Reprint of *A Study of Industrial Fluctuation* by Dennis H. Robertson (London School of Economics and Political Science).

Reprint of *Money* by Dennis H. Robertson (revised with additional chapters, London: Nisbet & Co).

1949   Second edition of *Banking Policy and the Price Level* by Dennis H. Robertson (New York: Augustus Kelly; London: Staples Press).

1959   Death of Arthur C. Pigou at Cambridge, on 7 March.

1963   Death of Dennis H. Robertson at Cambridge, on 21 April.

RICHARD F. KAHN

THE MAKING OF KEYNES' GENERAL THEORY

The six *Raffaele Mattioli Lectures* were delivered by Lord Kahn at the
Luigi Bocconi University, in Milan, from 5th to 14th June 1978.

FIRST LECTURE
Some comments on the earlier economists
up to early Keynes

1. *Say's Law: Adam Smith to John Stuart Mill.* – 2. *Say's Law: Alfred Marshall.* – 3. *Dennis H. Robertson in his 'A Study of Industrial Fluctuation'.* – 4. *Dennis H. Robertson in his 'Money'.* – 5. *The impact of young Piero Sraffa on the Cambridge of the Twenties.*

1. Say's Law: Adam Smith to John Stuart Mill

The classical doctrine, which used to be expressed categorically in the statement that 'Supply creates its own Demand', requires the underlying assumption that saving promotes the accumulation of national wealth. But expositions by classical economists of the public virtues of thrift often suffered from obscurity. For example, Adam Smith:

> Capitals are increased by parsimony, and diminished by prodigality [. . .]
> Whatever a person saves from his revenue he adds to his capital, and either employs it himself [. . .] or enables some other person to do so, by lending it to him for an interest, that is, for a share of the profits [. . .]

NOTE: *Lord Kahn introduced his Lectures with the following remarks:*

It is an honour which I deeply appreciate to have been invited to give the second series of Raffaele Mattioli Lectures. It gives me particular pleasure because Dr Mattioli was Piero Sraffa's oldest and greatest friend, whom I met on a number of occasions. He was a wonderful man. At one time he was a Lecturer at the Luigi Bocconi University. Piero Sraffa is both my oldest friend and the first economist with whom I established a close relationship, which has been maintained ever since 1929 until the present day. To Sraffa we all owe the fertile gift of the Italian – Cambridge school of economics, to the great advantage of Cambridge economics – and perhaps I may add of Italian economics. I used to meet Sraffa's father, Angelo, a man of charm and a great commercial lawyer. He was at one time Rector of the Luigi Bocconi University and Professor of Commercial Law.

Soon after the end of the First World War Sraffa visited England. He had been given an introduction to Keynes, on whom he made a very favourable impression. Keynes invited him to write a contribution on 'Italian Banking To-day' for the *Manchester Guardian*, Reconstruction Supplement, of which Keynes was the General

What is annually saved is as regularly consumed as what is annually spent, and nearly in the same time too; but it is consumed by a different set of people.[1]

The first half of the final sentence called for an apologetic editorial note by Cannan, Adam Smith's editor:

This paradox is arrived at through a confusion between the remuneration of the labourers who produce the additions to the capital and the additions themselves. What is really saved is the additions to the capital, and these are not consumed.[2]

Malthus was, of course, the great heretic of the classical age. But the extent of his heresy is, I suggest, less than Keynes attributed to him.

Editor. It was published in English on 7 December 1922. It was also published in Italian. Sraffa described how "the industrial crisis of 1921 had a grave repercussion on the ordinary [commercial] banks, all of which [. . .] found themselves loaded with doubtful credits and worthless securities, and at the same time compelled to agree to fresh advances to save what could be saved. [. . .] through the Consortium [of commercial banks] the banks of issue have been gradually extending their credit operations [. . .] in part taking the place of the ordinary banks and fulfilling functions properly theirs. [. . .] It will be interesting to follow the later developments in these tendencies" (PIERO SRAFFA, 'Italian Banking To-Day' *Manchester Guardian*, Supplement 'Reconstruction in Europe', 7 December 1922, pp. 675-6).

Mussolini was angry. Piero Sraffa was urged by his father to leave the country — at least temporarily. Keynes arranged for him to stay in Cambridge, England. But Sraffa was in no sense an exile. He paid frequent visits to Italy to maintain his connections and meet his friends.

At the end of the First Lecture I shall be discussing Sraffa's famous article 'On the Relations between Cost and Quantity Produced', published by this University in *Annali di Economia* in 1926 (PIERO SRAFFA, 'Sulle relazioni fra costo e quantità prodotta', *Annali di Economia*, vol. II, 1925-1926. Milano: Università Bocconi Editrice, 1926, pp. 277-328). On the strength of this article Keynes persuaded our Faculty to appoint Sraffa to a post. He has been with us ever since — a most important influence in our Faculty and much beloved.

The first time that I visited Italy after the war was in 1948 when Joan Robinson, Sraffa and I stayed on the Passo Sella in the Dolomites. It was early in the summer and there was too much snow. Our rock climbing was restricted. Roy Harrod's book *Towards a Dynamic Economics* was in page proof and Harrod lent me a proof, which we read when we were not walking or climbing. So far as Cambridge is concerned this was the origin of the economics of growth.

1. ADAM SMITH, *The Wealth of Nations*, Edited by Edwin Cannan. Fourth Edition. London: Methuen, 1925, vol. I, p. 320.

2. *Ibid.*, p. 320 note.

In the Introduction to the *Principles*, Malthus wrote:

Adam Smith has stated, that capitals are increased by parsimony, that every frugal man is a public benefactor, and that the increase of wealth depends upon the balance of produce above consumption. That these propositions are true to a great extent is perfectly unquestionable [. . .] but it is quite obvious that they are not true to an indefinite extent, and that the principle of saving, pushed to excess, would destroy the motive to production [. . .] The two extremes are obvious; and it follows that there must be some intermediate point, though the resources of political economy may not be able to ascertain it, where, taking into consideration both the power to produce and the will to consume, the encouragement to the increase of wealth is the greatest.[1]

Ricardo felt obliged to concede qualified agreement:

But the argument is not about the motive to production, in that every body is agreed – the accumulation of capital may go on so much faster, than labourers can be increased, that productions must cease increasing in the same proportion as capital, from want of hands [. . .].[2]

In a letter to Ricardo, Malthus wrote:

an attempt to accumulate very rapidly which necessarily implies a considerable diminution of unproductive consumption, by greatly impairing the usual motives to production must prematurely check the progress of wealth.[3]

In his reply Ricardo protested against Malthus' view that 'an increase of consumption' was a 'remedy' for 'stagnation of trade, in a want of employment for our labourers, &c. &c.'.[4]

---

1. THOMAS R. MALTHUS, *Principles of Political Economy*. First Edition. London: John Murray, 1820, Introduction, pp. 8-9; quoted by KEYNES, vol. x, p. 102 and vol. VII, p. 363.

2. DAVID RICARDO, *Works and Correspondence*, vol. II, *Notes on Malthus's Principles of Political Economy*. Edited by PIERO SRAFFA with the collaboration of M. H. Dobb. Cambridge: Cambridge University Press, 1951, p. 8.

3. DAVID RICARDO, *Works and Correspondence*, vol. IX, *Letters July 1821-1823*. Cambridge: Cambridge University Press, 1952, p. 10, from a letter dated 7 July 1821; quoted by KEYNES, vol. VII, pp. 362-3.

4. DAVID RICARDO, *Works and Correspondence*, vol. IX, p. 16, from Ricardo's letter to Malthus, 9 July 1821.

Ricardo was confused. Keynes wrote that he 'was stone-deaf to what Malthus was saying'.[1]

Ricardo took refuge in two quite separate lines of defence. One I have already indicated – if 'accumulation of capital may go on so much faster, than labourers can be increased, that productions must cease increasing in the same proportion as capital, from want of hands'.[2]

The other line of defence is indicated in the following passage:

With very low profits the motives for saving would cease, and therefore the motives for increased production would also cease. Do you not then say that increased production is often attended with evil consequences to mankind, because it destroys the motives to industry, and to the keeping up of the increased production? Now in much of this I cannot agree with you. I indeed allow that the case is possible to conceive of saving being so universal that no profit will arise from the employment of capital, but then I contend that the specific reason is, because all that fund which should, and in ordinary cases does, constitute profit, goes to wages, and immoderately swells that fund which is destined to the support of labour. The labourers are immoderately paid for their labour, and they necessarily become the unproductive consumers of the country. I agree too that the capitalists being in such a case without a sufficient motive for saving from revenue, to add to capital, will cease doing so – will, if you please, even expend a part of their capital; but I ask what evil will result from this? none to the capitalist, you will allow, for his enjoyments and his profits will be thereby increased, or he would continue to save. None to the labourers, for which we should repine; because their situation was so exceedingly favourable that they could bear a deduction from their wages and yet be in a most prosperous condition. Here it is where we most differ. You think that the capitalist could not cease saving, on account of the lowness of his profits, without a cessation, in some degree, of employment to the people. I on the contrary think that with all the abatements from the fund destined to the payment of labour, which I acknowledge would be the consequence of the new course of capitalists, enough would remain to employ all the labour that could be obtained, and to pay it liberally, so that in fact there would be little diminution in the quantity of

1. KEYNES, vol. VII, p. 364.
2. DAVID RICARDO, *Works and Correspondence*, vol. II, p. 8.

commodities produced, – the distribution only would be different; more would go [to] the capitalists, and less to the labourers.

I do not think that stagnation is a proper term to apply to a state of things in which for a time there is no motive to a further increase of production.[1]

Heretic Malthus certainly was. But he was traditionalist in his belief in *laissez-faire*:

if, in reality, saving is a national benefit, or a national disadvantage, according to the circumstances of the period; and, if these circumstances are best declared by the rate of profits, surely it is a case in which individual interest needs no extraneous assistance.

Saving, as I have before said, is, in numerous instances, a most sacred private duty. How far a just sense of this duty, together with the desire of bettering our condition so strongly implanted in the human breast, may sometimes, and in some states of society, occasion a greater tendency to parsimony than is consistent with the most effective encouragement to the growth of public wealth, it is difficult to say; but whether this tendency, if let alone, be ever too great or not, no one could think of interfering with it, even in its caprices. There is no reason, however, for giving an additional sanction to it, by calling it a public duty. [...] [Thus] we shall best conform to that great principle of political economy laid down by Adam Smith, which teaches us a general maxim, liable to very few exceptions, that the wealth of nations is best secured by allowing every person, as long as he adheres to the rules of justice, to pursue his own interest in his own way.[2]

Ricardo's innocent comment on Malthus' final sentence was: 'Who has ever proposed to leave it to any other?' [than the pursuit of individual self-interest].[3]

It was Keynes' belief that, 'The last echo of the controversy [between Ricardo and Malthus] is to be found in John Stuart Mill's discussion of his wages-fund theory'[4] in his *Principles*, published in 1848 (Book I, Chapter v).

1. *Ibid.*, vol. IX, pp. 24-5, from Ricardo's letter to Malthus, 21 July 1821.
2. THOMAS R. MALTHUS, *Principles of Political Economy*, pp. 517-18; DAVID RICARDO, *Works and Correspondence*, vol. II, pp. 449-50.
3. DAVID RICARDO, *Works and Correspondence*, vol. II, p. 450.
4. KEYNES, vol. VII, p. 364. See DON PATINKIN, 'Keynes's Misquotation of Mill: Comment', in *Economic Journal*, June 1978, pp. 341-2, on a learned discussion

Mill was emphatic:

every increase of capital gives, or is capable of giving, additional employment to industry [. . .] without creating an impossibility of finding them [the labourers] employment [. . .] This proposition [. . .] is also very much opposed to common doctrines. There is not an opinion more general among mankind than this, that the unproductive expenditure of the rich is necessary to the employment of the poor. Before Adam Smith, the doctrine had hardly been questioned; and even since his time, authors of the highest name and of great merit (for example, Mr. Malthus, Dr. Chalmers, M. de Sismondi) have contended, that if consumers were to save and convert into capital more than a limited portion of their income, and were not to devote to unproductive consumption an amount of means bearing a certain ratio to the capital of the country, the extra accumulation would be merely so much waste, since there would be no market for the commodities which the capital so created would produce. I conceive this to be one of the many errors arising in political economy [. . .][1]

In another part of his book Mill included a chapter specifically entitled 'Of Excess of Supply'[2] from which Keynes quoted the following passage at the opening of his *General Theory* as expressly setting forth the doctrine that supply creates its own demand:

meaning by this in some significant, but not clearly defined, sense that the whole of the costs of production must necessarily be spent in the aggregate, directly or indirectly, on purchasing the product.[3]

The passage runs as follows:

what [. . .] constitutes the means of payment for commodities. It is, simply, commodities. Each person's means of paying for the productions

on the question whether Keynes quoted from the original source initiated by J. RONNIE DAVIS and FRANCIS J. CASEY Jr., 'Keynes's Misquotation of Mill', *Economic Journal*, June 1977, pp. 329-30. Don Patinkin agrees that Keynes quoted from Alfred and Mary Marshall's early book (1879), that it does not follow that he had not read Mill, but that his 'carelessness of interpretation' (in the view of Don Patinkin) was not due to a few minor verbal discrepancies.

1. JOHN STUART MILL, *Principles of Political Economy*. First published, London: John W. Parker, 1848. People's Edition, London: Longmans, Green, 1891, Book I, Chapter V, Section 3, pp. 41-2.

2. *Ibid.*, People's Edition, Book III, Chapter XIV, Section 2, pp. 337-8.

3. KEYNES, vol. VII, p. 18.

of other commodities consists of those which he himself possesses. All sellers are inevitably, and by the meaning of the word, buyers. Could we suddenly double the productive power of the country, we should double the supply of commodities in every market; but we should, by the same stroke, double the purchasing power. Everybody would bring a double demand as well as supply: everybody would be able to buy twice as much, because every one would have twice as much to offer in exchange.[1]

John Stuart Mill regarded the point as

fundamental; any difference of opinion on it involves radically different conceptions of political economy, especially in its practical aspect. On the one view, we have only to consider how a sufficient production may be combined with the best possible distribution; but on the other there is a third thing to be considered – how a market can be created for produce [. . .] Besides, a theory so essentially self-contradictory cannot intrude itself without carrying confusion into the very heart of the subject [. . .].[2]

The error Mill attributed in the same passage to Malthus, Chalmers and Sismondi

[their] fatal misconception has spread itself like a veil between them and the more difficult portions of the subject, not suffering one ray of light to penetrate [. . .] the merit of having placed this most important point in its true light, belongs principally, on the Continent, to the judicious J. B. Say, and in this country to Mr. Mill [James, John Stuart's father] [. . .].[3]

Even Mill could not fail to notice that there were occasional periods of heavy unemployment and business losses which appeared as 'general over-supply'. This he accounted for as a commercial crisis.

At such times there is really an excess of all commodities above the money demand: in other words, there is an under-supply of money. From the sudden annihilation of a great mass of credit, every one dislikes to part with ready money [. . .] Almost everybody therefore

---

1. JOHN STUART MILL, *Principles of Political Economy*. People's Edition, Book III, Chapter XIV, Section 3, p. 338.
2. *Ibid.*, Section 4, p. 340.
3. *Ibid.*, Section 4, p. 341.

is a seller, and there are scarcely any buyers: [. . .] it is a great error to suppose, with Sismondi, that a commercial crisis is the effect of a general excess of production. It is simply the consequence of an excess of speculative purchases [. . .] the remedy is [. . .] the restoration of confidence [. . .] this temporary derangement of markets is an evil only because it is temporary.[1]

Mill then went on to a different theme – the secular fall of profits and interest – a concession similar to, but not identical with, the concession to Malthus made by Ricardo:

Low profits, however, are a different thing from deficiency of demand; and the production and accumulation which merely reduce profits, cannot be called excess of supply or of production.[2]

Keynes wrote:

Mill's successors rejected his wages-fund theory but overlooked the fact that Mill's refutation of Malthus depended on it. Their method was to dismiss the problem from the *corpus* of economics not by solving it but by not mentioning it [. . .] Theories of under-consumption hibernated until the appearance in 1889 of *The Physiology of Industry*, by J. A. Hobson [the economist] and A. F. Mummery [the mountaineer] [. . .].[3]

---

1. JOHN STUART MILL, *Principles of Political Economy*. People's Edition, Book III, Chapter XIV, earlier in Section 4, pp. 339-40.
2. *Ibid.*, p. 340.
3. KEYNES, vol. VII, p. 364.

2. Say's Law: Alfred Marshall

Pigou, Marshall's great disciple, and successor as Cambridge Professor of Political Economy, in the course of his highly critical review of Keynes' *General Theory*,[1] chided the author for quoting the following two sentences[2] from a little book published in 1879 by Marshall and his wife two years after their marriage:

it is not good for trade to have dresses made of material which wears out quickly. For if people did not spend their means on buying new dresses, they would spend them on giving employment to labour in some other way.[3]

Of course the Marshalls intended to be interpreted to mean that thrift results in labour being employed on the construction of capital goods. But they failed to say so. We are reminded of Adam Smith's form of words, quoted above, which called for an apology from his editor, Cannan: 'What is annually saved is as regularly consumed as what is annually spent.'

Pigou drew attention to a very much later passage in the Marshalls' little book: 'though men have the power to purchase, they may not choose to use it.'[4] Pigou pointed out that Keynes had quoted this sentence in his previous footnote. Actually Keynes was quoting from the book which I have mentioned by Hobson and Mummery, who continued:

But he [Marshall] fails to grasp the critical importance of this fact, and appears to limit his action to periods of 'crisis'.[5]

1. ARTHUR C. PIGOU, 'Mr. J. M. Keynes' General Theory of Employment, Interest and Money', *Economica*, May 1936, pp. 115-32.

2. *Ibid.*, p. 116; referring to KEYNES, vol. VII, p. 20, note 1.

3. ALFRED MARSHALL and MARY PALEY MARSHALL, *The Economics of Industry*. London: Macmillan, 1879, p. 17 (Second Edition – less rare – 1884). Italian Edition by GIACOMO BECATTINI, *Economia della produzione*. Milano: ISEDI, Istituto Editoriale Internazionale, 1975. Professor Becattini's Introduction is most interesting. Not to be confused with ALFRED MARSHALL, *Elements of Economics of Industry*. London: Macmillan, 1932.

4. ALFRED MARSHALL and MARY PALEY MARSHALL, *The Economics of Industry*, p. 154.

5. ALBERT F. MUMMERY and JOHN A. HOBSON, *The Physiology of Industry*. London: John Murray, 1889, p. 102, note 1.

Keynes added, 'This has remained fair comment, I think, in the light of Marshall's later work.'[1]

In the same year, 1879, Marshall printed for private circulation his *Pure Theory of Domestic Values*.[2]

The following passage is quoted by Keynes:

> The whole of a man's income is expended in the purchase of services and of commodities. It is indeed commonly said that a man spends some portion of his income and saves another. But it is a familiar economic axiom that a man purchases labour and commodities with that portion of his income which he saves just as much as he does with that which he is said to spend. He is said to spend when he seeks to obtain present enjoyment from the services and the commodities which he purchases. He is said to save when he causes the labour and the commodities which he purchases to be devoted to the production of wealth from which he expects to derive the means of enjoyment in the future.[3]

It is quite unambiguous. What is lacking is any indication of the machinery by means of which a man's saving can be made available to others for the purpose of the production of wealth.

The nature of a crisis was described by the young Marshalls in their book. After the words 'But though men have the power to purchase they may not choose to use it' the paragraph runs on:

> For when confidence has been shaken by failures, capital cannot be got to start new companies or extend old ones [. . .] there is but little occupation in any of the trades which make Fixed capital. Those whose skill and capital is Specialised in these trades are earning little, and therefore buying little of the produce of other trades [. . .] the disorganisation of one trade throws others out of gear, and they react on it and increase its disorganisation.

The chief cause of the evil is a want of confidence. The greater part of it could be removed almost in an instant if confidence could re-

1. KEYNES, vol. VII, p. 19, note 2.
2. ALFRED MARSHALL, *The Pure Theory of Domestic Values* (and also *The Pure Theory of Foreign Trade*). Published by the London School of Economics and Political Science. Scarce Tracts in Economic and Political Science, No. 1. London: 1930.
3. *Ibid.*, p. 34; quoted by Keynes, vol. VII, p. 19.

turn [. . .] If all trades which make goods for direct consumption agreed to work on [. . .] they would supply one another with the means of earning a moderate rate of profits and of wages. The trades which make Fixed capital might have to wait a little longer [. . .] Confidence by growing would cause itself to grow; credit would give increased means of purchase, and thus prices would recover [. . .] the revival of industry comes about through the gradual and often simultaneous growth of confidence among many various trades; it begins as soon as traders think that prices will not continue to fall: and with a revival of industry prices rise.[1]

That was Mr and Mrs Marshall in 1879. This is similar to Mill on 'over-supply' but the causation is different. Mill attributed the crisis to a reduction in credit while the Marshalls attributed it to an unexplained failure of confidence in future profits. Marshall had nothing to add either in 1890, or in 1920, the dates of the first and last edition of his *Principles of Economics*.

When in 1890 Marshall published the first edition it was entitled Vol. 1.[2] His intention was to publish further volumes, including one on *Industry and Trade* (published eventually in 1919);[3] and one on *Money, Credit and Employment* (eventually published in 1923, a year before his death at the age of almost 82) under the title *Money, Credit and Commerce*.[4] (The substitution of the word 'Commerce' for the word 'Employment' is significant.)

By 1907, with the appearance of the fifth edition, Marshall felt obliged to accept the prospect of delay over publication of his book on *Money*. He consequently inserted into the text of his concluding Chapter XIII, on 'Progress in Relation to Standards of Life', a new Section 10.[5] The whole of the passage from John Stuart Mill and the following two paragraphs were taken from the Marshalls' little book of 1879,[6] which Marshall had come

1. ALFRED MARSHALL and MARY PALEY MARSHALL, *The Economics of Industry*, pp. 154-5.
2. ALFRED MARSHALL, *Principles of Economics*. First Edition. London: Macmillan, 1890.
3. ALFRED MARSHALL, *Industry and Trade*. London: Macmillan, 1919.
4. ALFRED MARSHALL, *Money, Credit and Commerce*. London: Macmillan, 1923.
5. ALFRED MARSHALL, *Principles of Economics*. Fifth Edition. London: Macmillan, 1907, Book VI, Chapter XIII, Section 10, pp. 709-11.
6. ALFRED MARSHALL and MARY PALEY MARSHALL, *The Economics of Industry*, p. 154.

to regard with disfavour and which, after the publication of his *Principles,* he withdrew from circulation on the grounds that 'You cannot [. . .] tell the truth for half a crown'.[1]

Of considerable analytical interest is the young Marshalls' suggestion that confidence 'would return almost in an instant if all trades which make goods for direct consumption agreed to work on'. If they bought 'each other's goods as in ordinary times, they would supply one another with the means of earning a moderate rate of profits and of wages. The trades which make Fixed capital might have to wait a little longer.'[2]

In *Money, Credit and Commerce,* Marshall seemed to attribute a decline of activity mainly to a preceding speculative boom:

Prompt action by the Bank of England in regard to the rate of discount often checks unreasonable expansions of credit; which might otherwise grow, after the manner of a fall of snow on a steep mountain side. [. . .]

Those causes of discontinuity which lie within our scope, and are remediable [unlike harvest fluctuations], are chiefly connected [. . .] with the want of knowledge; [. . .]

Better and more widely diffused knowledge is a remedy for that excessive confidence which causes a violent expansion of credit and rise of prices; and it is also a remedy for that excessive distrust that follows. One of the chief sources of disturbance is the action of the general public in providing funds for joint-stock companies [. . .] many of them trust just where they should not [. . .].[3]

And there, on this particular subject of the causation of the level of demand, I leave Marshall – the great Cambridge economist, who counted Keynes and Dennis Robertson among his devoted disciples.

1. See ALFRED MARSHALL, *Principles of Economics,* Ninth (Variorum) Edition. With Annotations by CLAUDE W. GUILLEBAUD. London: Macmillan, 1961, vol. II, *Notes,* p. 12.

2. ALFRED MARSHALL and MARY PALEY MARSHALL, *The Economics of Industry,* p. 155.

3. ALFRED MARSHALL, *Money, Credit and Commerce,* pp. 258-61.

3. Dennis H. Robertson in his 'A Study of Industrial Fluctuation'

Immediately before the outbreak of the First World War in Cambridge, England, the thinking of Dennis Robertson was in advance of that of Keynes. His *Study of Industrial Fluctuation*[1] was published in 1915 at the age of 25. In his Preface he acknowledged Keynes' assistance and criticism. But Robertson at that date had developed his economic thinking well ahead of Keynes. His references to Marshall, though critical, are mainly on points of detail; similarly his references to Pigou, although as a disciple he worshipped them both, and was a close personal friend of Pigou. He was influenced also by Aftalion and Tugan-Baranowsky.

One passage is of particular interest as showing the influence of Say's Law even upon the study of the trade cycle:

the relapse in constructional industry is seen to be due to the existence or imminence of an over-production of instrumental as compared with consumable goods. Whether or not this over-production is indicated by an actual shortage of consumable goods which renders it impossible to maintain investment on the scale which has prevailed during the preceding years or months, and whether it is due to miscalculation or to the inevitable characteristics of modern large-scale production, its essential nature is the same, – a failure to secure the best conceivable distribution through time of the community's consumption of consumable goods. The aggregate satisfaction of the community over time is thereby diminished [. . .]

But [. . .] there is no reason for the consumptive trades as a whole to be adversely affected by the constructional collapse. [. . .] all that is needed is for the consumptive trades to produce upon the largest scale for one another's consumption. The classical objection to the possibility of a 'general over-production' [. . .] seems so far to be substantially valid.[2]

---

1. DENNIS H. ROBERTSON, *A Study of Industrial Fluctuation*. London: P. S. King & Son, 1915; reprinted by the London School of Economics and Political Science, Series of Reprints of Scarce Works on Political Economy, No. 8. London: 1948.
   2. *Ibid.*, pp. 187-8.

In this limited sense Say's Law still ruled in Cambridge. But in the Preface to the Reprint Robertson wrote that:

I do not think I had been brought up with any exaggerated respect for Say's Law of Markets, which is subjected to some rough handling on pp. 198-200.[1]

He quoted the young Marshalls' statement that 'though men have the power to purchase they may not choose to use it'.[2]

Robertson produced evidence that in some cycles the decline in the production of consumer goods led to the decline in the production of capital goods. Keynes, in criticising this passage,

seems inclined to doubt a fall even in the monetary demand price for consumable goods, and to refer the decline in employment in the consumptive trades to a diversion of productive energy into constructional industry.[3]

Robertson 'in large mesasure' agreed.

In a footnote to the reprint of his book Robertson tentatively recalled that Keynes' 'views at that date were of a more uncompromisingly "under-saving" type than my own'.[4]

The argument appeared to Robertson to be untouched by current statements of the doctrine of 'repercussion' based on the idea of 'the communication of prosperity from one industry to another in an endless chain'.[5]

Robertson failed to dispel obscurity by his statement that

there seems at first sight no sort of reason why I should be depressed if the marginal utilities of all commodities I possess are lowered provided their total utilities are increased, and provided there is no alteration in the ratio of exchange against my own particular products.[6]

---

1. DENNIS H. ROBERTSON, *A Study of Industrial Fluctuation*, p. xii.
2. *Ibid.*
3. *Ibid.*, pp. 220-1, note 6.
4. *Ibid.*, reprinted Edition 1948, p. xiv, note 1.
5. *Ibid.*, p. 125.
6. *Ibid.*, p. 188, note 2.

However, a few pages further on, Robertson wrote:

Nevertheless it is apparent that in spite of the survival of consumptive industry there are certain years [. . .] which are marked by something which may fairly be called a general depression of trade [. . .] We have, therefore, to discover some satisfactory reason for the diminished activity and restricted output of consumptive industry in these years.[1]

It seems astonishing that in Cambridge it was thought necessary in 1914 to ask that question. Keynes could not help.

In his Preface Robertson stated that to Keynes he owed more than it would be possible to acknowledge.

Robertson was certainly a pioneer, in a somewhat perverse sense (and for some years after the end of the war was ahead of Keynes in pioneering new lines of thought).

In his Preface, dated November 1915, he wrote:

Above all, the co-existence of brisk trade and employment with a war expenditure of £ 3,000,000 a day has compelled clear thinking on the real nature of saving and investment in the most unlikely quarters.[2]

The appearance of the Report of the Royal Commission on the Poor Laws had led to lively discussion of the question whether State expenditure in providing work for the unemployed would be effective. Pigou was heavily involved. No doubt it led to the publication in 1913 of his popular little book on *Unemployment*.[3] His first serious work, *Wealth and Welfare*,[4] the pre-War version of *The Economics of Welfare*,[5] devoted considerable attention to it.

Robertson, as I have stated, was critical of Pigou. In the course of Chapter XI of Pigou's book on *Unemployment*, on 'Direct State Action to Lessen Unemployment', Pigou wrote:

It may well be held, however, that remedial action by public authorities need not be confined to these indirect measures, but that there is room also for direct attack through policies deliberately designed to

1. *Ibid.*, p. 198.
2. *Ibid.*, p. xx.
3. ARTHUR C. PIGOU, *Unemployment*. New York: Henry Holt; London: Williams and Norgate, 1913.
4. ARTHUR C. PIGOU, *Wealth and Welfare*. London: Macmillan, 1912.
5. ARTHUR C. PIGOU, *The Economics of Welfare*. First Edition. London: Macmillan, 1920.

lessen the fluctuating character of the demand for labour. It, therefore, becomes important to inquire what success may be expected to attend action of this character.

At the outset of the inquiry a preliminary objection has to be overcome. It is sometimes urged that the aggregate wage-fund at any moment is rigidly fixed, and that, therefore, though it is, of course, possible in various ways to increase the demand for labour in any particular part of the industrial field, this can only be done at the expense of lessening, in a corresponding degree, the demand in other parts. This is equally true, it is maintained, whether the increase in demand in the particular part is brought about by means of a bounty to private employers, or through the employment of labour by the public authorities themselves. The argument in this latter aspect is forcibly expressed in the report of the Transvaal Indigency Commission. 'Wealth,' the Commission declares, 'is the only source from which wages are paid, and the State must levy taxation in order to pay wages to its workmen. When, therefore, a Government gives work to the unemployed, it is simply transferring wage-giving from the individual to itself. It is diminishing employment with one hand, while it increases it with the other. It takes work from people employed by private individuals and gives it to people selected by the State.'[1] Now, if the general type of reasoning, of which the above sentences are a particular example, is valid, it is clearly impossible for any governmental authority, either by direct action or indirectly through fiscal devices, to lessen the fluctuating character of the demand for labour as a whole. Such reasoning, however, is not valid. It is, indeed, true that the State is unable, by action of the kind contemplated, to increase the demand for labour on the whole on the average of good and bad times together. This consideration is, furthermore, exceedingly important; for it is fatal to all schemes designed to diminish unemployment by the devotion of a fixed annual sum to the conduct of new industries, such as planting forests or building military roads. But it is not true that the State is unable to increase the demand for labour in bad times at the cost of diminishing it to a more or less corresponding extent in good times. To establish this point, it is necessary to look behind the machinery of money payment to the real transactions which these payments represent and facilitate. When this is done, we perceive that, in any country at any moment, there

1. TRANSVAAL INDIGENCY COMMISSION, *Report. 1906-1908*. Presented to both Houses of Parliament by Command of His Excellency the Governor. Pretoria: Government Printing and Stationery Office, 1908, p. 129.

is flowing into warehouses and shops from various centres of production a continuous stream of goods. At the same time there are
flowing out two other continuous streams, embodying, respectively,
the goods about to be consumed by the propertied classes and the
goods about to be handed over by members of these classes as payments to induce Labour to perform further services. The argument
of the Transvaal Commission, and other like arguments, imply that
the volume of the stream flowing out towards Labour is rigidly determined by the volume of the stream flowing into warehouses and
shops. In reality, however, it depends, not only upon this, but also
upon the volume of the other outflowing stream, together with the
depth of the reservoir of goods standing in store between the inflowing and the outflowing streams. To simplify the discussion, let us
suppose – a supposition which tells against the case I am endeavouring to establish – that the consumption of the propertied classes is
absolutely constant. In this case, if commodities passed immediately
from the seat of their production to the hands of consumers, so that
there was no reservoir of stored goods intermediate between the two,
no means would exist by which governmental or any other authority
could modify the stream flowing out towards Labour, when once
the volume of the inflowing stream was given. But, since, as a matter
of fact, there is always and necessarily a very large intermediate fund
of goods temporarily in store, such means do exist. If it is desired to
make the outflowing stream more constant than it would normally
be, all that the public authority needs to do is to borrow (in effect)
from warehouses and shops, when the demand for labour is low, resources with which to increase the demand, and to pay back its bor-
rowings at the expense of the outflowing stream when the demand
again becomes high.[1]

This astonishing quotation from Pigou suggests, in the light of
my quotation from Robertson about war expenditure of £3 million a day, disillusionment on the part of Robertson with the
existing state of scepticism about the possibility of reducing unemployment. Robertson continued to criticise Pigou. But he
ended his book on an eloquent note of hope, and I quote the
concluding passage:

Another method of approaching the whole difficulty is by an artificial
elevation of the demand for constructional goods. The proposal of the

1. ARTHUR C. PIGOU, *Unemployment*, pp. 170-4.

Minority Report of the Poor Law Commissioners that Government contracts for structural work should be concentrated upon times of bad trade has found favour in many quarters, and seems to be deserving of cordial support.

It must be observed finally that all such proposals for increasing the volume of consumption during depression are, like a steady price level and the more equal distribution of wealth, open to the objection that they will tend to check that accumulation of consumable good upon which industrial progress depends. How much weight we attach to this objection depends upon more ultimate judgements, and upon the solution which we are prepared to give of the ambiguity latent [in the concept of maximising the community's aggregate of net consumption through time].

What is meant by the most desirable distribution of the community's income through time? Is the assumption valid upon which western civilisation seems to proceed, – that it is desirable so to manipulate one's income-stream that it shall flow in with an ever-rising tide? From some points of view the whole cycle of industrial change presents the appearance of a perpetual immolation of the present upon the altar of the future. During the boom sacrifices are made out of all proportion to the enjoyment over which they will ultimately give command: during the depression enjoyment is denied lest it should debar the possibility of making fresh sacrifices. Out of the welter of industrial dislocation the great permanent riches of the future are generated. How far are we bound to honour the undrawn bills of posterity, and to acquiesce in this never-closing hyperbola of inter-secular exchange? Shall we sacrifice ourselves as willing victims to the

> Urge and urge and urge
> Always the procreant urge of the world?
> [Walt Whitman]

Or shall we listen to the words of one of the wisest of English philosophers [Samuel Butler], who counsels us to eat our grapes downwards, and who always washed up the knives first in case it should please God to take him before he got to the forks? The question is one of ethics, rather than of economics: but let us at least remember that we belong to an age which is apt to forget the [things which really matter among the things which we cannot do without[1]], and immolate ourselves, if we must, with our eyes open and not in a trance.[2]

1. Based on Aristotle, *Physica* 194a 27 (τὸ οὗ ἕνεκα).
2. Dennis H. Robertson, *A Study of Industrial Fluctuation*, pp. 253-4.

4. Dennis H. Robertson in his 'Money'

On his return to Cambridge after serving in the Army Robertson got to work on an elementary book on *Money*. It was published in 1922, and after numerous revisions it was finally revised with additional chapters in 1948.[1] It immediately became the leading text-book on the subject. Robertson's brilliant and amusing literary style made it highly readable. In fact it was more than a text-book – it marked a new start in the development in Cambridge of monetary thought. He received no encouragement from his Professor and close friend, Pigou, who in an essay published in 1921[2] actually quoted from the young Marshalls, writing in 1879, that 'the greater part of the evil associated with an industrial depression could be removed almost in an instant if confidence could return'[3] and wrote about the post-War slump: 'The fundamental thing needed [. . .] is [. . .] a recovery of business confidence.'[4]

Keynes had remained a Treasury Civil Servant after the end of the War, and served at the Versailles Peace Conference in January 1919, until his resignation, in protest, in June 1919. He immediately began writing his *Economic Consequences of the Peace*,[5] which he completed in November.

On his return to Cambridge he was again in touch with Robertson, who in the Preface to his revised edition of *Money* of 1928 wrote:

My debt to Mr. J. M. Keynes, already very large when the first edition [1922] of this book was published, has reached a sum which is no longer capable of expression in words.[6]

1. DENNIS H. ROBERTSON, *Money*. London: Nisbet & Co. First published 1922. Second Edition (revised and reset), 1928. Revised with additional chapters, 1948.

2. ARTHUR C. PIGOU, 'Unemployment', *Contemporary Review*. July-December 1921, pp. 737-42; reprinted and revised: 'Unemployment and The Great Slump', in *Essays in Applied Economics*. London: P. S. King & Son, 1923, pp. 34-40.

3. ARTHUR C. PIGOU, 'Unemployment', *Contemporary Review*, July-December 1921, p. 742.

4. ARTHUR C. PIGOU, 'Unemployment and The Great Slump', in *Essays in Applied Economics*, p. 40.

5. KEYNES, vol. II.

6. DENNIS H. ROBERTSON, *Money*, Second Edition, 1928, p. ix.

Of the final chapter especially, on the 'Questions of the Cycle', Robertson wrote, referring to Keynes' co-operation:

[It] ought scarcely, even in such a book as this, to see the light over any other signature than his until his forthcoming work on the theory of money has been published.[1]

That statement calls for quotation from the final paragraphs of this revised edition of the book:

The Scope for Government Intervention. Even so, however, it is, in the author's view, unlikely that the monetary system will ever be able to cope unaided with a trade slump (or phenomena akin to a trade slump) as efficiently as with a trade boom (or phenomena akin to a trade boom). It is likely to require the assistance of a more powerful ally – the Government of the country itself [. . .] If the public's desire to save is increasing so fast, or the processes of manufacture and salesmanship are being speeded up so rapidly, that private industry is left bothered and bewildered as to how to harness the productive forces thus released, what can be more sensible [than] that the Government, using the monetary system as its handmaid, should intervene to turn them to good account [. . .] But of that this much only can be said here. Among the half-truths left us as a legacy by the Great Muddle is the doctrine that a banking system must at all costs be 'independent of the Government.' If this means [. . .] that the monetary policy of a country should be carried on *in vacuo*, without reference to the problem of the development of the vast national estate, then it is a sterile and a dangerous doctrine indeed.

And so we are led back to where we began – the fact that money is a servant and not a master – a means and not an end. The real economic evils of society – inadequate production and inequitable distribution – lie too deep for any purely monetary ointment to cure. An unwise monetary policy can wreak unmerited hardship and engender unnecessary confusion and waste: not even a wise one can turn a world which is unjust and poor into a world which is rich and just.[2]

A passage very similar to the final paragraph had already appeared at the end of Robertson's first edition of 1922.

1. DENNIS H. ROBERTSON, *Money*, Second Edition, 1928, p. ix.
2. *Ibid.*, Revised Edition, 1948, pp. 178-9.

5. The impact of the young Piero Sraffa on the Cambridge of the Twenties

Another aspect of prevailing orthodoxy was Marshall's conception of a system of prices depending upon the 'laws of increasing and diminishing returns'. The alliance between Italian and Cambridge economists began with the famous article by Piero Sraffa 'On the Relations between Cost and Quantity Produced'.[1] It was published in 1926 by the Luigi Bocconi University. A shorter, but more developed, version was published in English in the *Economic Journal* in 1926.[2] The impact of the article, which was not confined to the English version, was tremendous, particularly in Cambridge. I can devote only ridiculously little space to the subject.

The section of particular interest to Cambridge economists was that on increasing returns. Marshall's treatment of the subject rested on very thin ice, but nobody liked to mention the point, least of all his pious disciple, Pigou, and Pigou's disciple, Dennis Robertson.

The question, of course, is how a perfectly competitive industry can be subject to conditions of falling costs with rising output. If the individual firms are assumed to have falling costs as the output of each rises, there arises an obvious difficulty of which Marshall was well aware. As he put it:

the ultimate output corresponding to an unconditional demand at even current prices would be theoretically infinite.[3]

Marshall resorted to various devices.

Firstly, the industries in which the firms are subject to rapidly falling costs 'are the very industries in which each firm is likely to be confined more or less to its own particular market'.[4] Second,

1. PIERO SRAFFA, 'Sulle relazioni fra costo e quantità prodotta', *Annali di Economia*, vol. II (1925-1926), pp. 277-328.

2. PIERO SRAFFA, 'The Laws of Returns under Competitive Conditions', *Economic Journal*, December 1926, pp. 535-50.

3. ALFRED MARSHALL, *Principles of Economics*. Eighth Edition. London: Macmillan, 1920, pp. 456-7, and immediately earlier edition.

4. *Ibid.*, p. 458.

Marshall also referred to each management being afraid 'of spoiling his own peculiar market, or incurring odium from other producers for spoiling the common market',[1] by cutting prices at a time of recession. Thirdly, Marshall resorted to the device of what he called the 'trees of the forest'.[2] Having reached its full maturity each tree loses vitality and gives place to others. His point was that it took time for firms to grow and before any firm had reached the minimum on its average cost curve, decline would set in and growth would cease. Marshall did, however, admit that this analogy broke down with 'the great recent development of vast joint-stock companies, which often stagnate, but do not readily die'.[3] In an appendix Marshall admitted that:

The unsatisfactory character of these results is partly due to the imperfections of our analytical methods, and may conceivably be much diminished in a later age by the gradual improvement of our scientific machinery.[4]

All this Sraffa underlined in a completely dispassionate way.

Sraffa explained that when Marshall noticed that he was in a difficulty under conditions of free competition, he covered himself by emphasising the importance of external economies. He did not develop this escape route at all amply but his disciple Pigou made much of it in his *Economics of Welfare*. Sraffa's own comment is as follows:

In essence, the foundations were replaced without the building standing above receiving a single jolt from it all, and it was the great ability of Marshall which allowed the transformation to pass unnoticed. If he had given the originality of the new conception the prominence it deserved, perhaps it would not have been received without opposition. By presenting it as something very well-known and lacking novelty, almost as a commonplace, he was able to have it accepted as a tacit compromise between the necessities of the theory of competition, which are incompatible with the decrease of individual cost,

1. ALFRED MARSHALL, *Principles of Economics*, Eighth Edition, 1920, pp. 458-9.
2. *Ibid.*, pp. 315-16.
3. *Ibid.*, p. 316.
4. *Ibid.*, p. 809.

24

and the necessity not to stray too far from reality that (being far from perfect competition) presents numerous cases of individual decreasing costs of this kind. The fact that the 'external economies' peculiar to an industry, which make possible the desired reconciliation between scientific abstraction and reality, are themselves a purely hypothetical and unreal construction, is something that is often ignored.[1]

The Cambridge Faculty of Economics, which for so many years had been in a state of quiescence, was aroused. When I first took up the subject at the end of 1927, the questions raised by Sraffa were being eagerly discussed by the best students. The occasion was comparable with the effect a few years later of the publication of Keynes' *Treatise on Money*.

Pigou published four editions of the *Economics of Welfare*,[2] which in essence had originally appeared under the title *Wealth and Welfare* in 1912. His first edition was published in 1920, his second in 1924 and his third and fourth in 1929 and 1932. These two last editions show the impact of Sraffa's article and the discussions to which it led. He introduced into an appendix a footnote to the effect that:

Marshall's statements about his 'representative firm' show that this is conceived as an 'equilibrium firm'.[3]

This is, of course, complete nonsense, but Pigou was unaware of that fact and it simply indicated his self-protection mechanism against any loss of faith in his great hero. There was also a profusion of articles in the *Economic Journal*. The most important one was the 'Symposium', to which Sraffa, Robertson and Gerald Shove contributed, on 'Increasing Returns and the Representative Firm'.[4] The article is preceded by a list, prepared by Keynes, the editor, of other articles in the same field. His note ends as follows:

1. PIERO SRAFFA, 'Sulle relazioni fra costo e quantità prodotta', Section III, 'Costi decrescenti', pp. 306-7. I am grateful to Professor Alessandro Roncaglia and Dr John Eatwell for the translation of this passage.
2. ARTHUR C. PIGOU, *The Economics of Welfare*. London: Macmillan, Editions in 1920, 1921 (reprinted), 1924, 1929, 1932.
3. *Ibid.*, 1929, p. 788 note and 1932, p. 790 note.
4. See *Economic Journal*, March 1930, pp. 79-116.

We begin with a partial rehabilitation of Marshallian orthodoxy on conservative lines by D. H. Robertson, proceed with some negative and destructive criticisms by Piero Sraffa, and conclude with constructive suggestions by G. F. Shove.[1]

Economists throughout the world owe to Sraffa's articles and to Sraffa himself the idea that if economics is to become more realistic it is most important to develop the economics of imperfect competition.

Keynes brought Sraffa to Cambridge. It was in Cambridge that he worked on his great edition of the works of Ricardo, and his *Production of Commodities by Means of Commodities*, published in 1960,[2] which is today the subject of so much vigorous discussion.

Mention of his published works completely understates the enormously influential part which he has played in the development of Cambridge economics. To some extent this is attributable to the number of Italian economists who have studied in Cambridge and to the close link between Italian and Cambridge economists. For many years Sraffa was largely responsible himself for bringing Italians to Cambridge.

1. *Economic Journal*, March 1930, p. 79.
2. PIERO SRAFFA, *Production of Commodities by Means of Commodities*. Cambridge: Cambridge University Press, 1960.

SECOND LECTURE
The Quantity Theory of Money

1. *Introduction.* – 2. *The basic logic.* – 3. *Quantity Theory: Locke and Hume.* – 4. *Quantity Theory: John Stuart Mill.* – 5. *Quantity Theory: Alfred Marshall.* – 6. *Quantity Theory: Cambridge versus Yale. Pigou and Irving Fisher.* – 7. *Quantity Theory: Dennis H. Robertson in his 'Money'.* – 8. *Quantity Theory: Keynes in his 'Tract'.* – 9. *Quantity Theory: Keynes in his 'Treatise'.* – 10. *Quantity Theory: Keynes in his 'General Theory'.*

1. Introduction

These lectures opened on the subject of Say's Law. The discussion was concerned with the forces which determine physical output. The determination of the price-level has traditionally been regarded as a subject for a separate department of economics. In that department money played the dominant role.

I do not concern myself with the period of history, which ended only quite recently in advanced countries, in which metallic money if melted down became bullion, so that the value of money in terms of commodities – the reciprocal of the price-level – tended towards the cost in terms of commodities of producing the bullion and its value in use; and, to be more realistic, if the bullion was produced overseas, adjusted for the terms of trade and the rate of exchange with the bullion-producing countries. I will consider only a closed economy in which the quantity of money is determined by the action of the banking system, except in the earlier periods with which I deal.

The algebra will involve the following symbols. It is based on some definite unit of time – say a year. The total volume of transactions which in that unit of time are effected with the use of money is T. M is the total quantity of money and V the weighted average velocity of circulation. P_y is an index representing the weighted average of the prices of the commodities which enter into transactions.

So
$$MV = P_y T$$

The total quantity of money, M, is made up of M_1, that part which circulates actively as a means of exchange, and M_2, that part which is held inactive as a form of wealth – for a variety of reasons which Keynes summarised in his *General Theory* by the terms 'precautionary' and 'speculative' motives.

V_1 is the velocity of circulation of M_1. V_2, the velocity of circulation of M_2, is zero.

V, the *weighted average* velocity of circulation of the total quantity of money, M, is

$$V = \frac{M_1 V_1 + M_2 V_2}{M}$$

or

$$V = \frac{M_1 V_1}{M}$$

This reduces to the truism $MV = M_1 V_1$; both MV and $M_1 V_1$ are equal to the value of transactions in the period of time $P_y T$.

This form of the Quantity Theory is conveniently, though proleptically, known as the Yale equation, in honour of Irving Fisher, though it was used by earlier economists. Hence the price-index P_y. The word 'rapidity' was often used instead of 'velocity'.

The Theory is also presented in the form of the proportion, k, of the value of what Pigou called the 'total resources enjoyed by the community' which the public desire to hold in the form of money. These 'total resources' Pigou denoted by R, so that

$$M = k\, P_c\, R,$$

where P_c is the index number appropriate for valuing 'resources' in terms of consumption-goods. This form of the Quantity Theory is conveniently, though again proleptically, known as the Cambridge equation, in honour of Marshall and Pigou (see Sections 5 and 6). Hence the price-index P_c.

Although the Cambridge identity can be algebraically transformed into the Yale identity (see the following section), the underlying concepts are rather different. Irving Fisher, and his predecessors, thought of money as a means of effecting transactions; Pigou thought of money as a form of holding wealth necessary for effecting the ordinary transactions of life without trouble.

As I shall demonstrate in Sections 5 to 8, there was not complete agreement among the Cambridge economists as to the meaning of 'total resources' R. Indeed, Pigou himself did not make clear his interpretation of R. Marshall was inclined to think of an amalgam of personal income and personal wealth. Keynes followed Marshall.

In Sections 3 and 4, I refer to earlier economists to some of whom is to be attributed the 'Yale' form of the Theory, to some the 'Cambridge' form. Marshall made use of both forms (Section 5).

2. The basic logic

A little should be said about the question of causation in relation to identities.[1]

To use the word 'truism' in the same sense as 'identity' is to commit a solecism. According to the 1926 edition of the Oxford English Dictionary, a truism is 'a self-evident truth especially of slight importance; a statement so obviously true as not to require discussion'. According to the 1976 Supplement to this Dictionary, an identity 'is an element in a set which, if combined with any element by a (specified) binary operation, leaves the latter element unchanged'.

The fact that a relation is rightly described as an identity does not necessarily rule out its depicting a causal process. It depends what question is asked. It is widely agreed that the magnitude of PT cannot be causally attributed directly to the magnitude of MV.

The belief that the magnitude of PT cannot be causally attributed to the magnitude of MV remains valid if M_1 and V_1 are substituted for M and V. But the magnitude of M_1 is causally attributable to the value of transactions, PT, given by the equation $M_1 = \dfrac{PT}{V_1}$. If the total quantity of money is constant the magnitude of the inactive circulation, M_2, is also causally attributable to PT.

To take another example, the identity between the aggregate rate of investment, I, and the aggregate rate of saving, S, is not the basis of a definition. I and S are defined quite independently.

When there is complete freedom from supply constraints (both by plant and by labour), an attempted higher rate of saving does not result in a higher rate of aggregate saving. In so far as the saving of some is at a higher rate, that of others is lower to a compensatory degree. It does result in a lower rate of con-

---

1. I am grateful for help on this issue to my colleague, Dr Ross Harrison, one of our University philosophers.

sumption. That result is a case of cause and effect. Still more so, if the lower rate of consumption – lower incomes and profits, and more surplus capacity – causes a lower rate of investment.

A higher rate of aggregate investment results in a higher rate of aggregate saving. If it is the case that, at fairly high levels of capacity utilisation, prices measured in wage-units are higher, the higher rate of saving would be caused, not only by higher output, but also by some redistribution of income from wage-earners to capitalists – the former save a lower proportion of their incomes than the latter.

Or take a movement through time from a lower to a higher rate of investment. At each moment of time aggregate saving and aggregate investment are equal. But which classes in the economy, at each moment, are doing the additional saving involves the difficulties of sequence analysis, which is clearly an investigation into a process of causation.

The Cambridge equation expresses the real value of the stock of money which, in a particular situation, it is desired, in the aggregate, to hold as an alternative to other forms of wealth. The word 'wealth' has the advantage of having a fairly definite meaning (though some of it needs specification), and is preferable to vague phrases such as Pigou's 'total resources that are enjoyed by the community'.

Whatever the term, it is usually denoted by R. k is the proportion of R that is held in money, measured in real terms, as a form of wealth as opposed to serving as a vehicle for transactions.

The composition of the commodities, the transactions in which are the subject of the Yale equation, is quite different from that of the commodities which constitute wealth. It is clear what system of index numbers should be used to arrive at the average price-level which enters into the Yale equation.

It is impossible in the Cambridge equation. If the system of index numbers is that required to arrive at the average price-level of the constituents of wealth, it means that the sacrifice involved in holding money rather than other forms of wealth is conceived as taking the form of an average slice of the national wealth. This is absurd.

That difficulty is not one with which I intend to be concerned. Brushing it ruthlessly on one side, I conceive of two price-levels, P_c and P_y, relevant to the Cambridge and Yale concepts. It is astonishing how few writers on the Quantity Theory appreciate the index-number problem on this simple level, and how small the number who have considered the abstruse index-number problem which the Cambridge concept raises and which I am ignoring.

Irving Fisher[1] included a number of interesting appendices on the index-number problem, but he did not discuss the Cambridge concept as an alternative to his.

We then have

$$M = k\,P_c\,R \quad \text{(Cambridge)}$$

or

$$\frac{M}{k} = P_c\,R$$

$$MV = P_y\,T \quad \text{(Yale)}$$

Hence

$$kV = \frac{T}{R}\,\frac{P_y}{P_c}$$

The fact that it is logically impossible, because of the index-number problem, to calculate precise and unique measures of T, R, P_y and P_c, does not prevent $k\,P_c\,R$ and $\dfrac{P_y T}{V}$ from being definite quantities of money. The explanation is that there is an appropriate affinity between the form of the index-number problem in the measurement of P_y and of T, and equally of P_c and of R.

I come now to the essence of my line of thought. I put forward a causal relation between M_2 and the prices of certain forms of wealth. This relation bears some family resemblance to the Cambridge form of the Theory. And it supports the view of

1. See Section 6 below.

those who claim that the Cambridge form, properly presented, points to the causative influence on prices of the quantity of money – or rather of M_2 – unlike the Yale form.

But the prices on which I claim a causative influence of M_2 are of a very narrow range of forms of wealth. What I am putting forward is not a form of the Quantity Theory, in any sensible use of the phrase. It is a version of Keynes' Liquidity Preference Theory of the determination of the rate of interest. But it is more generalised than the version put forward in his *General Theory* (1936) and carries the seed of modern portfolio analysis. In the *General Theory* Keynes confined himself to the choice between holding money, in inactive form, M_2, and holding fixed-interest securities. It is easy to widen the concept so as to bring in equities, as in effect Keynes had done in his *Treatise on Money* (1930).

There are also certain other assets which are close substitutes for money. Their prices are, to varying degrees, related to the quantity of M_2. These assets are confined in character to a very narrow range: fixed-interest securities, equities, a very small number of commodities – particularly those quoted on organised produce markets – dwellings, rare works of art.

But the prices of constituents of wealth as a whole are related to the quantity of M_2 to a negligible extent.

This is my reason for maintaining that the only sense in which the so-called Quantity Theory can be given a causal interpretation is not really a Quantity Theory at all but an exercise in portfolio analysis.

There is a simple method of elucidating the relationship between M_2 and the prices of those forms of wealth which, being liquid, are potential substitutes for money. As a basis of comparison it is necessary only – with a constant total quantity of money, M – to compare two different levels of output, entailing different values of PT and therefore of M_1, and therefore of M_2.

With the lower level of output M_1 is lower and M_2 higher than with the higher level of output. In the latter case compared with the former, some holders of money do not need it as a form of exchange and hold it as a form of liquidity. If the prices of substitute forms of wealth were not sufficiently higher, the holders of this inactive money would want to convert some of it into other forms of wealth. It is the case – so familiar on the Stock Exchange – of prices having to be adjusted to the level of demand to the extent required to prevent any transaction from taking place.

To put the issue in a slightly different light, for this higher amount of M_2 there has to be a demand. The demand is provided by appropriately higher prices of those forms of wealth which are substitutes for money. These prices have to be just sufficiently higher as to result in the necessary higher demand for M_2.

In the following sections, which deal with the attitude towards the Quantity Theory of a few economists, I shall take it as read that the Yale equation is a truism, and the Cambridge equation a delusion.

Before I proceed further, there are a few points to be mentioned.

1. In Section 5 on Marshall, I shall refer to a number of passages in which Marshall related the amount of money held not only to wealth but to income as well. This seems perfectly logical. The smaller a man's income the less is he induced to hold money rather than income-earning assets.

In his *Tract*, the only actual quotation from Marshall made by Keynes – the great interpreter of Marshall – is one in which Marshall related the holding of money to *income* as well as to *property*.

2. Keynes, in his Obituary of Marshall,[1] relied largely on an unpublished draft, written in about 1871,[2] on which I elaborate in Section 5. Although, in this early work, Marshall drew no distinction between 'active' and 'inactive' money – to use adjectives introduced by Keynes much later, Keynes much preferred it to *Money, Credit and Commerce*, published in Marshall's very old age.

In this draft, money was regarded as homogeneous. Instead of

1. Reprinted in KEYNES, vol. x, pp. 161-231.
2. See note 2 on page 42. The draft has been published in JOHN K. WHITAKER, *The Early Economic Writings of Alfred Marshall, 1867-1870*. London: Royal Economic Society, 1975, vol. 1, pp. 164-77.

separating 'hoards' from money in active circulation, Marshall
relied on the average interval between receipts and payments
to determine the average velocity of circulation, and the influence on it of an average person's desire to hold a certain proportion of his wealth in the form of money. The point emerges
only in an Addendum to this 1871 draft, from which the following
is a quotation (not quoted by Keynes in his Obituary):

> Suppose a man's money income comes in at times beyond his own
> control say half yearly. Then if he chooses to have but little cash
> about him he must defer satisfying his wants as far as possible till
> Xmas and midsummer.
>
> He may indeed meanwhile 'buy on credit': but that is not properly
> buying. He pays interest (practically at a high rate: but this is not of
> the essence). The main point is that he has not the advantage that the
> possession of cash gives of buying exactly what he wants.[1]

Although logically the contention is a sound one, young Marshall would have made it easier to accept by assuming weekly
rather than half-yearly wage payments.

3. Thirdly, a point of importance. The distinction between
'active' and 'inactive' holdings of money is usually to-day a
purely notional one, devised for the sake of convenience, at any
rate in Britain. Nowadays the distinction between *current* and
deposit accounts does not have a one-one relationship with the
distinction between *active* and *inactive* deposits. Apart from the
deposit rate of interest paid on deposit accounts, bank charges
depend on the average balance held on current account and the
degree of activity of the account.

Of course, inactive balances are often held in the form of three-
month Treasury Bills, with finance companies, local authorities
and the like. But once the 'word' money ceases to have the precise meaning of currency and deposits with the banks, the Quantity Theory is deprived of its foundation.

In the extreme case there is no difference of character between
one currency note or bank deposit and another. There is no
need to adopt young Marshall's device of altering the interval
between receipts and payments in response to a desire to be

---

1. *Ibid.*, p. 176.

logical. All it means is, in the formal and meaningless language of the crude Quantity Theory, that, if the total quantity of money remains constant, the weighted average velocity of circulation, V, changes.

For the purposes of exposition, clarity is provided by assuming two different stocks of money, 'active' and 'inactive'. But the same results are achieved by going to the opposite extreme.

3. Quantity Theory: Locke and Hume

There are a few passages in John Locke's Chapter on *Money* which sound remarkably modern (though most do not). For example:

> ready Money must be constantly exchang'd for Wares and Labour, or follow within a short time after.

> This shows the necessity of some *Proportion of Money* to Trade; but what that Proportion is, is hard to determine, because it depends not barely on the quantity of Money, but the quickness of Circulation.[1]

'Locke explains', wrote Keynes, 'that money has two values: 1) its value in use which is given by the rate of interest "and in this it has the Nature of Land" [. . .] and 2) its value in exchange "and in this it has the Nature of a Commodity" [. . .] But [. . .] he was confused.'[2]

Professor Arthur H. Leigh takes the view that 'Keynes overstates the extent to which Locke anticipated his own ideas on interest, money, and employment and underrates the quality of Locke's theoretical system.'[3] Locke's 'theory of money's value in exchange contains all of the elements of Fisher's equation of exchange [. . .] To interpret his theory of the demand for money the "Cambridge" equation is also useful.'[4]

David Hume, sixty years later, was not really a quantity theorist at all. In his treatment there is a causal factor. It is an increasing stock of money, which, so long as the increase continues, raises the level of demand.

> 'tis only in this interval [. . .] betwixt the acquisition of money and rise of prices, that the encreasing quantity of gold and silver is favourable to industry [. . .]

1. JOHN LOCKE, *Some Considerations of the Consequences of the Lowering of Interest and Raising the Value of Money*. London: Printed for Awnsham and John Churchill, 1692, p. 32.

2. KEYNES, vol. VII, p. 343.

3. ARTHUR H. LEIGH, 'John Locke and the Quantity Theory of Money', *History of Political Economy*, Summer 1974, pp. 200-19 (the quotation on p. 217).

4. *Ibid.*, p. 202.

'tis of no manner of consequence, with regard to the domestic happiness of a state, whether money be in a greater or less quantity. The good policy of the magistrate consists only in keeping it, if possible, still encreasing; because, by that means, he keeps a spirit of industry alive in the nation [. . .]

It seems a maxim almost self-evident, that the prices of every thing depend on the proportion betwixt commodities and money [. . .]

'Tis also evident, that the prices do not so much depend on the absolute quantity of commodities and that of money [. . .] as on that of the commodities, which come or may come to market, and of the money which circulates. If the coin be lockt up in chests, 'tis the same thing with regard to prices, as if it were annihilated: If the commodities be hoarded in granaries, a like effect follows [. . .] 'Tis only the overplus, compar'd to the demand, that determines the value.[1]

Somewhat obscure. But well ahead of Hume's time.

Far from being the originator of the Quantity Theory, Hume believed that prices were determined by the forces of supply and demand.

---

1. DAVID HUME, 'Of Money', in *Political Discourses*. Edinburgh: R. Fleming, 1752; reprinted in ALAN A. WALTERS (ed.), *Money and Banking. Selected Readings*. Harmondsworth: Penguin Books, 1973, pp. 28-32. See KEYNES, vol. VII, p. 343, note 3.

4. Quantity Theory: John Stuart Mill

In its modern form, the Quantity Theory was attributed by Marshall to John Stuart Mill. Schumpeter endorses John Stuart Mill's claim to be the first strict quantity theorist in the modern sense, but considers that of his father, James, as almost as strong; the claims of Ricardo and McCulloch fail on account of their occasional deviations from the doctrine of a *strict* inverse proportionality between the quantity of money and its value.[1]

The following passage from John Stuart Mill's *Political Economy* expands the doctrine as he saw it:

the value of money [. . .] varies inversely as its quantity; every increase of quantity lowering the value, and every diminution raising it, in a ratio exactly equivalent. [. . .]

If we assume the quantity of goods on sale, and the number of times those goods are resold, to be fixed quantities the value of money will depend upon its quantity, together with the average number of times that each piece changes hands in the process. The whole of the goods sold (counting each resale of the same goods as so much added to the goods) have been exchanged for the whole of the money, multiplied by the number of purchases made on the average by each piece. Consequently, the amount of goods and of transactions being the same, the value of money is inversely as its quantity multiplied by what is called the rapidity of circulation. And the quantity of money in circulation, is equal to the money value of all the goods sold, divided by the number which expresses the rapidity of circulation.[2]

Mill was somewhat perplexed about the concept of the rapidity of circulation (nowadays called velocity).

It is habitually assumed that whenever there is a greater amount of money in the country, or in existence, a rise of prices must necessarily follow. But this is by no means an inevitable consequence. In no commodity is it the quantity in existence, but the quantity offered

1. Joseph A. Schumpeter, *History of Economic Analysis*. New York: Oxford University Press; London: George Allen and Unwin, 1954, pp. 703-4.
2. John Stuart Mill, *Principles of Political Economy*. Second Edition. London: John W. Parker, 1849, vol. II, Book III, Chapter VIII, Sections 2 and 3, pp. 16-18.

for sale, that determines the value. Whatever may be the quantity of money in the country, only that part of it will affect prices, which goes into the market of commodities, and is there actually exchanged against goods. Whatever increases the amount of this portion of the money in the country tends to raise prices. But money hoarded does not act on prices. Money kept in reserve by individuals [. . .] to meet contingencies which do not occur, does not act on prices.[1]

In taking the view that the quantity of money that influences prices is not the same thing as the quantity in existence, Mill followed the line set out in Section 1 above.

Marshall, quite unreasonably, as will be seen in the following Section, regarded the concept of 'rapidity of circulation' as a weakness in Mill's system and found an escape from it. But this did not prevent him on occasion from using the concept himself.

1. JOHN STUART MILL, *Principles of Political Economy*, vol. II, Book III, Chapter VIII, Section 4, p. 20.

5. Quantity Theory: Alfred Marshall

Marshall's treatment of the Quantity Theory is best examined through the eyes of Keynes, his obituarist, partly because of the light thrown by the Obituary on Keynes' own early views. At the time at which it was written, he was a pious follower of Marshall.

As I shall show in Section 8, Keynes was then a fanatical believer in the Quantity Theory, in the full causal sense of the determination of the price-level by the quantity of money. In the Obituary Keynes expressed regret that Marshall did not publish his book on *Money* until extreme old age, when time had deprived his ideas of freshness and his exposition of sting and strength.

He wrote:

his main ideas became known to pupils in a general way, with the result that there grew up at Cambridge an oral tradition, first from Marshall's own lectures and after his retirement [in 1908] from those of Professor Pigou, different from, and (I think it may be claimed) superior to, anything that could be found in printed books until recently.[1]

In this old age, Marshall was cautious and ambivalent. To the following crucial passage Keynes made no reference:

This notion that the amount of ready purchasing power, required by the population of a country at any time, is a definite quantity, in any given state of her industry and trade, is implied, even when not explicitly stated, in the now familiar doctrine that the value of a unit of a currency varies, other things being equal, inversely with the number of the units and their average rapidity of circulation.

This 'Quantity doctrine' is helpful as far as it goes: but it does not indicate what are the 'other things' which must be assumed to be

1. The Memoir of Alfred Marshall by John Maynard Keynes was published in: *Economic Journal* ('Alfred Marshall, 1842-1924'), September 1924, pp. 311-72; in ARTHUR C. PIGOU, *Memorials of Alfred Marshall* ('Alfred Marshall, 1842-1924'), London: Macmillan, 1925, pp. 1-65; and also in *Essays in Biography* ('Alfred Marshall'), London: Macmillan, 1933, pp. 150-266. The *Economic Journal* version and the *Essays in Biography* version are identical; the latter preferred by Keynes himself and reprinted in KEYNES, vol. x, pp. 161-231, is referred to in these Lectures.

equal in order to justify the proposition: and it does not explain the causes which govern 'rapidity of circulation'.

It is almost a truism: for, if one column of a ledger recorded accurately all the transactions for money in a year with their values; while another column specified the number of the units of money employed in each transaction; then the two columns when added up would balance. The second column would of course represent the aggregate value of the total number of changes of ownership of all the units of money: and that is the same thing in other words as the total value of the money multiplied by the average changes of ownership (otherwise than by free gift, theft, etc.) of each unit.

The other things, that must remain equal for the purposes of this statement, include (a) the population; (b) the amount of business transacted per head of the population; (c) the percentage of that business which is effected directly by money; and (d) the efficiency (or average rapidity of circulation) of money. Only if these conditions are reckoned in, can the doctrine come under investigation: and if they are reckoned in the doctrine is almost a truism.[1]

The words 'almost a truism' Keynes must have attributed to senility. But Keynes was delighted to discover among Marshall's papers a manuscript – about 23 octavo pages long – in Marshall's handwriting entitled *Theory of Money, mss about 1871* – written when Marshall was only about 29 years old.[2] In it Keynes found 'the whole of the substance of Book I, Chapter IV [the relevant chapter] of his *Money, Credit and Commerce* [. . .] worked out with fair completeness and with much greater strength of exposition and illustration than he could manage fifty years later'.[3]

Keynes emphasised Marshall's exposition of the Quantity Theory of Money as a part of the General Theory of Value . . . 'He went on to explain how each individual decides how much to keep in a ready form as the result of a *balance* of advantage

1. ALFRED MARSHALL, *Money, Credit and Commerce*. London: Macmillan, 1923, p. 48.
2. Deposited in the Marshall Library, Faculty of Economics, University of Cambridge, England, in an envelope posted to Marshall on 7 April 1922. Published in JOHN K. WHITAKER, *The Early Economic Writings of Alfred Marshall, 1867-1870*. London: Royal Economic Society, 1975, vol. I, pp. 164-77.
3. KEYNES, vol. X, p. 190.

between this and alternative forms of wealth. "The exchange value of the whole amount of coin in the Kingdom [he wrote in the manuscript of 1871 mentioned above] is just equal to that of the whole amount of the commodities over which the members of the community have decided to keep a command in this ready form".'[1]

The point is made even more clearly in a passage from the 1871 draft that Keynes did not quote:

> when we come to the theory of money we are told that its value depends upon its amount together with the rapidity of circulation, and although from this account we should naturally be led to infer the presence of some other regulating conditions – although, on reading an exposition of the theory *in extenso* as it is given for instance in Mill, we find these conditions distinctly enunciated – we do not find a clear statement of that balancing of advantages which in the ultimate analysis must be found to determine the magnitude of every quantity which rests upon the will of man. If we seek for this we shall find that 'the rapidity of circulation' is not the most convenient thing to be made the basis of our investigations.[2]

Marshall used both the Cambridge and the Yale concepts. In his Obituary Keynes displayed an unqualified preference for the Cambridge concept. One of his objections to the exposition written in Marshall's dotage must have been that it was not confined to the 'Cambridge concept', but that towards the end it drifted without explanation into the 'Yale concept', involving use of the term 'rapidity of circulation'.

1. *Ibid.*, p. 191.
2. JOHN K. WHITAKER, *The Early Economic Writings of Alfred Marshall, 1867-1870*, p. 166.

6. Quantity Theory: Cambridge versus Yale. Arthur C. Pigou and Irving Fisher

The 'Cambridge' and 'Yale' concepts have been considered in the course of Section 1. This section is largely confined to consideration specifically of Pigou's and of Irving Fisher's treatment.

I have shown that Marshall (and, of course, many other economists) made use both of the Cambridge and of the Yale concepts, interchangeably, although they are derived from quite different processes of thought.

Both Marshall and Fisher allowed for hoarding, to use a new word with the same meaning as inactive balances. On the Yale concept money 'hoarded' offers no difficulty. It is that part of the total stock of money which is not used in the course of day-to-day transactions: it does not circulate (except at an infinitesimal rate) – to use Mill's words, it is 'kept in reserve for contingencies'.

In Marshall, the idea of hoarding offered a slight difficulty. This did not arise so long as Marshall operated on the Yale concept. But on the more typically Marshallian Cambridge concept, a distinction has to be drawn between the amount of his wealth which an individual decides to keep in a ready form 'to be spent as occasion may require' and the amount which he holds in ready form as a reserve. As Marshall in effect wrote, the distinction 'does not matter' on the Cambridge concept, but it does matter if the exposition is transferred to the Yale concept.

It is unnecessary to repeat the algebra of Section 1. But a brief summary in verbal form may be useful.

Fisher[1] is concerned with the flow of transactions, say per annum, involving expenditure on commodities, including capital goods; transactions in payment of wages and for other services are excluded.

The Cambridge equation is concerned with the wealth of the community in real terms. Pigou referred to it as 'total resources

1. IRVING FISHER, *The Purchasing Power of Money*. New York: The Macmillan Company, 1911.

[...] that are enjoyed by the community'[1]. It seems right to confine this to commercial wealth, as opposed to such things as churches and museums. But, clearly, valuable pictures should be included if held by individuals as opposed to museums. Possibly State-owned property, including roads, should be excluded. The real value of inactive money is weighed up against other forms of wealth. Although this was not made clear, it is M_2 that is relevant.

Though the two concepts are quite different, the equations can be algebraically translated into each other, as I showed in Section 1. But this is largely ignored even by Keynes, who in 1909 won the Adam Smith Prize with an Essay on Index Numbers.

The possibility of algebraic transformation set out in Section 2 does not mean that there is not a fundamental difference between the Cambridge and Yale concepts. That was not Keynes' view put forward in his *Tract*. 'It comes to the same thing in the end and it is easy to pass from the above formula to Professor Fisher's.'[2] In his Obituary of Marshall, Keynes described Fisher's ideas, published in book-form before Marshall's, as 'analogous to those which had been worked out by Marshall at much earlier dates'.[3]

Meanwhile I content myself with a few references which bear on this point to Pigou's 1917 article. Fisher had stated in his Preface that 'The purpose of [his] book is to set forth the principles determining the purchasing power of money'.[4]

Pigou purported not to be an '"opponent" of the "quantity theory" or a hostile critic of Professor Fisher's lucid analysis [...] All ways are merely devices for facilitating an orderly arrangement of ideas.' There is no 'fundamental disagreement [between us] about the real causes at work'.[5]

Then Pigou ventured cautiously out into the open.

1. ARTHUR C. PIGOU, 'The Value of Money', *Quarterly Journal of Economics*, November 1917, p. 42.
2. KEYNES, vol. IV, p. 63, note.
3. KEYNES, vol. X, p. 189, note 2.
4. IRVING FISHER, *The Purchasing Power of Money*, p. vii.
5. ARTHUR C. PIGOU, 'The Value of Money', p. 39.

the machinery that I shall suggest in the following pages is quite different from that elaborated by Professor Irving Fisher in his admirable *Purchasing Power of Money*, and, as I think, more convenient. I am not in any sense an 'opponent' of the 'quantity theory' or a hostile critic of Professor Fisher's lucid analysis.[1]

Pigou claimed for the Cambridge concept a 'real advantage, because it brings us at once into relation with volition – an ultimate cause of demand'.[2]

In conclusion, Pigou – with apparent modesty – suggested that 'less experienced craftsmen [than Professor Fisher] need, I think, a better – and more completely fool-proof tool'.[3]

My own interpretation is that Pigou attributed causal significance to the Cambridge, but not to the Yale, concept. But he was too polite to come into the open.

1. ARTHUR C. PIGOU, 'The Value of Money', p. 39.
2. *Ibid.*, p. 54.
3. *Ibid.*, p. 65.

7. Quantity Theory: Dennis H. Robertson in his 'Money'

Dennis Robertson's exposition of the Quantity Theory was more critical in the first (1922) edition and more complete in the 1928 and 1948 editions.[1]

In the 1922 edition but not in the later editions he wrote:

This tedious truism has sometimes, under the name of the 'quantity theory of money', been on the one hand elevated to the rank of a great discovery, and on the other hand denounced as a pernicious falsehood.[2]

And:

what interest does this bare stump of a quantity theory possess for us?[3]

Part, but only part, of Robertson's answer was that

long generations of controversy leave the modern writer little choice in the matter [. . .] No longer either a triumphant *Credo* or a pestilent heresy, the 'quantity theory of money' remains as a dowdy but serviceable platitude.[4]

I now turn to the 1928 and 1948 editions of Robertson's *Money*. These editions were clearly influenced by Keynes' *Tract*, published in 1923. The more critical attitude of the relatively young Robertson gave way to the more conservative attitude of the relatively less young Keynes. It was only over the writing of Keynes' *General Theory* that the positions were to be reversed.

And in the actual presentation of versions of the Quantity Theory Robertson was influenced by Keynes' *Tract*. This will become clear only when, in Section 8, I come on to Keynes' *Tract*.

In the 1928 and 1948 editions Robertson abandoned the

1. DENNIS H. ROBERTSON, *Money*. London: Nisbet & Co.; Cambridge: Cambridge University Press First published 1922; Second Edition (revised and reset), 1928; revised with additional chapters, 1948.
2. *Ibid.*, 1922, p. 32.
3. *Ibid.*, p. 34.
4. *Ibid.*

sceptical passages. He began by presenting the Yale concept in Fisher's form − in terms of the rate of transactions, arriving at the 'transaction-value' of money.

But he then proceeded to a meaningless form of the Yale concept, defining an 'income-velocity of circulation' as 'the average number of times [each piece of money] is spent in purchase of the goods and services which enter into ordinary consumption, during the week or other period of time', arriving at an 'income-value of money'.[1]

Robertson then turned to the Cambridge concept. But he had completely forgotten Marshall. He expressed the real value of the supply of money as a proportion of real national income. In dealing with Marshall in Section 5, I referred to one passage in which real income is brought in *as well as wealth*. Robertson did not allow for any influence of *wealth* on the demand for money. In his Obituary of Marshall, Keynes − I repeat − had explained Marshall's concept of 'a balance of advantage between [the holding of money] and alternative forms of wealth'. This part of the Obituary (published in September 1924) was presumably written after the completion of the *Tract*, but before the publication of the later editions of Robertson's *Money*. As an alternative to 'a proportion of real national income', Robertson suggested 'a proportion of *annual real turnover*', so as to secure symmetry between his exposition of the Yale and Cambridge concepts.

Robertson also, in the later editions, repeated Keynes' error (mentioned in the following section) of regarding 'increased consumption' as one of the alternatives to holding money.

The 1928 edition was revised in the period in which Robertson was helping Keynes with his *Treatise*. Reverting to the view emphasised in his pre-War *A Study of Industrial Fluctuation* he wrote that:

Money is after all a subject of secondary importance, in the sense that neither the most revolutionary nor the 'soundest' monetary policy can be expected to provide a remedy for those strains and dishar-

---

1. DENNIS H. ROBERTSON, *Money*. Second Edition 1928, p. 34. On p. 33 of the 1948 Edition the wording is slightly different.

monies whose roots lie deep in the present structure of industry, and perhaps in the very nature of man himself.[1]

The following passage from the later editions suggest that Robertson, as in his pre-War book, rather than Keynes, was the pioneering spirit.

Broadly speaking, the sitting money exercise is the more useful for enabling us to understand the underlying psychological forces determining the value of money; while the money on the wing exercise is the more useful for equipping us to watch with understanding the actual processes by which in real life the prices of goods and services change – for reminding us that the quantity of money and the quantity of goods do not affect the price-level by some kind of occult planetary influence, but by modifying the capacity or willingness of human beings to buy or refrain from buying, to sell or refrain from selling.[2]

1. *Ibid.*, Preface to 1928 Edition, p. viii, repeated in 1948 Edition, p. xii.
2. *Ibid.*, 1928, p. 39; and 1948 Edition, pp. 38-9.

8. Quantity Theory: Keynes in his 'Tract'

Keynes had no systematic education in economics. He took his degree in Mathematics, wrote his College Fellowship Dissertation on Probability, and was closely associated with the Cambridge philosophers who thrived in his youth – William E. Johnson (who did lecture also on economics), G. E. Moore and Bertrand Russell (and, a little later on, Ludwig Wittgenstein). However, as Roy Harrod put it, Keynes was 'absorbing Economics through every pore' while living with his parents in Cambridge.[1] Marshall was a family friend who won Keynes over to the study of economics. Economics was one of the papers which he took in the Civil Service Examination in 1906. For the next two years he was a civil servant in the Indian Office. In 1913 he was appointed a member of the Royal Commission on *Indian Finance and Currency*. Keynes played the major part in drafting an Annex on setting up a State bank. Marshall was much impressed by it. Keynes published his *Indian Currency and Finance* in 1913.[2] Harrod wrote:

Keynes [. . .] had imbibed in his early youth the late Victorian respect for first principles [. . .] He was a currency expert, believing in the importance of the currency question.[3]

In 1909 Keynes had begun to lecture in Cambridge on Money, Credit and Prices. To quote Harrod:

He at once made a great impression. He was evidently a theorist; he expounded Marshallian monetary doctrine, which still had not much publicity outside the Cambridge classrooms. He was evidently also a realist.[4]

Keynes was 40 years old when he published his *Tract on Monetary Reform* in 1923.[5] He was going to spend a considerable

---

1. Roy F. Harrod, *The Life of John Maynard Keynes*. London: Macmillan, 1951, p. 121, note 1.
2. Keynes, vol. i.
3. Roy F. Harrod, *The Life of John Maynard Keynes*, p. 163.
4. *Ibid.*, p. 145.
5. Keynes, vol. iv.

part of the next twelve years of his life in a struggle to escape from the stranglehold of the Quantity Theory – success being heralded by the publication at the beginning of 1936 of his *General Theory*, the *Treatise on Money* representing an intermediate phase.

The Preface to the *Tract* opens in promising style:

We leave saving to the private investor, and we encourage him to place his savings mainly in titles to money. We leave the responsibility for setting production in motion to the business man, who is mainly influenced by the profits which he expects to accrue to himself in terms of money.[1]

It sounds as though Keynes had been influenced by the passage in the original Preface to Robertson's pre-War book, in which Robertson remarked that the first few months of the War compelled 'clear thinking on the real nature of saving and investment'.[2] But, alas, no, he had not as yet. Keynes' Preface continues with some complacency:

Those who are not in favour of drastic changes in the existing organisation of society believe that these arrangements, being in accord with human nature, have great advantages. But they cannot work properly if the money, which they assume as a stable measuring-rod, is undependable. Unemployment, the precarious life of the worker, the disappointment of expectation, the sudden loss of savings, the excessive windfalls to individuals, the speculator, the profiteer – all proceed, in large measure, from the instability of the standard of value.[3]

The book was inspired by the importance of securing stability of the price-level, as a result of paying more heed to the lesson indicated by the Quantity Theory.

According to Keynes, writing in 1919 in his *Economic Consequences of the Peace*:[4]

Lenin is said to have declared that the best way to destroy the capi-

---

1. *Ibid.*, p. xiv.
2. DENNIS H. ROBERTSON, *A Study of Industrial Fluctuation*. London: P. S. King & Son, 1915, p. xx.
3. KEYNES, vol. IV, p. xiv.
4. KEYNES, vol. II, pp. 148-9.

talist system was to debauch the currency. [. . .] Lenin was certainly right.[1]

Keynes – until recently a Treasury civil servant – was writing under the shadow of the post-War hyper-inflations. In fact the German mark was not stabilised until after he had finished the book (by that remarkable confidence trick – the introduction in November 1923 of the Rentenmark, backed by German land). Keynes regarded the excessive issue of bank notes in Germany (and other countries) as mainly a form of taxation.

It is curious that the author of the *Economic Consequences of the Peace* did not refer to the sudden fall in the exchange-value of the mark in the second half of 1921, caused by the commencement of cash payments of reparations.[2]

(My own prejudice against the Quantity Theory dates from August 1923, when I was just 18 years old. My family was taking its summer holiday at a resort on the Baltic Sea. Towards the end of the month the German banknote printers went on strike. The banks severely rationed their customers. At my father's request I spent three hours every morning standing in a queue outside a bank, only to draw a sum in notes entirely inadequate to the family's needs. But the strike did not put any curb on the regular doubling of prices every 24 hours.)

I admit to prejudice against the Quantity Theory of Money but it does seem to me to have seriously impeded the development of monetary thought – with extremely serious consequences in the case of Keynes.

1. Professor Frank Fetter, in an interesting article, has made it clear that there is no evidence that Lenin did make such a statement, although it is quite plausible. See FRANK WHITSON FETTER, 'Lenin, Keynes and Inflation', *Economica*, February 1977, pp. 77-80.

2. Bresciani-Turroni did not accept this view, though he agreed that the initial shock was due to the heavy fall in the exchange-value of the mark. See COSTANTINO BRESCIANI-TURRONI, *The Economics of Inflation*. London: George Allen & Unvin [the Italian original *Le vicende del marco tedesco*. Milano: Università Bocconi Editrice. First Edition, 1931]. English Edition, 1937, substantially revised by the author, with a Foreword by Lionel Robbins. Reviewed by JOAN ROBINSON, 'The Economics of Inflation', *Economic Journal*, September 1938, pp. 507-13; reprinted in an enlarged version in 'The Economics of Hyper-Inflation', *Collected Economic Papers*. Oxford: Basil Blackwell, 1951, vol. 1, pp. 69-77.

The gradual change in Keynes' attitude towards the Quantity Theory of Money illustrates the development of his thought. In his *Tract*, he stated

My exposition follows the general lines of Professor Pigou [. . .] and of Dr Marshall [. . .], rather than the perhaps more familiar analysis of Professor Irving Fisher. [. . .] It comes to the same thing in the end and it is easy to pass from the above formula to Professor Fisher's; but the above method of approach seems less artificial than Professor Fisher's and nearer to the observed facts.[1]

Keynes showed himself in his *Tract on Monetary Reform* as a fanatical believer in the Quantity Theory, in the full causal sense of the determination of the price-level by the quantity of money.

In the *Tract*, Keynes is at one point as orthodox on the subject of the Quantity Theory as any earlier economist, and more orthodox than many. He was far more strictly monetarist than Marshall and Pigou.

The Quantity Theory, he wrote, was 'fundamental. Its correspondence with fact is not open to question.'[2] He quoted a saying of Goschen, of sixty years earlier – it could with much more justification be related to-day – that 'there are many persons who cannot hear the relation of the level of prices to the volume of currency affirmed without a feeling akin to irritation'.[3] Keynes in 1923 shared Goschen's contempt for such Philistines.

He chose the Cambridge concept, but he measured wealth in terms of consumption-goods so long as he was using his own words. (He made a slip by regarding *spending* as an alternative to holding money.)

Although he followed Marshall closely, when it came to using Marshall's words he quoted only the passage to which I have referred in which Marshall related the holding of money to *income* as well as to *property*.

It will simplify exposition to think in terms only of bank deposits (though Keynes complicates it by bringing in bank notes

---

1. KEYNES, vol. IV, p. 63, note 1.
2. *Ibid.*, p. 61.
3. *Ibid.*

53

held by the public and bank notes which form part of the reserves of the banks). His Quantity Theory would then be written:

$$M = Pk$$

where M is the quantity of bank deposits held by the public, P is the cost of living index and k is the number of consumption-units which the public require to hold as money.

Four pages after his statement that the 'theory is fundamental', Keynes denied the validity of the Quantity Theory, in the form in which it is normally presented, except *in the long run*, in which 'we are all dead'.[1] A change in the quantity of money, in a period shorter than that long run, may itself be the cause of a change in k.

It is often thought that Keynes, no sooner having nailed his flag to the Quantity Theory mast, hauled it down, presenting the usual simple exposition why, regarded as a statement of causation, the Theory is bogus.

Keynes was not thinking on these lines at all. (Even in the *Treatise on Money*, published in 1930, although savings deposits played an important role, the exposition of the consequences 'of a changed supply of money' did not result in the dethronement of the Quantity Theory.)[2]

The considerations that Keynes had in mind were simply these:

1) Policy over the relative size of the reserves of the banks varies from time to time.

2) In agricultural countries

where peasants readily hoard money, an inflation, especially in its early stages, does not raise prices proportionately, because when [. . .] more money flows into the pockets of the peasants, it tends to stick there; deeming themselves that much richer, the peasants increase the proportion of their receipts that they hoard.[3]

Keynes concluded this section of the *Tract* by pointing out to

1. KEYNES, vol. IV, p. 65.
2. KEYNES, vol. V, pp. 235-38.
3. KEYNES, vol. IV, p. 66.

'the reader what a long way we may be led by an understanding of the implications of the simple quantity equation with which we started'.[1]

To the reader of the *General Theory*, the Preface to the *Tract* ends on a curious note:

Nowhere do conservative notions consider themselves more in place than in currency; yet nowhere is the need of innovation more urgent. One is often warned that a scientific treatment of currency questions is impossible because the banking world is intellectually incapable of understanding its own problems. If this is true, the order of society, which they stand for, will decay. But I do not believe it. What we have lacked is a clear analysis of the real facts, rather than ability to understand an analysis already given.[2]

Keynes concluded:

If the new ideas, now developing in many quarters, are sound and right, I do not doubt that sooner or later they will prevail. I dedicate this book, humbly and without permission, to the Governors and Court of the Bank of England, who now and for the future have a much more difficult and anxious task entrusted to them than in former days.[3]

1. *Ibid.*, pp. 69-70.
2. *Ibid.*, pp. xiv-xv.
3. *Ibid.*, p. xv.

9. Quantity Theory: Keynes in his 'Treatise'

In the early drafts of the *Treatise on Money*, the Quantity Theory of Money continued for a time to dominate Keynes' thinking. Keynes' long struggle over a period of six years to produce a version of the *Treatise* worthy of publication was directed partly to an escape from the stranglehold of the Quantity Theory of Money in its crude form. In the end Keynes was able to write that 'The forms of the quantity theory [. . .] on which we have all been brought up [. . .] are but ill adapted for this purpose' of exhibiting 'the causal process by which the price level is determined, and the method of transition from one position to another. [. . .] they do not, any of them, have the advantage of separating out those factors through which [. . .] the causal process actually operates during a period of change.'[1]

Five pages further on, Keynes wrote that the conclusions that he drew from his Fundamental Equations

are, of course, obvious and may serve to remind us that all these equations are purely formal; they are mere identities; truisms which tell us nothing in themselves. In this respect they resemble all other versions of the quantity theory of money. Their only point is to analyse and arrange our material in what will turn out to be a useful way for tracing cause and effect, when we have vitalised them by the introduction of extraneous facts from the actual world.[2]

Keynes did not explain how the introduction of facts could convert a truism into a causal relationship.

This is the first occasion on which Keynes admitted that the Quantity Theory is a truism. Nevertheless, Keynes seems to have been so much under the spell of the Quantity Theory that he could write about his Fundamental Equations as though they were 'versions' of the Quantity Theory; although, up to this point in his book, the quantity of money does not figure in them in any sense.

1. KEYNES, vol. v, p. 120.
2. *Ibid.*, p. 125.

Seven pages further on, Keynes attempted a reconciliation with the Quantity Theory. It was not successful. But in it can be seen the seed of what in the *General Theory* was to flourish under the name of the Liquidity Preference Theory. This Theory explains how the quantity of money exercises a causative influence by helping to determine the rate of interest – or, more generally, as we would put it now, the state of credit and the price-levels of securities, both fixed-interest and equities.

And yet, another three pages on, Keynes insisted on a symbolic presentation, which to most readers of the time must have appeared to have been a reaffirmation of the Quantity Theory in its simple form.

Chapter 14 on 'Alternative Forms of the Fundamental Equations'[1] is of interest exclusively for a historical comparison of the Cambridge and Yale forms of the Quantity Theory. But it demonstrates Keynes' continued fascination with the Theory.

1. *Ibid.*, pp. 198-214.

In May 1933, half way through the evolution of the *General Theory*, Keynes made his position very clear in a letter to Dennis Robertson, rejecting an article submitted for the *Economic Journal*:

this is a case – my fault not yours – where you are addressing yourself to one of the deader of my dead selves. I think there is a good deal in what you say, though I think I should still stick to my own view. In my present state of mind, however, I doubt that either version of the Cambridge equation is of any serious utility, and I can't remember that I have ever come across a case of anyone ever using either of them for practical purposes of interpretation. Thus, whether my version is slightly better than yours, or whether I ought to yield to your criticisms, I am not prepared to put up a serious case in defence of either. All this section is really a survival of the time when I was trying to make some practical use of the Cambridge equation, an attempt I have long since given up.[1]

(Keynes was confused in referring to 'either version of the *Cambridge* equation'. Robertson in his letter had referred to the 'old K-and-V method', obviously meaning either the Cambridge or the Yale concept.)

Towards the end of his *General Theory*, Keynes provided a symbolic expression, involving four elasticities of response, which he wrote 'can be regarded as a generalised statement of the Quantity Theory of Money'. He added: 'I do not myself attach much value to manipulations of this kind [. . .] I doubt if they carry us any further than ordinary discourse can.'[2] He referred to a warning which he had given a few pages back:

It is a great fault of symbolic pseudo-mathematical methods of formalising a system of economic analysis [. . .] that they expressly assume strict independence between the factors involved [. . .] whereas, in ordinary discourse [. . .] we can keep 'at the back of our heads' the necessary reserves and qualifications [. . .] Too large a proportion of

---

1. *Letter* to D. H. Robertson, *3 May 1933*; published in KEYNES, vol. XXIX, pp. 17-19 (the quotation on p. 18).
2. KEYNES, vol. VII, p. 305.

recent 'mathematical' economics are merely concoctions, as imprecise as the initial assumptions they rest on, which allow the author to lose sight of the complexities and interdependencies of the real world in a maze of pretentious and unhelpful symbols.[1]

And that was the end of the Quantity Theory until its recent resuscitation. Keynes in his long fight for release had conquered.

A most uncompromising statement of Keynes' complete release was provided in the Preface to the French edition to the *General Theory*, dated February 1939:

I have called this book the *General Theory of Employment, Interest and Money*; and the third feature to which I may call attention is the treatment of money and prices. The following analysis registers my final escape from the confusions of the Quantity Theory, which once entangled me. I regard the price level as a whole as being determined in precisely the same way as individual prices; that is to say, under the influence of supply and demand. Technical conditions, the level of wages, the extent of unused capacity of plant and labour, and the state of markets and competition determine the supply conditions of individual products and of products as a whole. The decisions of entrepreneurs, which provide the incomes of individual producers and the decisions of those individuals as to the disposition of such incomes determine the demand conditions. And prices – both individual prices and the price-level – emerge as the resultant of these two factors. Money, and the quantity of money, are not direct influences at this stage of the proceedings [...] The quantity of money determines the supply of liquid resources, and hence the rate of interest, and in conjunction with other factors (particularly that of confidence) the inducement to invest, which in turn fixes the equilibrium level of incomes, output and employment and (at each stage in conjunction with other factors) the price-level as a whole through the influences of supply and demand thus established.[2]

1. *Ibid.*, pp. 297-8.
2. *Ibid.*, pp. xxxiv-xxxv.

THIRD LECTURE
The *Treatise* and economic policy issues, 1928-1931

1. Keynes' 'Treatise on Money'. – 2. Economic policy issues, 1928-1931.

1. Keynes' 'Treatise on Money'

Work on the *Treatise on Money* was started in July 1924. It was not completed until September 1930.

One of the difficulties of tracing the development of Keynes' thought is to identify the influence of Robertson. His *Banking Policy and the Price Level* was finished late in 1925 (published in January 1926).[1] There is an overlap of over a year in the writing of the two books.

Chapters v and vi of Robertson's book are crucial. Of them Robertson wrote:

> I have had so many discussions with Mr. J. M. Keynes on the subject-matter of Chapters v and vi, and have re-written them so drastically at his suggestion, that I think neither of us now knows how much of the ideas therein contained is his and how much is mine. I should like to, but cannot, find a form of words which would adequately express my debt without seeming to commit him to opinions which he does not hold. I have made a few specific acknowledgements in footnotes: happily there is the less need for meticulous disentanglement as his own version of the Theory of Credit is to be published very soon.[2]

The correspondence between Keynes and Robertson makes it clear that Keynes was not only helpful but encouraging, though far from completely satisfied. It is true that, in a letter dated 28 May 1925, Keynes wrote, having read the whole of the draft:

> I [...] remain just as unhappy about the whole thing as I was before. [...] I think that you ought [...] to get another opinion.[3]

---

1. Dennis H. Robertson, *Banking Policy and the Price Level*. London: P. S. King, 1926. Revised Edition 1932. Reprinted New York: Augustus M. Kelley, and London: Staples Press, 1949.

2. *Ibid.*, p. 5.

3. *Letter* to D. H. Robertson, *28 May 1925*; published in Keynes, vol. xiii, pp. 34-6 (the quotation on p. 34).

But, as a result of changes made by Robertson, by 28 September Keynes wrote a far more encouraging letter though he still felt that 'the whole thing can be put *much* simpler and shorter'.[1]

Robertson's use of economic terms – related in some way to the concept of saving – remained a bone of contention with Keynes.

The main issue was what Robertson meant by *hoarding* and how, if at all, it related to Keynes' *saving* (however defined).[2]

Chapter 5 of Robertson's book is entitled 'The Kinds of Saving'. The word 'saving' is not, however, used. (Eight years later, in the course of a controversy in the *Economic Journal* with Keynes about 'Saving and Hoarding', Robertson defined 'saving' as the excess of 'yesterday's' income over 'to-day's' consumption, a 'day' being a certain period of time which is 'so short that the income which a man receives on a given day cannot be allocated during its course to any particular use'.[3])

In Chapter 5 of Robertson's *Banking Policy and the Price Level* the word 'lacking' took the place of the word 'saving'.[4] Lacking is either Spontaneous, Automatic, or Induced.

It is all very ingenious. It is difficult, however, to pretend that Robertson's tortured writing and Keynes' tortured collaboration over *Banking Policy and the Price Level* were conducive to clarity of thought.

In the course of his Preface to his 1949 edition, Robertson wrote, *inter alia*:

(ii) As recorded on p. 5, these chapters were closely discussed with Keynes, and drastically re-written at his suggestion. I have not preserved my original draft; and at this time of day it is not possible to carry the question of our mutual indebtedness much further than is

---

1. *Letter* to D. H. Robertson, *28 September 1925*; published in KEYNES, vol. XIII, pp. 39-40 (the quotation on p. 40).

2. The voluminous correspondence is to be found in KEYNES, vol. XIII (see the Index to vol. XIV, under 'Hoarding, Definitions, Robertson's') and in vol. XXIX, pp. 16-28.

3. DENNIS H. ROBERTSON, 'Saving and Hoarding', *Economic Journal*, September 1933, pp. 399-413 (the quotation on p. 399); reprinted in *Essays in Monetary Theory*. London: P. S. King & Son, 1940, pp. 65-82.

4. DENNIS H. ROBERTSON, *Banking Policy and the Price Level*, p. 41 (Chapter v: 'The Kinds of Saving').

done on p. 5. As recorded on p. 49, Induced Lacking (defined on that page), which plays a large part in the story, was contributed by Keynes. It is true that in his *Treatise on Money* (1930), vol. 1, p. 300, he went far towards repudiating his own offspring, dismissing it as 'too precarious a source of additional savings to deserve separate mention'. But I make no complaint of that [...][1]
Though I could wish he had not invited confusion by inadvertently contrasting Induced Lacking not with Automatic Lacking but with Imposed Lacking, of which in my classification it was a sub-species.[2]

And

(iv) While Keynes must at the time have understood and acquiesced in my step-by-step method, it is evident that it never, so to speak, got under his skin; for in his two successive treatments of the savings-investment theme in his two big books he discarded it completely. This was naturally a great personal disappointment to me; and it is, I think, being increasingly recognised that it was also a misfortune for the smooth progress of theory. I do not think that anybody who had really grasped the method of the Appendix to Ch[apter] v of this book need have been puzzling his head in 1930 over the problem of 'where the savings went to', or have stood in need of the crowning revelation that 'savings' and 'investment', if defined so as to be identical, are indeed always necessarily equal, – a phenomenon which was the starting-point, not the culmination, of the analysis attempted in this little book![3]

It is a mystery how two economists, employing radically different methods of analysis, could collaborate for so many years.

Keynes when writing the *Treatise* was still heavily under the influence of Dennis Robertson. The collaboration – now of Robertson with Keynes – continued throughout the whole period.

The continued collaboration over the writing of Keynes' *General Theory* I discuss in Section 3 of Lecture IV.

Keynes began working on the *Treatise* during the summer of 1924 at Tilton, his country house. Dennis Robertson visited him during the early stages.

1. DENNIS H. ROBERTSON, *Banking Policy and the Price Level*, Second Edition 1949, p. x.
2. *Ibid.*, note 3.
3. *Ibid.*, pp. xi-xii.

As late as January 1928 Keynes wrote from Cambridge to his wife, Lydia:

Dennis [Robertson] came in last night and we had a long talk about the new theory. I think it will do, and that it is very important. But it owes a great deal to him.[1]

On 24 November 1929 he reported to his wife that 'it looks as if my proof sheets are going to get through the criticism of Dennis and Pigou without any serious damage'.[2] The Preface was signed on 14 September 1930 and the book was published before the end of the year.

In the Preface to the *Treatise* Keynes admitted that:

there is a good deal in this book which represents the process of getting rid of the ideas which I used to have and of finding my way to those which I now have. There are many skins which I have sloughed still littering these pages. It follows that I could do it better and much shorter if I were to start over again. I feel like someone who has been forcing his way through a confused jungle.[3]

I turn now to consider what are the fundamental distinctions between the *Treatise* started in 1924 and published in 1930, and the *General Theory* started in 1931 and published in 1936.

In Section 9 of my last Lecture I showed how Keynes deceived himself into thinking that he had carried the Quantity Theory into the *Treatise*. All this turned out a delusion. The breach, as I shall show in a moment, was agonising. After all had not Frank Ramsey, the great mathematical logician, written to Keynes: 'how exciting your quantity equation seemed; I wish I was sufficiently used to thinking about banking to appreciate it fully and to make better criticisms. But I could see that it was a great advance' [in 1928!].[4]

Nevertheless, the great innovation of the *Treatise* was the abandonment of the Quantity Theory of Money – apart from

1. From a *Letter* to Lydia Keynes, *20 January 1928*; excerpt published in KEYNES, vol. XXIX, p. 2.
2. From a *Letter* to Lydia Keynes, *24 November 1929*; excerpt published in KEYNES, vol. XXIX, p. 4.
3. KEYNES, vol. v, p. xvii.
4. From a *Letter* from Frank P. Ramsey, *3 August 1918*; excerpt published in KEYNES, vol. XIII, pp. 78-82 (the quotation on p. 78).

some few parting gestures – in favour of the idea of the flow of expenditure – both on consumption-goods and on investment-goods – determining outputs, employment and price-levels (in terms of wage-units).

Superficially the *Treatise* seems more concerned with price-levels than with levels of output and employment; the *General Theory* very little with price-levels and primarily with levels of output.

Keynes pointed out, concerning his 'Fundamental Equations' for the price-levels of consumption-goods and investment-goods, that 'These conclusions are, of course, obvious [. . .] they are mere identities; truisms which tell us nothing in themselves. In this respect they resemble all other versions of the quantity theory of money.'[1] (At this point Keynes still suffered from the Quantity Theory virus.) The equations merely state that each price-level is equal to the money cost of production per unit of output *plus* any element of abnormal profit per unit of output.

The Fundamental Equations are truisms in the sense that they determine *abnormal profit*. *Profits* are defined as 'the difference between the actual remuneration of the entrepreneurs [. . .] and their normal remuneration';[2] defined as

that rate of remuneration [at any time] which, if they were open to make new bargains with all the factors of production at the currently prevailing rates of earnings, would leave them under no motive either to increase or to decrease their scale of operations.

Thus when the actual rate of entrepreneurs' remuneration exceeds (or falls short of) the normal as thus defined, so that profits are positive (or negative), entrepreneurs will [. . .] seek to expand (or curtail) their scale of operations.[3]

Keynes resisted suggestions made to him that he should describe 'profits' as 'windfalls', but on at least two occasions he erred himself.[4]

1. KEYNES, vol. v, p. 125.
2. *Ibid.*, p. 112.
3. *Ibid.*, pp. 112-13.
4. *Ibid.*, pp. xxiii and 155.

But later in the book, Keynes wrote:

it is obviously the anticipated profit or loss on new business, rather than the actual profit or loss on business just concluded, which influences [entrepreneurs] in deciding the scale on which to produce [. . .] it is the *anticipated* profit or loss which is the mainspring of change.[1]

One of the peculiarities of the *Treatise* was Keynes' refusal to treat *abnormal profits* as belonging to the same category as *saving*, as defined in the *Treatise*. He regarded them as 'the difference between the value of the increment of the national wealth in any period and the aggregate of individual savings'.[2] This is only another way of saying that abnormal profits are, by definition, the excess of investment (increment of value of wealth) over saving, as defined in the *Treatise*.

Definitions apart, Keynes' great discovery was that everything turned on the extent to which the division of the community's earnings between expenditure on consumption-goods and on savings differed from its division between earnings derived from the production of consumption-goods and from investment-goods. If the two ratios are equal, the price-level of consumption-goods will be in equilibrium with their cost of production. To the extent that they differ, there will be abnormal profits or losses on the production of consumption-goods, and the position will be one of disequilibrium.[3]

Keynes felt that only definitions which resulted in the existence of a *difference* between the rates of investment and of saving would bring home to his readers the fundamental cause of disequilibrium.

The reason for Keynes' choice of definitions is made clearer in the Preface to the Japanese edition of the *Treatise*, especially in the following passage:

those who object to these definitions have not, I think, followed out to the end the consequences of rejecting them. For if windfall profits

1. KEYNES, vol. v, p. 143.
2. *Ibid.*, p. 114.
3. *Ibid.*, p. 121.

and losses [Keynes had forgotten his rejection of the use of the word 'windfall' in favour of 'abnormal'] are included in income [. . .] and saving [is defined] as the excess of income thus defined over expenditure on consumption, it follows that saving is in all cases exactly equal to the value of current investment. That is to say the total volume of saving ceases to be a factor having any independent existence. Its amount cannot be affected by the voluntary decision of the various recipients of income as to how much of their income they will spend on consumption; and it solely depends on what the value of current investment happens to be. This seems to me not less paradoxical than my use of these terms.[1]

In the course of a review of the *Treatise* in the *Economic Journal*, Robertson described Keynes' terminology as 'extremely confusing, and [. . .] liable to lead even practised thinkers into error'.[2] In his Rejoinder published in the same issue, Keynes wrote:

I think I might do better than in my *Treatise*, but it is not very easy. [. . .] Does Mr. Robertson, in practice, mean by 'savings' exactly the same as what he means by 'the value of new investment'?[3]

There is one strong argument in favour of the *Treatise* definitions. It is not, however, strong enough to justify their retention.

A rise in the rate of investment is implicitly divided into two parts. At any particular moment of time after it has taken place it will have resulted partly in an increase of output, partly in a rise in prices. The rise in the rate of saving is determined by the increase of output, valued at unchanged prices. The rise in the rate at which abnormal profits are being earned is equal to the rise in prices multiplied by output. The rise in the rate of increase of national wealth is equal to the increase in the rate of saving (defined in the *Treatise* sense). The rise in the rate at which ab-

---

1. From the Preface to the Japanese Edition (April 1932), reprinted in KEYNES, vol. v, p. xxiii. The Preface to the German Edition (October 1931) is less clear on this point.

2. DENNIS H. ROBERTSON, 'Mr. Keynes' Theory of Money', *Economic Journal*, September 1931, pp. 395-411 (the quotation on p. 407).

3. JOHN MAYNARD KEYNES, 'A Rejoinder' to Mr D. H. Robertson, *ibid.*, pp. 412-23; reprinted in KEYNES, vol. XIII, pp. 219-36 (My 'multiplier' article – 'The Relation of Home Investment to Unemployment', described in Section I of Lecture IV – had been published in *Economic Journal*, June 1931, pp. 173-98).

normal profits are earned represents redistribution of income in favour of entrepreneurs at the expense of wage-earners.

Here can be seen the embryo of the modern post-*General Theory* post-Keynesian Theory of Distribution.

Keynes himself never saw this. The *General Theory* is – in a sense which I shall qualify in Lecture v – a short-period theory, whereas the Theory of Distribution is long-period. The *Treatise* is essentially long-period; Keynes expressed reluctance to be led 'too far into the intricate theory of the economics of the short period'.[1]

Somewhat later in Volume I of the *Treatise* Keynes takes the case of a reduction of consumption, implicitly over a period too short for any appreciable reduction of output to take place. The result is a fall in the prices of consumption-goods:

the saving, instead of resulting in an increase of aggregate wealth, has merely involved a double transference – a transference of consumption *from* the savers to the general body of *consumers*, and a transference of wealth *to* the savers from the general body of *producers*, both total consumption and total wealth remaining unchanged. Thus, in Mr Robertson's language, the saving has been 'abortive'.[2]

I do not want to spend too much time on Keynes' Fundamental Equations. Keynes himself wrote:

These conclusions are, of course, obvious and may serve to remind us that all these equations are purely formal; they are mere identities; truisms which tell us nothing in themselves. In this respect they resemble all other versions of the quantity theory of money [it had not yet entirely lost its grip]. Their only point is to analyse and arrange our material in what will turn out to be a useful way for tracing cause and effect.[3]

At the outset we are faced with a slight difficulty. Keynes chose his 'units of quantities of goods in such a way that a unit of each has the same cost of production at the base date'.[4]

The Fundamental Equation for the price-level, *P*, of con-

1. KEYNES, vol. v, p. 145.
2. *Ibid.*, p. 156.
3. *Ibid.*, p. 125.
4. *Ibid.*, pp. 121-2.

sumption-goods, when the remuneration of entrepreneurs is, on the average, normal, is

$$P = \frac{E}{O} \tag{1}$$

where E is total money earnings or income and O total output (including investment-goods).

This becomes
$$P = \frac{W}{e} \tag{2}$$

where W is the rate of money earnings per unit of human effort and e the coefficient of efficiency (output per unit of human effort).

In preparing this Lecture I was rather puzzled. But I cannot remember having being puzzled before on this point or that the point arose at the 'Circus', which I come on to in Section 2 of Lecture IV. But I have now come across Appendix 2 to Volume I of the *Treatise* in the Royal Economic Society edition.[1] In the *American Economic Review* of September 1932, Alvin Hansen pointed out what he described as a fundamental error.[2] Keynes, in the December number, admitted it.[3] Actually the point at issue is rather trivial. Keynes corrected the 'fundamental error' by substituting for the words which I have just quoted about the choice of units of output the words:

Let us choose our unit of goods consumed as the quantity which had unit cost of production in the base year and our unit of goods invested in any year as the quantity which has in that year the same cost of production as a unit of goods consumed.[4]

(Apparently I made a feeble attempt to get Keynes to make an amendment just before completion of the final draft of the *Treatise*.)

1. 'Appendix 2. Definitions of the Units Employed', in KEYNES, vol. v, pp. 329-31. In this Appendix are reprinted the central passages of Alvin Hansen's note and Keynes' reply to which reference is made in the text. On this point see also ROY HARROD, *The Life of John Maynard Keynes*. London: Macmillan, 1951, pp. 433-4, note 1.

2. ALVIN H. HANSEN, 'A Fundamental Error in Keynes's "Treatise on Money"', *American Economic Review*, September 1932, p. 462; reprinted in KEYNES, vol. v, pp. 329-30.

3. JOHN MAYNARD KEYNES, 'Keynes's Fundamental Equations: A Note', *American Economic Review*, December 1932, pp. 691-2; reprinted in KEYNES, vol. v, pp. 330-1.

4. KEYNES, vol. v, p. 331.

If we leave pedantry on one side, it should be recognised that equation (2) represents a remarkable breakthrough. The price-level of consumption-goods is equal to – Keynes actually wrote 'determined' by[1] – under normal conditions – money-costs per unit of output. Quite abruptly the Quantity Theory of Money was jettisoned (though its ugly head made another short and half-hearted appearance twelve pages further on). One of the outstanding tenets of the *General Theory* has emerged. Moreover, when the state of demand is such that profits are abnormal or subnormal, the effect on the price-level of consumption-goods is given by the term $\dfrac{I' - S}{R}$, so that $P = \dfrac{E}{O} + \dfrac{I' - S}{R}$, Keynes' first Fundamental Equation.

I' is the cost of production of new investment-goods, S saving (in the *Treatise* sense) and R the output of consumption-goods. This displays the second basic feature of the *General Theory*, the role of investment and thrift in determining the degree of prosperity of the economy as a whole. As Keynes put it:

the price-level [of consumption-goods], as determined by the first term, is upset by the fact that the division of the output between investment and goods for consumption is not necessarily the same as the division of the income between savings and expenditure on consumption.[2]

I am not going to discuss the second Fundamental Equation for the price-level of output as a whole. This involves the value, I, as distinguished from the cost, I', of new investment-goods.

The determination of the value of new investment-goods – and also of old ones in so far as there is a market for them – is a subject which is developed both in the *Treatise* – and later in the *General Theory*. The treatment is path-breaking but leaves room for further development.

One influence on the prices of investment-goods is the degree of confidence of entrepreneurs in the profitability of using them in the future. This influence is developed more extensively in the

1. KEYNES, vol. v, p. 123.
2. *Ibid.*

General Theory than in the *Treatise*. Most of the *Treatise* analysis is a forerunner of the treatment of the Theory of Liquidity Preference of the *General Theory*.

> The price level of investments as a whole, and hence of new investments, is that price level at which the desire of the public to hold savings deposits is equal to the amount of savings deposits which the banking system is willing and able to create.[1]

At the same time an individual's

> distaste for other securities is not absolute and depends on his expectations of the future return to be obtained from savings deposits and from other securities respectively.[2]

And:

> the value of capital goods depends on the rate of interest at which the prospective income from them is capitalised.[3]

Other securities include all the securities (equities) of which the underlying assets are investment-goods.

I shall be developing this subject in Lecture v (on the *General Theory*) and I shall refer back to the analysis in the *Treatise*.

One great problem arises from the ambiguity of the word *investment* – it may either relate to securities, and in particular to equities, or to real capital-goods. Both in the *Treatise* and in the *General Theory* the two are confused. Don Patinkin agrees with me as to obscurity in the *Treatise*. He suggests that Keynes

> implicitly assumes that the ratio between the market value of the equity securities of any firm and the net book value of the firm's assets is always unity.[4]

I agree with Don Patinkin that the adoption of such an assumption would facilitate interpretation of Keynes, even though the assumption is invalid. But later in Volume i of the *Treatise*, Keynes wrote:

---

1. *Ibid.*, p. 129.
2. *Ibid.*, pp. 127-8.
3. *Ibid.*, p. 139.
4. Don Patinkin, *Keynes' Monetary Thought. A study of its development*. Durham, North Carolina: Duke University Press, 1976, pp. 37-8, note 4.

Nor does the price of existing securities depend at all closely over short periods either on the cost of production or on the price of new fixed capital [. . .] The investment boom in the United States in 1929 was a good example of an enormous rise in the price of securities as a whole which was not accompanied by any rise at all in the price of the current output of new fixed capital.[1]

Keynes laid great emphasis, and devoted a large amount of space, to the influence of the banking system on investment, partly through the influence of the rate of interest on the rate of investment, partly through the influence of the quantity of bank deposits on the prices of capital goods.

There is, indeed, no possibility of intelligent foresight designed to equate savings and investment unless it is exercised by the banking system; for it is the facilities allowed by the banks which are the marginal factor determining the precise degree to which entrepreneurs will be in a position to carry out their enterprises. Yet hitherto the banking system has been mainly preoccupied with a different objective.[2]

Keynes did *not* rely on an expansion of bank advances to finance the excess of investment over saving. The abnormal profits precisely fill this gap.

He was conscious of the danger of being misunderstood on this issue, as a result of the teaching of certain foreign economists, and to some extent of Robertson. In the course of his Preface to the German edition (October 1931) (as amended in his Preface to the Japanese edition [April 1932]) he wrote:

My definition of *income* is thought paradoxical because I exclude from it [. . .] windfall profits and losses, and my definition of *saving*, being the excess of income thus defined over expenditure on consumption, corresponds to my definition of *income*. But those who object to these definitions have not, I think, followed out to the end the consequences of rejecting them [. . .].

All the theories, other than my own, consider that 'forced' saving (in their terminology) is a phenomenon due to some action on the part of the banking system, which is variously described as an act of inflation, an expansion of credit or a departure of the banking system

1. KEYNES, vol. v, p. 222.
2. *Ibid.*, p. 251.

from 'neutrality'. Sometimes the amount of 'forced' saving is considered to be equal to the increase in the volume of money or of credit or in the volume created in excess of what is required to maintain 'neutrality' [. . .] The conception is, if I understand it aright, that the money value (or, alternatively the money cost of production – it is not always clear which) of current investment, i.e. the money-value (or cost) of the current increment of the community's capital, is made up of two parts added together, the first of which is equal to the 'voluntary' savings of the public and the second (which may be either positive or negative) to the change in the volume of currency and bank money created by the banking system after allowing for certain offsets.

Now what I wish to emphasise is that this is not the theory of Book III below, though it may have certain affinities with it. I believe that the ideas, which I have just endeavoured to sketch, are essentially unclear and that, if a thorough attempt is made to render them clear, they will undergo a series of modifications which will gradually have the effect of bringing them into conformity with my own theory. My primary purpose in this place, however, is not to argue which is right and which is wrong, but to call the reader's attention to the fact that my theory is *different* from the theory outlined above. For whilst I hold that the policy of the banking system influences the difference between saving and the value of investment, I do not hold that there is any direct, necessary or invariable relationship between this difference and the amount of credit, whether after allowing for various specific offsets or not, which could be deduced from a knowledge, however complete, of banking and currency statistics.[1]

In a footnote in the *Treatise* itself Keynes gave priority to a few economists for his path-breaking distinction between *saving* and *investment*. He already here objected to the concept of 'forced saving', as used by Schumpeter. The term had become a familiar feature especially of the very newest German writings on money. And of course he objected to Robertson's 'automatic lacking'. Subject to that Keynes gave priority to Mises and Schumpeter and, above all, to Dennis Robertson.[2] He mentioned also Hans Neisser.[3]

1. *Ibid.*, pp. xxiii-xxiv.
2. *Ibid.*, p. 154, note 1.
3. *Ibid.*, p. 178.

The *Treatise* is closely associated in the minds of economists with the name of Wicksell. Wicksell was of course a great pioneer: his *Geldzins und Güterpreise* was published in 1898. But I doubt whether his influence on Keynes amounted to much more than adopting his distinction between the *natural rate* of interest and the *market rate*.

the natural rate of interest is the rate at which saving and the value of investment are exactly balanced, so that the price level of output as a whole [. . .] exactly corresponds to the money rate of the efficiency earnings of the factors of production.[1]

My translation of Wicksell's book was not published until 1936.[2] I quote one passage from it:

There is a certain rate of interest on loans which is neutral in respect to commodity prices, and tends neither to raise nor to lower them. This is necessarily the same as the rate of interest which would be determined by supply and demand if no use were made of money.[3]

Not a concept likely, for the purpose at issue, to commend itself to Keynes.

Don Patinkin has settled the issue so far as I am concerned, and no doubt many other economists.

Keynes failed to realize – and hence failed to apply – the full meaning of Wicksell's basic distinction between these two rates. In particular, for Wicksell the 'natural rate' represented the marginal productivity of capital [. . .][4]

In his *General Theory* Keynes stated that in the *Treatise* he

had [. . .] overlooked the fact that in any given society there is, on this definition, a *different* natural rate of interest for each hypothetical level of employment [. . .] [He] had not then understood that, in certain conditions, the system could be in equilibrium with less than full employment.[5]

1. KEYNES, vol. v, p. 139.
2. J. G. KNUT WICKSELL, *Geldzins und Güterpreise*. Jena: Gustav Fischer, 1898. Translation by Richard Kahn: *Interest and Prices*. London: Macmillan, 1936.
3. *Ibid.*, p. 102.
4. DON PATINKIN, *Keynes' Monetary Thought*, p. 47.
5. KEYNES, vol. VII, pp. 242-3.

It is impossible to tell whether Keynes was aware that in Wicksell's Chapter on 'The Quantity Theory and its Opponents' Wicksell wrote:

The Theory provides a real explanation of its subject matter, and in a manner that is logically incontestable; but only on assumptions that unfortunately have little relation to practice, and in some respects none whatever.[1]

We have the great authority, Bertil Ohlin, to tell us in 1937 that Wicksell's

Geldzins und Güterpreise of 1898 and his later books and papers on money contained the embryo of 'a theory of output as a whole', although this fact was not clearly perceived until the late 'twenties, when Professor Lindahl presented his elaboration of Wicksell.[2]

The two volumes of the *Treatise* cover a wide field. Apart from the small part of the book to which I have referred, they deal mainly with the Management of Money, including the important chapter on 'The "Modus Operandi" of Bank Rate', and with fluctuations in the rate of investment and the credit cycle.

Of particular importance are the four chapters in Volume 2 on Problems of International and Supernational Management of the Banking System particularly as – for the sake of simplicity – the *General Theory* was to be written almost entirely in terms of a closed system.

In the course of discussing his Fundamental Equations, Keynes wrote:

A principal object of this treatise is to show that we have here the clue to the way in which the fluctuations of the price level actually come to pass, whether they are due to oscillations about a steady equilibrium level or to a transition from one equilibrium to another.[3]

This is one matter of fundamental importance which it will be easier to discuss later in Section 2 of Lecture IV on the Cambridge 'Circus', in order to secure a proper historical perspective.

1. J. G. KNUT WICKSELL, *Interest and Prices*, p. 41.
2. BERTIL OHLIN, 'Some Notes on the Stockholm Theory of Savings and Investment', *Economic Journal*, March 1937, Part 1, p. 53.
3. KEYNES, vol. v, p. 137.

On finishing the book on 14 September 1930, Keynes wrote to his mother:

Artistically it is a failure – I have changed my mind too much during the course of it for it to be a proper unity. But I think it contains an abundance of ideas and material.[1]

The book made a great impact on publication. It certainly was not regarded as a failure. But parts of it presented difficulties to the reader.

1. *Letter* to Florence A. Keynes, *14 September 1930*; reprinted in KEYNES, vol. XIII, p. 176.

2. Economic policy issues, 1928-1931[1]

Keynes was far happier writing for a non-academic audience – whether members of the intelligent public, politicians or bankers. His popular and other non-academic writings were unlaboured, in contrast to the elements of strain and torture that entered into his academic writing.

To secure conviction he relied on sincerity and commonsense. He could deploy his skill at advocacy without arousing the resentment displayed by his academic economics. When it came to the more precise logic of the *General Theory*, he had to demand from his readers the abandonment of firmly ingrained theoretical ideas. It was not difficult to arouse resentment and Keynes deliberately wanted to provoke in order to secure basic rethinking.

Keynes, the propagandist, was always forging ahead of Keynes, the author of theoretical academic works. Indeed, it was Keynes' zeal as a reformer, and his facility in putting his ideas into shape, that set the pace for the writing of the *General Theory*.

His work for the Liberal Party had started in 1923. Through the *Nation* (which later became the *New Statesman and Nation*), on which he exercised a strong financial and moral influence, and the Liberal Party Summer Schools he had taken an active part in Liberal Party politics. From 1925 he was involved in the preparation of *Britain's Industrial Future*, published in 1928.[2] The crucial period of intense popular activity was from March 1929 (when the Liberal Manifesto was published) – about six and a half years before the completion of the *General Theory* – to June 1931 (with the signature of the Macmillan Report) – when thinking about the *General Theory* began.

Keynes was a member of the Macmillan Committee (appointed by the new MacDonald Labour Government), which sat from November 1929 to June 1931, an original member of the standing Economic Advisory Council, set up in February

---

1. See the Chronology, pp. XXIV, XXV.

2. *Britain's Industrial Future*. Report of the Liberal Industrial Inquiry, London: Ernest Benn, 1928. Among the members of the Executive Committee, in addition to Keynes, were Lloyd-George, Hubert D. Henderson, Herbert Samuel and John Simon; see also KEYNES, vol. XIX, Part II, pp. 731-8.

1930, and especially of its Sub-Committee of Economists, which sat from July to October 1930.

Over this period, Keynes was engaged with academic economists, bankers and other practical men – both in discussion and in drafting reports. The result was two-way. Keynes had to admit to himself that the concepts and methods of the *Treatise* were not adapted to dealing with the major policy problem – serious economic recession and heavy unemployment.

The problems which he had to face led him over a period of two years slap into the conceptual structure of the *General Theory*, which only in the very late stages began to solidify. At the same time the natural development of the structure of his thinking was in tune with the challenges with which he was faced. His economic instincts took charge of his popular activities as an economist. His thinking and energies rapidly carried him into the climate which culminated in the *General Theory*. They were helped by liberation from the corset of the Quantity Theory of Money.

Keynes was becoming a strong public advocate of capital development. With a General Election approaching, Keynes took an active part in the operations of the Liberal Party.

He had helped to draft parts of the Liberal 'Programme for National Development', which advocated a policy of capital spending on public account. In March 1929 the Liberals issued their electioneering Programme:

We Can Conquer Unemployment. We Mobilised for War, Let us Mobilise for Prosperity.[1]

The Liberal Party Manifesto resulted in May 1929 in the publication by the Conservative Government of a White Paper on *Certain Proposals Relating to Unemployment*,[2] and, in the same month, the publication of *Can Lloyd George Do It?* by Keynes and Henderson.[3]

1. LIBERAL PARTY, *We Can Conquer Unemployment*. London: Cassell, 1929.

2. *Memoranda on Certain Proposals Relating to Unemployment*. Presented by the Minister of Labour to Parliament. May 1929. Cmd. 3331. London: His Majesty's Stationery Office, 1929.

3. JOHN MAYNARD KEYNES and HUBERT D. HENDERSON, *Can Lloyd George Do It?*. London: The Nation and Athenaeum, 1929 (12 May). Reprinted in KEYNES, vol. IX, pp. 86-125.

Five of the Memoranda contained in the Government White Paper were each signed by the Ministerial head of the Department involved. But the Treasury Memorandum was described as 'prepared by the Treasury under the direction of the Chancellor of the Exchequer' (Winston Churchill), but was not signed.

The Treasury Memorandum had, of course, not been seen by Keynes and Henderson when they completed *Can Lloyd George Do It?* but they exploited the Budget Statement of the Chancellor, delivered a few weeks earlier on 16 April.

The Chancellor had said in the course of his Budget Statement:

It is the orthodox Treasury dogma, steadfastly held, [. . .] that whatever might be the political or social advantages, very little additional employment and no permanent additional employment, can, in fact, and as a general rule, be created by State borrowing and State expenditure.[1]

The Chancellor admitted that 'Some State expenditure' was 'inevitable, *but not as a cure for unemployment*'.[2] Keynes' rejoinder, in the Pamphlet, was:

In relation to the actual facts of today, this argument is, we believe, quite without foundation.

In the first place, there is nothing in the argument which limits its applicability to State-promoted undertakings. If it is valid at all, it must apply equally to a new works started by Morris, or Courtaulds, to any new business enterprise entailing capital expenditure. If it were announced that some of our leading captains of industry had decided to launch out boldly, and were about to sink capital in new industrial plant to the tune, between them, of £100 millions, we should all expect to see a great improvement in employment. And, of course, we should be right. But, if the argument we are dealing with were sound, we should be wrong [. . .] Indeed, we should be driven to a still more remarkable conclusion. We should have to conclude that it was virtually out of the question to absorb our unemployed work-people by any means whatsoever (other than the unthinkable inflation).[3]

And a little further on:

1. KEYNES, vol. IX, p. 115.
2. *Ibid.*
3. *Ibid.*, pp. 115-16.

We are using our savings to pay for unemployment, instead of using them to equip the country. The savings which Mr Lloyd George's schemes will employ will be diverted not from financing other capital equipment, but partly from financing unemployment. From the Unemployment Fund alone we are now paying out £50 million a year; and this is not the whole of the cost of supporting the unemployed.[1]

And so

We are left with a broad, simple, and surely incontestable proposition. Whatever real difficulties there may be in the way of absorbing our unemployed labour in productive work, an inevitable diversion of resources from other forms of employment is not one of them.[2]

Can Lloyd George Do It? ended as follows:

It is not an accident that the Conservative government have landed us in the mess where we find ourselves. It is the natural outcome of their philosophy:
[. . .]
You must not try to employ everyone, because this will cause inflation.
You must not invest, because how can you know that it will pay?
You must not do anything, because this will only mean that you can't do something else.
Safety first! The policy of maintaining a million unemployed has now been pursued for eight years without disaster. Why risk a change?
We will not promise more than we can perform. We, therefore, promise nothing [. . .].
Fears and doubts and hypochondriac precautions are keeping us muffled up indoors. But we are not tottering to our graves. We are healthy children [. . .].
And over against us, standing in the path, there is nothing but a few old gentlemen tightly buttoned-up in their frock coats, who only need to be treated with a little friendly disrespect and bowled over like ninepins.
Quite likely they will enjoy it themselves, when once they have got over the shock.[3]

Keynes must have forgotten how clever Treasury officials

1. KEYNES, vol. IX, p. 117.
2. *Ibid.*, p. 120.
3. *Ibid.*, pp. 124-5.

were (as they still are), although he had worked as an important Treasury official in the War, and in 1929 knew the leading ones personally, including especially Sir Richard Hopkins, a Second Secretary.

Keynes had made an elementary blunder. In a few popular articles[1] published immediately after the Budget Statement was delivered on 16 April, he gave away the fundamental case against the Treasury which he was going to make in *Can Lloyd George Do It?* against the 'Treasury view', as put forward on behalf of Winston Churchill, in the passage which I have quoted. Sir Richard Hopkins was warned and the 'Treasury view' no longer appeared in the White Paper as fundamental and decisive, taken by itself, as Winston Churchill had made it appear in his Budget Statement.

Its force was reduced by the introduction of a considerable amount of subsidiary argument, partly based on a bewildering mass of statistics.

The real 'Treasury view' makes its appearance only one and a half pages from the end in the following form:

The large loans involved, if they are not to involve inflation, must draw on existing capital resources. These resources are on the whole utilised at present in varying degrees of active employment; and the great bulk is utilised for home industrial and commercial purposes. The extent to which any additional employment could be given by altering the direction of investment is therefore at the best strictly limited.[2]

Earlier in the Treasury Memorandum the contention of *We Can Conquer Unemployment*

that the additional £125 millions a year required for new State or local authority borrowing can be found without impinging on the supply of capital for other home requirements[3]

---

1. For example, JOHN MAYNARD KEYNES on 'A Cure for Unemployment', *Evening Standard*, 19 April 1929; letters from Keynes on 'National Schemes for Unemployment', *Evening Standard*, 30 April and 7 May 1929; reprinted in KEYNES, vol XIX, Part II, pp. 808-16.

2. *Memoranda on Certain Proposals Relating to Unemployment*, p. 53.

3. *Ibid.*, p. 49.

was dismissed by a quite different, and much weaker, line of argument than that used by the Chancellor of the Exchequer in his Budget Statement. The argument was:

This, on the face of it, appears to be highly improbable. There is not the least reason to suppose that works under Government auspices would be more remunerative or have more success in attracting capital than any other works.[1]

The final two sentences of the Treasury Memorandum run as follows:

Seeing that the national savings are less, allowing for the altered level of prices, than before the war, and capital is therefore comparatively scarce and dear, it follows that we cannot afford investments which yield only an uneconomic, or a very distant, return, or are of a purely luxury nature. Judged by this test, it is difficult to believe that the greater part of the expenditure proposed would increase the power of industry to provide remunerative employment.[2]

I shall now show that Richard Hopkins, under cross-examination by Keynes before the Macmillan Committee, placed more reliance on these last two lines of argument than on the 'Treasury view' proper, which he did not seem very anxious to defend.

Among the members of the Macmillan Committee on Finance and Industry (appointed on 5 November 1929 by the Chancellor of the Exchequer of the new Labour Government, Philip Snowden), in addition to Keynes, were Professor Theodore Gregory, of the London School of Economics, Ernest Bevin (Secretary of the most powerful trade union of the country), R. H. Brand (a Banker), Reginald McKenna (Chairman of the Midland Bank), other bankers, several industrialists and representatives of other interests.

In his *Treatise*, to be published in a year's time, Keynes presented, in sardonic vein, his own account of how bankers thought changes in Bank Rate affected the economy.[3] On the Macmillan Committee he secured confirmation, and made Governor Norman of the Bank of England look rather ridiculous.

1. *Memoranda on Certain Proposals relating to Unemployment*, p. 49.
2. *Ibid.*, p. 54.
3. KEYNES, vol. v, pp. 166-97.

Norman was cross-examined on 26 March 1930, and emerged in a somewhat chastened mood from Keynes' clutches. Keynes had to pay a price. Hopkins was already on his guard. The guard was now doubled.

Hopkins was examined on a number of occasions. The relevant one was on 22 May. By then he realised what a severe cross-examiner he was up against.

In the available space it is possible to provide only a very few extracts from the proceedings:[1]

Chairman   I think the next matter on which you were going to offer some observations was on the question whether industry might be set going by the initiation, with Government aid, of a large programme of public works?

Hopkins   Yes. Perhaps you will allow me, Mr Chairman, to try and express my view at some little length with regard to this. It is a topic which is associated with a document which has come to be known as 'The Treasury View' [...]

Chairman   I have in front of me the document in question [...][2]

Hopkins   [Quoting from the White Paper] 'The scale of State capital expenditure is therefore not a question of principle, but of degree [...] the economic justification of all schemes ought to be very thoroughly examined before they are put in hand'.[3]

Then later on:

Keynes   There are two separate propositions. There is the proposition that schemes of capital development are of no use for reducing unemployment?

Hopkins   Yes.

Keynes   And there is the proposition that it is difficult to find good schemes?

Hopkins   Yes.

Keynes   Would it be a misunderstanding of the Treasury view to say that they hold to the first proposition?

1. MACMILLAN COMMITTEE ON FINANCE AND INDUSTRY, *Minutes of Evidence*, vol. II. Oral evidence of Sir Richard V. N. Hopkins, 16 and 22 May 1930. London: His Majesty's Stationery Office, 1931, pp. 1-26; question nos. 5310-5710. See also KEYNES, vol. XX, pp. 166-79.

2. *Memoranda on Certain Proposals Relating to Unemployment.*

3. *Ibid.*, p. 44.

Hopkins The first proposition goes much too far. The first proposition would ascribe to us an absolute and rigid dogma, would it not?

Keynes Well, there might be various reasons. One reason which, when I misunderstood the Treasury view, I thought would be advanced was, that quite apart from the utility of the schemes they would not help on balance because it was the nature of the economic machine that any capital that could be found for those schemes would be diverted from other uses. That is a misunderstanding?

Hopkins Yes. That is much too rigid an expression of any views that have come from us.

Keynes You do not express in your evidence to-day any view remotely resembling that?

Hopkins No. I would not say that. As I see the position it is this, that we should pay regard to the economic justification of schemes wherever it be possible [. . .][1]

Keynes So the issue between those who are in favour of these schemes and those who are against them is not whether they cure unemployment . . .?

Hopkins Do you wish me to agree?

Chairman I do not think you must take it that Sir Richard agrees.

Keynes What is the point where we differ?

Hopkins The capital for these schemes has got to come from somewhere.

Keynes That is equally true of good and bad schemes?

Hopkins Yes [. . .][2]

Keynes But do bad schemes make a larger hole than good schemes?

Hopkins Not intrinsically, of course; they may in their consequences [. . .]

Keynes I fail to see the logic of what you are saying?

Hopkins Well, it may divert capital from more useful schemes.

Keynes That is equally true of good and bad schemes? [. . .][3]

   Nearly all of what you have been saying to-day comes to this, that it is difficult to find good schemes?

Hopkins Yes.

Keynes And that bad schemes are open to indirect objections.

---

1. MACMILLAN COMMITTEE ON FINANCE AND INDUSTRY, *Minutes of Evidence*, vol. II, pp. 17-20; question nos. 5561, 5562, 5565; and 5600-5604.

 2. *Ibid.*, pp. 20-1, question nos. 5611-5613.

 3. *Ibid.*, p. 21, question nos. 5614-5616.

That is quite different from what I previously thought to be the Treasury view. It was not a view of that kind but a theoretical view, that the objection to these schemes was that they caused diversion on theoretical grounds. That was a misunderstanding on my part of what the Treasury intended, was it?

Hopkins Yes. Certainly in the case which we have been discussing, the main case, the Treasury view does come back to that. It is not a rigid dogma. It is the result of the views that we take as to the practical reactions of the scheme.

Keynes It bends so much that I find difficulty in getting hold of it?

Hopkins Yes; I do not think these views are capable of being put in the rigid form of a theoretical doctrine [. . .][1]

Keynes Is it your view that schemes which yield four per cent reduce unemployment while schemes which yield three per cent do not reduce unemployment?

Hopkins Oh! no. I see the logical dilemma into which you are endeavouring to drive me. I shall, of course, naturally come into it slowly and diffidently.

Chairman You are not obliged to answer, Sir Richard [. . .][2]

Keynes I have not any more questions on this point. I find, as a result of your evidence, Sir Richard, that the Treasury view has been gravely misjudged?

Hopkins But I should be very sorry if Mr Keynes thought that all his strictures on the Treasury were quite unjustified. Many of them were very fully earned!

Chairman I think we may characterise it as a drawn battle![3]

The Macmillan Committee reported in June 1931, three months before we were forced off the Gold Standard.[4] The Committee had allowed Keynes a great deal of time – both in cross-examining witnesses and, in private, in presenting his own views – not confined to arguing his case for increasing public investment.

1. *Ibid.*, p. 21, question nos. 5624-5625.
2. *Ibid.*, p. 22, question no. 5650.
3. *Ibid.*, p. 24, question nos. 5689-5690.
4. MACMILLAN COMMITTEE ON FINANCE AND INDUSTRY, *Report*. Presented to Parliament by the Financial Secretary to the Treasury, June 1931. Cmd. 3897. London: His Majesty's Stationery Office, 1931.

Their terms of reference were wide. The Committee was not only 'to enquire into banking, finance and credit', but also 'to make recommendations calculated [. . .] to promote the development of trade and commerce and the employment of labour'.[1]

In spite of some opposition to Keynes' advocacy of public expenditure, there was a general desire to provide Keynes with an opportunity for publicly arguing his views. It was, therefore, decided to annex to the Report a number of Addenda signed by some of the members.

One Addendum represented an important victory for Keynes.[2] It was signed not only by Keynes, but by Ernest Bevin, the prominent trade-union leader, McKenna, and three other members of the Committee, but not the economist, Theodore Gregory – six out of a total of fourteen. They discussed the 'Treasury view', but they 'gathered [. . .] from the evidence of Sir R. Hopkins that it would be a mistake to attribute this view to the Treasury at the present time'.[3] In the view of the signatories of this Addendum as against that of their Chairman, Keynes had won the long drawn-out battle with Hopkins. It was recommended that 'the task of capital development in this country' should now be attacked 'in a much more systematic and far-sighted manner than hitherto'.[4]

I shall describe in Section 4 of Lecture v Keynes' success, both in the main Report and in this Addendum, in opposing a general reduction of money-wages.

Devaluation was rejected in the Addendum, in agreement with the main Report,[5] but Mr Bevin and one other member expressed carefully qualified dissent.

Keynes' own view was that, having suffered the agonies of returning to the pre-War dollar parity of sterling, against which

1. MACMILLAN COMMITTEE ON FINANCE AND INDUSTRY, *Report*. 'Minute of Appointment. Treasury Minute dated 5th November, 1929', p. vi.
2. COMMITTEE ON FINANCE AND INDUSTRY, *Report, Addendum I*, pp. 190-209; reprinted in KEYNES, vol. xx, pp. 283-309.
3. *Ibid.*, p. 204; KEYNES, vol. xx, p. 302.
4. *Ibid.*, p. 207; KEYNES, vol. xx, p. 306.
5. *Ibid.*, pp. 110-11 and 199; KEYNES, vol. xx, p. 296.

he had been bitterly opposed, it would be foolish, for the great financial international centre of London, lightly to abandon the benefits of a fixed parity.

This was in line with the view taken in October 1930 by Keynes' Committee of Economists of the Economic Advisory Council, to which I refer in Section 1 of Lecture IV.

Included in the Addendum was a proposal, as an alternative to devaluation, of a tariff on all imports balanced by an equal subsidy on all exports, thus improving the country's competitive position (both overseas and at home) without sacrificing the benefits of Free Trade. (Keynes had already, on 7 March 1931, published this proposal in an article in the *New Statesman and Nation*.)[1]

By the beginning of August 1931 Keynes had changed his mind on the subject of devaluation. In a letter to the Prime Minister, Ramsay MacDonald, on 5 August he had to admit that it was now his view

and this is the new fact within the last two months – it is now nearly *certain* that we shall go off the existing gold parity at no distant date. Whatever may have been the case some time ago, it is now too late to avoid this [. . .].

[Devaluation] might quite well be taken by the country as a whole, not as a disaster, but with an extraordinary sense of relief and of hope. The 'inner opinion' – what everyone believes at the bottom of his heart but never realises until the last moment – is a mighty force in this country.[2]

Keynes came out in public in a letter to the *Evening Standard* on 10 September.[3] He wrote that he 'personally now believe[d] [devaluation] to be the right remedy',[4] but he still put forward

1. 'Proposals for a Revenue Tariff', *New Statesman and Nation*, 7 March 1931, reprinted with the same title in KEYNES, vol. IX, pp. 231-8.

2. SUSAN HOWSON and DONALD WINCH, *The Economic Advisory Council 1930-1939. A Study in Economy Advice during Depression and Recovery*. Cambridge: Cambridge University Press, 1977, p. 89.

3. JOHN MAYNARD KEYNES, 'We Must Restrict our Imports', *Evening Standard*, 10 September 1931; reprinted as 'On the Eve of Gold Suspension', in KEYNES, vol. IX, pp. 238-42.

4. *Ibid.*, p. 242.

as an alternative 'direct measures to restrict imports (and, if possible, subsidise exports)'.[1]

On 21 September the country did not so much devalue as get forcibly pushed off the pre-War parity.

Six days later, in an article in the *Sunday Express*, Keynes wrote that 'there are few Englishmen who do not rejoice at the breaking of our gold fetters'.[2] *Force majeure* was, in the eyes of international financiers, quite different from a cold-blooded decision.

Between the publication of *Can Lloyd George Do It?* and the appointment of the Macmillan Committee, the General Election of 30 May 1929 had been fought. The Liberals fared disastrously. As a result of an Election dominated by unemployment, the Liberals were left with only 49 seats – out of a total membership of the House of Commons of over 600.

Ironically, the new minority Labour Government ran into immediate trouble over economic policy. 'Jimmy' Thomas, who had been a leading trade-union leader, was responsible for the co-ordination of Government unemployment policies. At the start he made it clear that the Government had no intention of infringing orthodox canons of investing only in projects which were remunerative in a commercial sense as 'no useful purpose would be served by adopting extravagant and indefensible proposals'.[3]

The Treasury were already dominant over the new Government. This was too much for Oswald Mosley, a member of the Left Wing group of the Labour Party, a junior Minister, working under Thomas, who was a strong supporter of Keynes' ideas and a rapidly rising politician.

The sad sequence is told in Robert Skidelsky's biography.[4] Completely frustrated, he resigned after a year. 'Of the sixty-odd

1. KEYNES, vol. IX, p. 241.
2. JOHN MAYNARD KEYNES, 'The Future of the World', *Sunday Express*, 27 September 1931; reprinted as 'The End of the Gold Standard' in KEYNES, vol. IX, pp. 245-9.
3. SUSAN HOWSON and DONALD WINCH, *The Economic Advisory Council 1930-1939*, p. 19.
4. ROBERT SKIDELSKY, *Oswald Mosley*. London: Macmillan, 1975, pp. 209-12.

ministers who have resigned their offices this century, Mosley was the only one to do so over unemployment.'[1]

After his triumphant resignation speech of 28 May, the Editor of *The Times*, in a leading article on 2 June, condemned his 'panic policy of reckless extravagance'.[2]

Defence came from an unexpected quarter. In a letter published in *The Times* on 6 June, Pigou wrote:

When [...] as at the present time, there is an enormous mass of unemployment, their virtue and their relevance [of the arguments against State action designed to stimulate employment] are lost. If employment is 'artificially created' in these conditions, men are available to come into it, not merely from more useful occupations elsewhere, but from soul-destroying idleness.[3]

In December 1930, Mosley published a Manifesto, signed by seventeen Labour Members of Parliament. Keynes published in the *Nation and Athenaeum* a comment which was, for the most part, highly favourable.[4]

Keynes was given another opportunity of trying out his ideas by his appointment as a member of the Economic Advisory Council, set up by Ramsay MacDonald in February 1930, three months after the Macmillan Committee. Over the following nine years he took full advantage of the opportunity of developing his ideas on issues of economic policy.

On 24 July 1930 a Committee of Economists of the Economic Advisory Council was appointed, with Keynes in the Chair. It reported on 24 October 1930. I discuss the Committee in the course of Section 1 of my next Lecture.

Keynes' preoccupation with practical questions of economic policy for over a year resulted in the realm of theory in the making of a fresh start, with muscles unbound. In the summer of 1931 he began serious thinking about what was to be the

1. *Ibid.*, p. 209.
2. *Ibid.*, p. 211.
3. *Ibid.*, pp. 211-12.
4. JOHN MAYNARD KEYNES, *Sir Oswald Mosley's Manifesto*, London: The Nation and Athenaeum, 1930 (13 December); reprinted in KEYNES, vol. XX, pp. 473-6.

General Theory. He had made some progress when in March 1933 he published four articles in *The Times*, which soon took the form of a pamphlet, entitled *The Means to Prosperity*. It is reproduced in *Essays in Persuasion.*[1] It is interesting to compare this pamphlet with *Can Lloyd George Do It?* The passage of four strenuous years had, to a remarkable degree, lubricated the operation of his mind and his pen.

1. KEYNES, vol. IX, pp. 335-66.

FOURTH LECTURE
From the 'multiplier' to the *General Theory*

1. The 'multiplier'. – 2. The Cambridge 'Circus'. – 3. From the 'Treatise' to the 'General Theory'.

1. The 'multiplier'

I began work on my so-called 'multiplier' article in the Austrian Tyrol in August 1930. I cannot recall whether or not I was influenced by being a Joint Secretary of the Committee of Economists (appointed on 24 July).

I was inspired by *Can Lloyd George Do It?* partly because this marked a milestone in the development of thought, but also because of certain arithmetical and logical problems which it raised.

The article was eventually published in the *Economic Journal* in June 1931.[1] It is normally regarded as a simple statistical enquiry, and this is confirmed by its title 'The Relation of Home Investment to Unemployment'. Indeed, the title appears further to restrict its scope – as does much of its drafting – to the arithmetical question which faced Keynes and Henderson when they were writing *Can Lloyd George Do It?*

They had used the words 'direct' and 'indirect' employment as in the Liberal Party manifesto *We Can Conquer Unemployment* – to distinguish between employment on the site from employment in the production of the necessary materials and their transfer.[2]

A high proportion of the additional employment proposed in the Liberal Party manifesto was on roads and bridges.[3]

---

1. RICHARD KAHN, 'The Relation of Home Investment to Unemployment', *Economic Journal*, June 1931, pp. 173-98; reprinted in RICHARD KAHN, *Selected Essays on Employment and Growth*. Cambridge: Cambridge University Press, 1972, pp. 1-27.
2. LIBERAL PARTY, *We Can Conquer Unemployment*. London: Cassell, 1929, p. 21.
3. *Ibid.*, p. 52.

Keynes and Henderson accepted the Liberal claim that each additional million pounds spent annually on road improvements would employ, directly or indirectly, 5,000 work people – 2,000 to 2,500 directly and the remainder indirectly.

They were able to quote a 'reluctant admission' that these figures were correct, extracted in the House of Commons by a Parliamentary Question addressed to the Minister of Transport.

In *We Can Conquer Unemployment* only a page is devoted to the 'Indirect Effects on Employment'.

In all this, so far, we have taken no account of the large increase in employment everywhere resulting indirectly from the addition to the national purchasing power represented by the wages of the workers directly employed in this way.[1]

The word 'indirect' was confusing. It had been used to distinguish between employment on the site and employment in the production of the necessary materials and their transfer. To avoid this confusion, the words used in my article, and later by Keynes in the *General Theory*, are 'primary' and 'secondary' employment. Primary employment included 'direct' and 'indirect'; 'secondary' employment resulted from the addition to national purchasing power.

Keynes and Henderson were confusing in a different sense. They referred to the 'general stimulus of trade' caused by the substitution of wages for unemployment pay. They continued:

the greater trade activity would make for further trade activity; for the forces of prosperity, like those of trade depression, work with a cumulative effect. When trade is slack there is a tendency to postpone placing orders [. . .] a general hesitation to go forward or take risks. When, on the other hand, the wheels of trade begin to move briskly the opposite set of forces comes into play, a mood favourable to enterprise and capital extensions spreads through the business community, and the expansion of trade gains accordingly a gathering momentum.[2]

1. LIBERAL PARTY, *We Can Conquer Unemployment*, p. 52.
2. JOHN MAYNARD KEYNES and HUBERT D. HENDERSON, *Can Lloyd George Do It?*. London: The Nation and Athenaeum, 1929 (12 May); reprinted in KEYNES, vol. IX, pp. 106-7.

The favourable influence on the state of confidence – on the expectations and spirits of entrepreneurs – of a rise in demand is a most important cumulative factor. It is difficult to assess its order of magnitude, and in any case it is, up to a point, a progressive movement through time. The additional employment provided in this way depends, *inter alia*, on whether the rise in Government expenditure on capital development is likely to be maintained, or – as a result perhaps of a high probability of a General Election resulting in power passing to a Government hostile to its predecessor's policy – is likely to be brought to an end. But, of course, the 'shot in the arm' argument is not to be ignored.

The state of confidence about the near future – and both the factors which influence it and the influences which it exercises – is a difficult subject to assess, still more to quantify. It plays a prominent part in the *General Theory*.

Towards the end of my article I was careful to state that it was based on the assumption that 'the state of general confidence [was] not affected'.[1] I did not mean that this was at all probable – but merely that in the study of one type of causation it is necessary to abstract from others. I then devoted only three concluding paragraphs to the subject: it was not the subject of the article.

Keynes and Henderson, unlike the authors of *We Can Conquer Unemployment*, took the opposite course. No attempt was made to separate out the ratio of secondary to primary employment, on the assumption of a given state of confidence.

Naturally enough, they wrote that: 'It is not possible to measure effects of this character with any sort of precision.' The sentence goes on 'and little or no account of them is, therefore, taken'[2] in this pamphlet. They continued:

But, in our opinion, these effects are of immense importance. For this reason we believe that [. . .] [they] would be far larger than the Liberal pamphlet assumes.[3]

1. RICHARD KAHN, 'The Relation of Home Investment to Unemployment', p. 197.
2. KEYNES, vol. IX, p. 107.
3. *Ibid.*

They failed to realise that the authors of the Liberal pamphlet were discussing secondary employment in the strict sense – something as different as chalk is from cheese from the subject which Keynes and Henderson were trying to assess in this part of their pamphlet.

Further on in their pamphlet, Keynes and Henderson wrote:

Mr Lloyd George has given a pledge that the execution of his programme will not mean an addition to taxation. He has added that, of course, this does not mean that it will cost nothing, but that the cost will be less than the money which it will save in other directions *plus* the buoyancy of the revenue attributable to it *plus* economies on such things as armaments.[1]

The suggestion that entirely irrelevant economies on armaments would be needed to secure fulfilment of the pledge strongly indicated that the pledge was not completely justified.

On the other hand, in this passage Keynes and Henderson, in contrast to the last passage but two quoted by me, were *tacitly* confining themselves to secondary employment in the strict sense, and taking no credit for the possible triggering off of a cumulative boom. Their rough estimate was that 'nearly a *half* of the *capital* cost would be recovered *at the time*', a quarter from the saving on the Unemployment Fund.[2]

The estimates made in my article led to the conclusion that the saving to the Unemployment Fund, together with the saving to the Exchequer on the cost of transitional benefit, should be just half of the total cost. The excess of my *half* over the Keynes – Henderson *quarter* is accounted for only partly by my bringing in the saving on the cost of transitional benefit.

My extremely conservative estimate of the increase in the yield of taxation was exactly the same – one eighth of the total cost – as that made by Keynes and Henderson.

It is remarkable that the inspired guesses of Keynes and Henderson turned out to be so accurate although, so far as is known, they made no estimate of the 'multiplier' – the ratio of the total

1. KEYNES, vol. IX, p. 110.
2. *Ibid.*, p. 112.

additional employment (primary and secondary) to the primary employment.

The superficially obvious object of my article was to estimate the 'multiplier' – Keynes' happier substitute for my 'ratio' of secondary to primary employment. My conclusion was that it lay between 0.56 and 0.94, and I suggested that the adoption of $\frac{3}{4}$ would be 'erring in the direction of under-statement'.[1] It was only after I had estimated this ratio that I could proceed to estimate the figures for the net cost to the Exchequer.

A member of the original staff of the Economic Advisory Council, set up in February 1930, was Colin Clark, a clever, flexible, courageous and practical statistician. Soon after, the staff were asked by Ministers to examine the effect on employment of expansion in the export trades. Colin Clark, in the note prepared by him, with the help of A. W. Flux of the Board of Trade, included no estimate of the secondary effects of this increase in employment on the following grounds:

It will be seen at once that any crude calculation [. . .] would lead to assuming an infinite series of beneficial repercussions. This clearly cannot represent the case, nor on the other hand can we categorically deny the possibility of beneficial repercussions. The limiting factors, however, are obscure and economic theory cannot state the possibilities with precision.[2]

That was in about April 1930. The odd thing is that in July I made the acquaintance of Colin Clark in my new capacity of co-Secretary of the newly appointed Committee of Economists of the Council, which was appointed on 24 July and reported on 24 October 1930, when the *Treatise* had just been completed.

I was not a statistician and it was in co-operation with Colin Clark that I produced, for the use of the Committee of Economists, a paper which might be regarded as a primitive draft

---

1. RICHARD KAHN, 'The Relation of Home Investment to Unemployment', p. 186.

2. SUSAN HOWSON and DONALD WINCH, *The Economic Advisory Council 1930-1939. A Study in Economic Advice during Depression and Recovery*. Cambridge: Cambridge University Press, 1977, p. 36, note.

of part of my article. Colin Clark not only provided the statistical basis. He helped me in the drafting. I cannot recall any doubt on his part that the sum of an infinite convergent series is finite.

My paper was circulated to the members of the Committee of Economists. Keynes was in the Chair. The other members were Hubert Henderson (economist), Pigou, Lionel Robbins (of the London School of Economics) and Sir Josiah Stamp (an eminent self-taught statistician and economist – at the time Chairman of the London, Midland and Scottish Railway, and a Director of the Bank of England), with Francis Hemming, a civil servant, and me as Joint Secretaries.

According to Susan Howson and Donald Winch (who confirm my own memory):

Keynes [. . .] attempted to incorporate the early results of Kahn's work on primary and secondary employment [. . .] to give some idea of the magnitudes involved in an expansionary programme, and to emphasise that the 'inflationary' effects on domestic prices of increases in employment would arise out of any scheme for increasing employment. Even so, Kahn's findings gave rise to controversy between Kahn, Pigou and Keynes on the validity of the exercise.[1]

They also state:

Keynes tried to use the [multiplier] idea to argue for public works in the report, but Pigou's and Henderson's objections ensured that there was no sign of this in the final product.[2]

I agree that Pigou and Henderson argued strongly against public works. I agree, in particular, that 'Henderson objected that the "conclusions reached . . . rest upon no appeal to fact at all"'.[3]

Nevertheless, in the Summary of the Committee's principal Conclusions it was stated that:

Under conditions of extensive unemployment such as prevail to-day, and have prevailed in lesser degree for some years, the policy of promoting useful schemes of capital development, either by pressing forward such work as lies within the direct control of the Government

1. SUSAN HOWSON and DONALD WINCH, *The Economic Advisory Council 1930-1939. A Study in Economic Advice during Depression and Recovery*, p. 59.
2. *Ibid.*, p. 49.
3. *Ibid.*, p. 69.

or by the offer of State subsidies to local authorities and public utility companies is a sound one for the State to pursue, since we do not accept the view that the undertaking of such work must necessarily cause a mere diversion from other employment.[1]

The argument was amplified in the body of the Report,[2] and, implicitly although not explicitly, full credit was given to the multiplier. It is true that it is qualified in various ways, summed up by the mild statement that 'The above conditions necessarily set limits to the extent to which it is possible to meet unemployment by the policy of public works'.[3]

Subject to the dangers involved in looking back half a century, my impression is that it was largely a matter of Keynes' success in genuinely convincing the sceptics, but to some degree their submission to Keynes' fervour and their desire to appear unanimous.

Robbins did not sign the Report but offered a Minority Report of his own. He was by no means completely damning on the subject of public works but he was 'more apprehensive [than his colleagues] that a continuance of this policy may definitely tend to delay the coming of recovery'[4] – this at a time when the number of unemployed amounted to about 2,300,000!

In a lecture which I delivered to the American Statistical Association on 'Public Works and Inflation' in Cincinnati in December 1932, I pointed out the obvious reasons why the multiplier for the USA was considerably higher than for the UK – a low ratio of imports to national income and a low level of subsistence for the unemployed. Timidly I did not go beyond suggesting that the USA multiplier was considerably in excess of 2.[5]

I sent Keynes an account of my visit to the USA. He replied:

1. *Ibid.*, p. 221.
2. *Ibid.*, p. 200, paragraph 63.
3. *Ibid.*, p. 201, paragraphs 65-7 (the quotation on paragraph 67).
4. *Ibid.*, p. 228.
5. RICHARD KAHN, 'Public Works and Inflation', *Journal of the American Statistical Association*, Supplement, March 1933, pp. 168-73; reprinted in RICHARD KAHN, *Selected Essays on Employment and Growth*, pp. 28-34.

Colin [Clark] was delighted with the multiplier for secondary employment, but I tell him that all it does is to increase slightly my confidence in the accuracy of his statistics [. . .] I tell him not to overcook it.[1]

Keynes, in his pamphlet *The Means to Prosperity*, estimated the UK multiplier at 'at least 2', and the USA multiplier to 'be greater than 2'.[2]

Although it was, and still is, my estimate of the multiplier with which my article is mainly associated, it was far more important for a quite different contribution. My main concern – from the start – was to prove that the various offsets – the increase in the yield of taxation, savings of various kinds to the Exchequer, or rather (as we should now put it) to the Public Sector, the increase in the excess of imports over exports, the increase in private savings (mainly out of profits), and the change in the rate of saving due to the rise in prices – added up to the cost of the investment. This I called the 'fundamental relation'.

I was fortunate that James Meade, of Oxford, was spending the academic year 1930-31 in Cambridge. He was working in somewhat the same field and he and I co-operated closely. I made use of some of his unpublished results and called the fundamental relation 'Mr. Meade's relation'. I pointed out that

this relation, far from being the logical consequence of summing an infinite geometrical progression, is in reality self-evident in nature and is merely a particular case of a general relation, due to Mr. J. E. Meade.[3]

In a footnote I stated:

It is to be noted that the word profits is here being employed in the ordinary sense of the difference between business men's receipts and

---

1. *Letter* to Richard F. Kahn, *29 January 1933*; reprinted in KEYNES, vol. XIII, p. 413.

2. JOHN MAYNARD KEYNES, *The Means to Prosperity*. London: Macmillan, 1933, reprinted in KEYNES, vol. IX, pp. 335-6. The version of the pamphlet published in the *Collected Writings* is not the original British version, published in March 1933, but the American version, published in the middle of 1933. The words 'at least 2' appear in the British version (see p. 341, note 1 of KEYNES, vol. IX). In the American version the words are an unqualified '2', and the estimate for the USA was added.

3. RICHARD KAHN, 'The Relation of Home Investment to Unemployment', p. 188.

their outgoings, and not in the sense in which Mr. Keynes employs the word. But it is clear that Mr. Meade's relation is merely a special statement of Mr. Keynes' general proposition [in his *Treatise*] that 'profits' are equal to the difference between investment and savings.[1]

I was here using the word 'savings' in the *Treatise* sense.

Of course what we had done – but failed completely to realise – was, by a very roundabout method, to establish the identity of saving and investment – if saving is defined on commonsense lines rather than on those of the *Treatise*.

I then set out 'Mr. Meade's relation' in its most general form:

Cost of investment = saving on dole + increase in excess of imports over exports + increase in unspent profits – diminution in rate of saving due to rise in prices.[2]

I suggested that:

This relation should bring immediate relief and consolation to those who are worried about the monetary sources that are available to meet the cost of the roads. The increase in the excess of imports over exports is equal, if gold is not flowing at an appreciable rate, to the reduction in foreign lending. So that if one is looking for sources *outside* the banking system, they are available to precisely the right extent. The cost of the roads is equal to the saving on the dole *plus* the reduction in foreign lending *plus* the increase in unspent profits *minus* the reduction in the rate of saving.[3]

In setting out 'Mr. Meade's relation' I accidently omitted the increase in Government revenue resulting from higher levels of output and input.

The article, as published, is in retrospect poorly ordered. The most important part of it is a small section, completely lost in the main body of the text. It opens:

The price-level and output of home-produced consumption-goods, just like the price and output of any single commodity, are determined

1. *Ibid.*
2. *Ibid.*, p. 188.
3. *Ibid.*, p. 189.

by the conditions of supply and demand. If the conditions of supply can be regarded as fixed, both the price-level and the output are determined by the demand; and there is a unique correlation between price-level and output.[1]

I failed to give clear expression to the idea that Keynes should be thinking of the demand for output as a whole – or, at least, for the output as a whole of consumption-goods and the output as a whole of capital-goods.

The following passage is important, even if we all at that time were too much exercised over the extent of the rise in the price-level associated with a rise in demand (the slope of the short-period supply curve) – certainly very small in a deep depression.

The relief of unemployment by means of national development is often objected to on the grounds that it will cause a rise in the cost of living. The extraordinary fatuity of this objection is, of course, quite apparent. There is nothing unnatural about the rise in prices caused by the building of roads. It will occur equally if employment in the production of consumption-goods is stimulated to an equal extent by more natural means (other than a reduction of costs). [. . .]

Even more fantastic is it to argue at the same time that road-building causes a rise in prices and yet that it is not responsible for any *net* addition to the volume of employment. The rise in prices, if it occurs at all, is a natural concomitant of increased output, to a degree indicated by the slope of the supply curve.[2]

I was handicapped by having to translate my thinking into the definitions of the *Treatise*. I had not sufficient independence of mind to abandon the *Treatise*.

In June 1932 Professor Jens Warming of Copenhagen University published an article on the same subject.[3] I commented in the following number of the *Economic Journal*.[4] Warming had seriously misunderstood me: he had failed to appreciate the distinction between expenditure on consumption and saving out of increased income.

1. RICHARD KAHN, 'The Relation of Home Investment to Unemployment', p. 177.
2. *Ibid.*, p. 178.
3. JENS WARMING, 'International Difficulties Arising out of the Financing of Public Works during Depression', *Economic Journal*, June 1932, pp. 211-24.
4. RICHARD KAHN, 'The Financing of Public Works: A Note', *Economic Journal*, September 1932, pp. 492-5.

However, Warming made an extremely important linguistic breakthrough. He pointed out that it is the extra saving made out of increased income which is 'the real source of investment';[1] 'the secondary employment must continue until the total created income causes so much saving that the original investment can be paid'.[2] But Warming had failed to realise that the equality of the increase in saving with the increase in investment insured him against what he called 'inflation'.

Warming was not using the word 'saving' in the sense used by Keynes in the *Treatise* (so as to exclude 'abnormal profits') but, I pointed out,

in the ordinary sense of the aggregate of the excess of individuals' receipts over their expenditure on consumption. But in this simple-minded sense of the term, savings are *always and necessarily* equal to investment: that is a mere truism, which emerges at once, as Mr. Keynes has demonstrated [a year earlier in the *Economic Journal*][3], from the simple-minded definition of savings. Whatever the level of investment, funds are always available to pay for it.[4]

Dennis Robertson deduced from my use of the adjective 'simple-minded' that I was opposed to these sensible definitions rather than strongly in favour. His own mind had already begun to move in the same direction. So had Keynes', but reluctantly.

Lack of space prevents me from commenting adequately on Professor Don Patinkin's recent article on 'Keynes and the Multiplier'.[5]

Nobody can suppose that there is anything new in the idea of the multiplier. When I was aged about 8, my father explained to me the cumulative effect of providing one extra man with employment. What he did not explain to me – and what I was too young to ask – is why the multiplier is not infinite.

1. JENS WARMING, 'International Difficulties Arising out of the Financing of Public Works During Depression', p. 214.

2. *Ibid.*, pp. 215-16.

3. KEYNES, 'A Rejoinder' to Mr. D. H. Robertson, *Economic Journal*, September 1931, pp. 412-23; reprinted in KEYNES, vol. XIII, pp. 219-36.

4. RICHARD KAHN, 'The Financing of Public Works: A Note', p. 494.

5. DON PATINKIN, 'Keynes and the Multiplier', *Manchester School of Economic and Social Studies*, September 1978, pp. 209-23.

Of the authors referred to by Don Patinkin the most interesting is Nicholas Johannsen. He was described by Keynes in
his *Treatise* as an 'American amateur economist (crank, some
might say)'.[1] In a footnote Keynes described him as seeming to
'come very near to the truth' in his book and subsequent pamphlets. But Keynes regarded his doctrine of 'impair savings' as
indicating a 'more or less permanent condition in the modern
world due to a saturation of the capital market'. Johannsen
overlooked 'the fact that a fall in the rate of interest would be
the cure'.[2] Don Patinkin refers to Johannsen's 'Multiplying
Principle'.[3]

He treated saving as the only leakage, so that the cumulative
effect of a downswing resulted in one-quarter of income being
obliterated.

Don Patinkin is fully justified in criticising the presentation
of the argument in my article for failure to make it clear that it
was, in effect, an exercise in comparative statics and not in sequence analysis. My failure has led to a vast amount of misunderstanding. The issue called for a much fuller exposition than
my footnote to which Don Patinkin refers:

I am here considering the position in the final position of equilibrium when everything has settled down [. . .] some time will [. . .]
elapse [before this point is reached] [. . .] I do not enter into the
question of this time-lag.[4]

My failure to enlarge on this issue would have led to endless
trouble had not Keynes come to the rescue. In the course of the

1. KEYNES, vol. VI, p. 90. (The American amateur economists were in fact two:
Keynes in the *Treatise* refers also to Colonel Rorty and his theory of 'over-commit-
ments'.)

2. *Ibid.*, note 2.

3. NICHOLAS A. L. J. JOHANNSEN, *A Neglected Point in Connection with Crises*. New
York: The Bankers Publishing Company, 1908, pp. 43 et seq. In his slightly earlier
book (*Keynes' Monetary Thought*. Durham, North Carolina: Duke University Press,
1976, p. 84), PATINKIN complains that, Keynes, having in his *Treatise* mentioned
Johannsen in these favourable terms, failed in his *General Theory* to classify him with
Karl Marx, Silvio Gesell and Major Douglas (KEYNES, vol. VII, p. 32), or indeed
to mention him at all.

4. RICHARD KAHN, 'The Relation of Home Investment to Unemployment',
p. 183, note 2.

American edition of *The Means to Prosperity*, published in the middle of 1933, Keynes, in a section on the multiplier, estimated the time-lags, and concluded that:

it will be seen that seven-eighths of the total effects come from the primary expenditure and the first two repercussions, so that the time-lags involved are not unduly serious.[1]

There is a widespread belief – stronger to-day than it was after the publication of the *General Theory* – that the case for public expenditure as a means of raising demand is not a matter of commonsense but an illustration of the Quantity Theory of Money. In other words, it is successful only to the extent that the necessary funds are secured from the banking system (entailing a danger of inflation) rather than from the non-banking Private Sector. A good example is provided in the course of a letter written by Robertson to Keynes on 1 April 1933, half-way through the writing of the *General Theory* (and incidentally a good example of Robertson's concern over the abandonment by Keynes of the Quantity Theory):

I hate always to appear in print as a controversialist with you, but it is because of the inexhaustible suggestiveness of the *Treatise*! And I don't see how progress is better made in these fundamental matters than by public discussion between the ½ dozen people who are wallowing in them.

I know I shall never reconvert you to old K-and-V method [the Quantity Theory]; but I can't refrain from suggesting how much stronger they make the *prima facie* case for public works. For on your and Kahn's s[hort] p[eriod] method, all new money inevitably becomes completely inert in the end, and most of it pretty quickly. Hence your arguments can do nothing to allay the objections of those who urge that the budgets *of future years* will be burdened by the interest charges on the loan. But surely *prima facie* money once effectively introduced into circulation may be expected to stay there, and to circulate (thus affecting prices or employment as the case may be) with a velocity approximating to that of existing money, unless and until it is withdrawn by taxation, deflation, etc.[2]

1. KEYNES, vol. IX, p. 343.
2. KEYNES, vol. XXIX, p. 17. I quoted Keynes' rejoinder in Section 10 of the Second Lecture. In the course of it he accused Robertson of 'addressing yourself to one of the deader of my dead selves'.

Even by that late date Robertson completely failed to appreciate that:

1. There was no reason why additional expenditure on public works needed to be financed by the creation of additional money as against borrowing from the public (though if a heavy programme was started off suddenly, some temporary help from the banking system would be useful for pump-priming purposes).

That was one of the lessons which I had tried to teach in my 'multiplier article' and is based on the rise in the rate of saving with the rise in the rate of Government expenditure.

The increase of employment was *not* the result of an increasing quantity of money.

2. However, to avoid a rise in the rate of interest, and tighter credit generally, it would be desirable that the total amount of money available for the active circulation should increase in proportion with the increase in the value of national output.

3. If the additional flow of expenditure were terminated, employment would fall to its previous level apart from:

a) the effectiveness of the temporary public works programme as a 'shot in the arm', resulting on a more or less lasting basis in a limited recovery of confidence and in the rate of investment;

b) the favourable influence on employment of a higher quantity of money, in excess of the needs of the active circulation, as a result of lower rates of interest and, generally, easier credit.

Robertson failed to realise that the lasting benefit which he in his letter was urging Keynes to claim could be achieved *without* any public works programme merely by using open-market operations to increase the quantity of money; and that the benefit was not attributable to the circulation of additional money but to lower rates of interest and easier credit.

2. The Cambridge 'Circus'

The publication of the *Treatise* on 31 October 1930 led almost immediately to a group of younger Cambridge economists getting together to discuss the basic issues, stimulated by the knowledge that Keynes would shortly be embarking on a new book. It operated during the academic year 1930-31. It consisted of James Meade, Joan and Austin Robinson, Piero Sraffa and myself. In addition to discussions among ourselves, we held a seminar – membership of this was severely restricted but it included students in their third (final) year.

The account of this 'Circus' in Vol. XIII of Keynes' *Collected Writings* was prepared in 1971 in time to be incorporated by Donald Moggridge in the Volume, published in 1973.[1] We were relying on forty-year-old memories. But we agreed on the published account. Donald Moggridge has in addition published useful comments in the course of an article.[2]

More recently our joint account has been usefully supplemented by Austin Robinson[3] and Joan Robinson.[4]

Purely personal memories I am reserving for my final Lecture. As I stated in the Introduction to these Lectures, I am not entering into personal controversy, partly because it would use up valuable space, partly because it would be unseemly to appear to be making a case for my friends and myself. Don Patinkin disputes the importance commonly attributed to us in assisting Keynes to write the *General Theory*. In so far as he relies on documents, he is fully entitled to make his case. Others can judge. For my own part I feel myself unable to arouse any feeling of passion over events which took place so long ago.

---

1. KEYNES, vol. XIII, pp. 337-43.

2. DONALD E. MOGGRIDGE, 'From the *Treatise* to *The General Theory*: An Exercise in Chronology', *History of Political Economy*, Spring 1973, pp. 72-88.

3. AUSTIN ROBINSON, *Keynes and his Cambridge Colleagues*, in DON PATINKIN and J. CLARK LEITH (eds.), *Keynes, Cambridge and 'The General Theory'*. Proceedings of a Conference held at the University of Western Ontario. London: Macmillan, 1977, pp. 25-38.

4. JOAN ROBINSON, *Contributions to Modern Economics*. Oxford: Basil Blackwell, 1978.

To anybody who did not know Keynes, it is astonishing that he was willing, week after week, to discuss with me, acting as the group's spokesman, the problems which had arisen and their implications. He could so easily have requested us to submit a comprehensive draft memorandum for his consideration. Austin Robinson has referred to Keynes' 'extraordinary magnanimity'.[1] And:

At no moment in his life, I think, did Keynes' greatness of character appear more strongly than at this time [. . .] Keynes never even appeared to hesitate. He was off with the rest of us in pursuit of truth with as enthusiastic a zest as if he were demolishing the work of his worst enemy.[2]

The age of each of us was under 34; Keynes was 47 years old.

The most important issue discussed by the Circus was what Austin Robinson called the '"widow's cruse" fallacy'[3] and the 'Danaid jar' fallacy.[4] The reference is to the following passage in Volume I of the *Treatise*:

There is one peculiarity of profits (or losses) which we may note in passing, because it is one of the reasons why it is necessary to segregate them from income proper, as a category apart. If entrepreneurs choose to spend a portion of their profits on consumption [. . .] the effect is to *increase* the profit on the sale of liquid consumption goods by an amount exactly equal to the amount of profits which have been thus expended [. . .] Thus, however much of their profits entrepreneurs spend on consumption, the increment of wealth belonging to entrepreneurs remains the same as before. Thus profits, as a source of capital increment for entrepreneurs, are a widow's cruse which remains undepleted however much of them may be devoted to riotous living. When, on the other hand, entrepreneurs are making losses, and seek to recoup these losses by curtailing

1. Austin Robinson, *Keynes and his Cambridge Colleagues*, p. 35.
2. Austin Robinson, 'John Maynard Keynes, 1883-1946', *Economic Journal*, March 1947, p. 40.
3. Holy Bible, I Kings xvii; Austin Robinson, *Keynes and his Cambridge Colleagues*, p. 34.
4. In Greek legend, Argos, founded by Danaus, suffered every summer from a drought. In the lower world the fifty daughters of Danaus (the Danaides) had to carry water in broken vases.

their normal expenditure on consumption, i.e. by saving more, the cruse becomes a Danaid jar which can never be filled up.[1]

The complaint of the members of the Circus was that Keynes was here implicitly assuming a fixed output of consumption-goods. If entrepreneurs responded to the abnormal profits by increasing the output of consumption-goods, the price-level of consumption-goods would progressively fall, and abnormal profits would fall, until either entrepreneurs earned no more than normal remuneration or some barrier was encountered – full-capacity utilisation or full employment of labour.

Donald Moggridge suggests that a 'fixed national output' is implied.[2] I can see no evidence for this. It would have been quite out of keeping with other parts of the *Treatise*, to which I am about to refer.

Keynes gave no reason for choosing any particular level of total output, O, and he did not attempt any explanation of the division of O between R, the sales of consumption-goods, and C, the output of capital-goods *plus* the increment of working capital and stocks.

Keynes could easily have explained that he was examining one point of time during a process of change. Towards the end of Section I of Lecture III, on the *Treatise*, I described the Fundamental Equations as representing 'a remarkable break-through', in drawing a distinction in price-determination between 'money-costs per unit of output' (in an equilibrium situation) and abnormal or subnormal profits.

But the text of my present Lectures was not available to the members of the Circus; and I like to suppose that my own thinking has advanced in the course of half a century.

The astonishing thing about the '"widow's-cruse" fallacy' is that a considerable section of the two volumes of the *Treatise* are devoted to fluctuations in the rate of investment and the credit cycle. For example, Chapter 20 is 'An Exercise in the Pure Theory of the Credit Cycle' –

1. KEYNES, vol. V, p. 125.
2. DONALD MOGGRIDGE, 'From the *Treatise* to *The General Theory*: An Exercise in Chronology', p. 76.

an essay in the internal mechanics of the price-wage-employment structure during the course of a cycle which represents a recovery in the volume of employment from a preceding slump which has reached an equilibrium between prices and costs of production, but is still characterised by unemployment.[1]

(This chapter comprises an elaborate sequence analysis. It explains why some economists regard the *Treatise* as – in some respects – superior to the *General Theory*.)

I do not see how we – members of the Circus – could have attributed to Keynes the assumption of inelastic supply, and I am completely mystified by the questions:

a) why we did not see this for ourselves;

b) why it did not come out in the course of the discussions between Keynes and me, on one of the occasions when I reported on difficulties which had arisen in discussions at the Circus – the upshot of which I would have reported back to the other members of the Circus.

The mystery is enhanced by Moggridge's discovery of a memorandum enclosed in a letter from Keynes to Ralph G. Hawtrey dated 28 November 1930, ten weeks after Keynes had completed the *Treatise* and less than a month after publication.[2] Keynes was dealing in the form of a nine-page memorandum with a large number of criticisms by Hawtrey of the proofs which Keynes had not had time to deal with before publication.

The question *how much* reduction of output is caused [. . .] is important, but not strictly a monetary problem. I have not attempted to deal with it in my book, though I have done a good deal of work at it. I am primarily concerned with what governs *prices*.[3]

And finally the following even more astonishing passage:

I repeat that I am not dealing with the complete set of causes which determine volume of output. For this would have led me an endlessly

---

1. KEYNES, vol. v, p. 274.

2. DONALD MOGGRIDGE, 'From the *Treatise* to *The General Theory*: An Exercise in Chronology', p. 78. Both the letter and the memorandum are reproduced in KEYNES, vol. XIII, pp. 139-49.

3. *Letter* to Ralph G. Hawtrey, *28 November 1930*; published in KEYNES, vol. XIII, pp. 139-49 (the quotation on p. 145).

long journey into the theory of short-period supply and a long way
from monetary theory; – though I agree that it will probably be
difficult in the future to prevent monetary theory and the theory of
short-period supply from running together. If I were to write the
book again, I should probably attempt to probe further into the difficulties of the latter; but I have already probed far enough to know
what a complicated affair it is.[1]

Of course the members of the Circus were completely unaware of this memorandum.

There is wide-spread agreement – though not universal – as
to the importance of the Circus in helping Keynes to make the
transition from the *Treatise* to the *General Theory*.

The Circus dissolved in May 1931 – the examination period.
In June, Keynes attended in Chicago a Conference organised by
the Harris Foundation and delivered three lectures on 'An Economic Analysis of Unemployment'.[2] The members of the Circus
were entitled to feel that Keynes was responding to their criticisms with remarkable speed and lucidity. A few quotations
will make this clear, although the main inspiration was, as described by Keynes in his opening sentence, the fact that they
were to-day 'in the middle of the greatest economic catastrophe –
the greatest catastrophe due almost entirely to economic causes –
of the modern world'[3] – a situation designed to give full play
to Keynes' eloquence.

Keynes emphasised the unprecedently high level of the rate
of investment through the world – in the United States 'something prodigious and incredible' which had prevailed in 1928.

It seems an extraordinary imbecility that this wonderful outburst of
productive energy should be the prelude to impoverishment and depression [. . .].

1. *Ibid.*, pp. 145-6.
2. JOHN MAYNARD KEYNES, 'An Economic Analysis of Unemployment', in QUINCY
WRIGHT (ed.), *Unemployment as a World Problem*. Chicago, Ill.: University of Chicago
Press, 1931, pp. 3-42; reprinted in KEYNES, vol. XIII, pp. 343-67.
3. KEYNES, vol. XIII, p. 343.

I see no hope of a recovery except in a revival of the high level of investment.[1]

[. . .] nothing, obviously can restore employment which does not first restore business profits. Yet nothing, in my judgment, can restore business profits which does not first restore the volume of investment, that is to say (in other words), the volume of orders for new capital goods [. . .].[2]

There can [. . .], I argue, be no secure basis for a return to an equilibrium of prosperity except a recovery of fixed investment to a level commensurate with that of the national savings in prosperous times [. . .].[3]

If our object is to remedy unemployment it is obvious that we must first of all make business more profitable. In other words, the problem is to cause business receipts to rise relatively to business costs [. . .].

The cumulative argument for wishing prices to rise appears to me, therefore, to be overwhelming, as I hope it does to you. Fortunately many if not most people agree with this view.[4]

Keynes proceeded to advocate constructive 'programmes under the direct auspices of the government or other public authorities'; and 'a reduction in the long-term rate of interest'.[5]

The drafting of these Harris Foundation lectures, delivered in June 1931, must of course have started while the Circus was operating. I repeat that the members of the Circus could claim that their influence was beginning to be revealed. As Moggridge has put it, 'the lectures saw Keynes giving much more attention to changes in output, rather than price levels, and giving hints of the idea of less than full employment equilibrium':[6] I would have written a much stronger word than 'hints'.

More than that, the lectures revealed a sense of mastery and confidence – inferior, however, to that achieved in March 1933 in *The Means to Prosperity*.[7]

1. KEYNES, vol. XIII, p. 349.
2. *Ibid.*, p. 355.
3. *Ibid.*, p. 358.
4. *Ibid.*, p. 362.
5. *Ibid.*, p. 364.
6. DONALD MOGGRIDGE, 'From the *Treatise* to *The General Theory*: An Exercise in Chronology', p. 79.
7. KEYNES, vol. IX, p. 335-66.

(During the Circus period Keynes, apart from his normal heavy load, and apart from coping with a host of critics of the *Treatise*, with the Circus and with preparing the Harris Foundation lectures, was helping to draft the Macmillan Report, including Addendum I, which was signed on 23 June 1931.)

In conclusion, there is a point of interest which Moggridge brings to light.[1] During the summer of 1931 Joan Robinson was working on her 'Parable on Saving and Investment', in which she dealt with some of the problems which had arisen at the Circus.[2] In the article she recorded that, as to the widow's cruse, Keynes had admitted the case against him. The proofs were not available to enable her to submit them to Keynes until 9 April 1932. Keynes encouraged her to publish without amendment. On the '"widow's cruse" fallacy', he wrote, on 14 April 1932:

I think you are a little hard on me as regards the assumption of constant output. It is quite true that I have not followed out the consequences of changes of output in the earlier theoretical part [. . .] I shall be doing it in my lectures; though that does not absolve me from being criticised for not having done it in my *Treatise*. But in my *Treatise* itself, I have long discussions with [?of] the effects of changes in output [. . .] Surely one must be allowed at a particular stage of one's argument to make simplifying assumptions of this kind.[3]

1. KEYNES, vol. XIII, p. 342.

2. JOAN ROBINSON, 'A Parable on Savings and Investment', *Economica*, February 1933, pp. 75-84. The article had been held up by the editor.

3. *Letter* to Joan Robinson, *14 April 1932*; published in KEYNES, vol. XIII, pp. 269-70 (the quotation on p. 270).

3. From the 'Treatise' to the 'General Theory'

This section is short – in relation to the importance and interest of the subject. The subject to which I wish to devote fairly adequate space is the next Lecture – on the *General Theory* as a finished book.

A great deal has been published on the subject of this section. First of all, there is Moggridge in Vol. XIII of Keynes' *Collected Writings*. Then – very useful for a short survey – there is Moggridge's article 'From the *Treatise* to *The General Theory*'. There are two chapters in Don Patinkin's *Keynes' Monetary Thought*, as well as useful references in *Keynes, Cambridge and the General Theory*, edited by him and J. Clark Leith. And of course a great deal more. I am not attempting a bibliography on the subject. For that I refer my reader to the first footnote in Moggridge's article.

Possibly the first public intimation that Keynes was launching out on a new book is to be found in his Preface to the Japanese edition of the *Treatise*, dated 5 April 1932.

I propose [. . .] to publish a short book of a purely theoretical character, extending and correcting the theoretical basis of my views as set forth in Books III and IV below ['The Fundamental Equations' and 'The Dynamics of the Price Level'].[1]

Such a book, taking the *Treatise* as its basis, would have been extremely unsatisfactory. And, of course, the *General Theory*, when finally completed in December 1935, was an entirely different kind of book, both in character and scope.

It is not perhaps so very surprising that, working on the kind of book envisaged in that Preface, Keynes was able on 18 September 1932 to write to his mother: 'I have written nearly a third of my new book on monetary theory.'[2]

Of course many of us became aware of Keynes' intention in

---

1. KEYNES, vol. V, p. xxvii.
2. From a *Letter* to Florence A. Keynes, *18 September 1932*; excerpt published in KEYNES, vol. XIII, p. 380.

the summer of 1932. In the course of a letter to Hawtrey dated 1 June 1932, Keynes wrote:

As I mentioned to you, I am working it out all over again [. . .] I now put less fundamental reliance on my conception of savings and substitute for it the conception of expenditure [. . .] since there are two senses in which income can be used, it is much preferable to use a term about which everyone agrees [. . .] The main object of my treatment, however, will be to fill in the gap of which you complain that I do not follow up the actual genesis of change and am too content with a purely formal treatment of the first and final truisms.[1]

At about the same time Joan Robinson was corresponding with Keynes on a point in one of his lectures about which she, Austin and I were worried. After an all-day discussion with Joan and me on 8 May, which had ended amicably,[2] Keynes wrote to Joan on the following day. In the course of this letter he wrote:

my present belief is that in general [. . .] your way would be much more difficult and cumbersome. At any rate I lack at present sufficient evidence to the contrary to induce me to scrap all my present half-forged weapons; – though that is no reason why you should not go on constructing your own.[3]

These lectures were the first University lectures delivered by Keynes since 1929. He retained the title 'Pure Theory of Money'. But by the October Term of 1932 he had changed the title to 'Monetary Theory of Production' – an indication of a marked change in emphasis. Moggridge very conveniently sets out the conclusions reached by the end of 1932, i.e. after delivering the October Term course of lectures.[4]

It is disconcerting in these October 1932 lecture notes to read of the rate of interest 'such as to cause saving to be in excess of investment'.[5]

---

1. From a *Letter* to Ralph G. Hawtrey, *1 June 1932*; excerpt published *ibid.*, pp. 172-3.

2. KEYNES, vol. XXIX, p. 48.

3. *Letter* to Joan Robinson, *9 May 1932*; published in KEYNES, vol. XIII, pp. 377-8.

4. DONALD MOGGRIDGE, 'From the *Treatise* to the *General Theory*: An Exercise in Chronology', pp. 80-1.

5. KEYNES, vol. XXIX, p. 56.

In the course of 1933 the drafting showed great progress. But here again it is at first sight disconcerting to come across a Section on 'Certain Fundamental Equations',[1] in which he sets out a modified version of the 'Fundamental Equations' of the *Treatise*. Keynes explained, however, that this is

not because I propose to pursue it further at this moment, but to help readers of my *Treatise on Money* to see at once the relationship between the method of exposition now adopted and that with which they are already familiar.[2]

By March 1934 clarity had been far from reached over the fundamental definitions.[3] Work must have been most intense in the Easter Vacation (part of which I spent with Keynes at Tilton).

For Moggridge states that

by the time Keynes went to America in the spring of 1934 to receive an honorary degree at Columbia, what one would recognize as the simple textbook version of the theory was well in place, except for the marginal efficiency of capital, and some chapters, such as chapter 12 ['The State of Long-Term Expectations'] had reached their final form.[4]

But of course the treatment of the marginal efficiency of capital still called for a great deal of work.

A draft table of contents prepared in the middle of June 1934 is presented by Moggridge,[5] who writes that the drafts of the chapters other than Chapter 12 were at that date significantly different from the final versions.

During the summer of 1934 Keynes was exceptionally active.[6] (I remember it well because it was the one summer between 1928 and 1939 part of which I did not spend climbing in the Alps. I spent much of it with Keynes at Tilton.)

Vol. XIII of Keynes' *Collected Writings* from p. 471 to the end of p. 652, is devoted to the redrafting, and to the immense volume

1. KEYNES, vol. XXIX, pp. 68-73.
2. *Ibid.*, p. 71.
3. *Letter* from Richard F. Kahn, *20 March 1934*; published *ibid.*, pp. 120-2.
4. DONALD MOGGRIDGE, 'From the *Treatise* to *The General Theory*: An Exercise in Chronology', p. 83.
5. KEYNES, vol. XIII, pp. 423-4.
6. *Ibid.*, p. 471.

of correspondence with which the redrafting was partly associated.

Naturally enough it is often asked why it took so long to
write the *General Theory*. Keynes was able to start in a climate of
thought far more developed than when he started on his *Treatise*.

The fact that Keynes was a very busy man is only a partial
answer. If, by temporarily discarding some of his normal activities, he had made more room available for work on his book, he
could have devoted more hours to it on an average day. But
Keynes would often emphasise that for a fast worker like himself
inspiration would languish after a hard morning's work. Also
the development in a man's mind of intricate ideas is partly a
function of the passage of time rather than of the cumulative
number of hours devoted to it. This is more especially the case
when the give-and-take of discussions with others is part of the
process.

The most important question is whether Keynes should have
cut down the time devoted to correspondence with Dennis
Robertson, Hawtrey and Harrod, partly by discouraging them
and partly by devoting less of his own time to considering and
answering their letters.

Keynes' close friendship with Robertson went back to 1910.
In Sections 3 and 4 of my first Lecture I commented on their
co-operation over Robertson's pre-War book and on his first
post-War book (*Money*); and in Section 1 of Lecture III over
Robertson's *Banking Policy and the Price Level* and subsequently
over Keynes' *Treatise*. I quoted published tributes of each to the
other.

It was natural for written and oral discussion between them to
continue on the progress of work on the *General Theory*. Although
the breach on the economic issues – especially on terminology –
became wider, the tone of the correspondence remained friendly, and often amusing. Keynes was desperately anxious to get
Robertson to understand, Robertson was desperately anxious
to save Keynes from error. For Keynes to have discouraged
Robertson earlier than he felt he had to would have been an
act of betrayal – entirely alien to Keynes' character.

Robertson, even more perhaps than Keynes, was devoting much anguished time to controversy which seems to me to have been counter-productive. It was not until 11 March 1935, only nine months before the completion of the book, that Robertson wrote:

I expect that it *will* be best that in the main I should wait now till I can see the completed work with a fresh eye.[1]

In a letter dated 14 March Keynes agreed.[2] By 10 October, on Keynes' initiative, correspondence on relatively trivial issues was resumed.[3] On 20 September 1936 Keynes, after referring to the publication of criticisms of the *General Theory* by Robertson, and others, wrote:

It's awfully difficult to keep off Economics but *I* don't, dear Dennis, feel differently, and we must try to come to closer touch again.[4]

In the course of a letter dated 13 December 1936, Keynes wrote:

I, perhaps, am too ready to take pleasure in feeling that my mind is changed; you too ready to take pain. But surely the truth is that both our minds have been changing continuously and enormously, though on parallel lines that all but, yet don't quite, meet, over the last eleven years. I certainly date all my emancipation from the discussions between us which preceded your *Banking Policy and the Price Level* [. . .] But you won't slough your skins, like a good snake! You walk about with the whole lot on from the earliest until the latest, until you can scarcely breathe, saying that, because your greatcoat was once your vest, your present vest and your greatcoat are the same.[5]

In his reply dated 29 December, Robertson expressed pleasure. As regarding bad snakehood he made various good-humoured comments, one of which is:

---

1. *Letter* from Dennis H. Robertson, *11 March 1935*; published in KEYNES, vol. XIII, p. 520.

2. *Letter* to Dennis H. Robertson, *14 March 1935*; published *ibid.*, pp. 522-3.

3. *Letter* to Dennis H. Robertson, *10 October 1935*; published *ibid.*, pp. 523-4.

4. *Letter* to Dennis H. Robertson, *20 September 1936*; published in KEYNES, vol. XIV, pp. 87-8.

5. *Letter* to Dennis H. Robertson, *13 December 1936*; published *ibid.*, pp. 89-95 (the quotation on pp. 94-5).

I do venture to think that with each new skin you are apt to put on a pair of blinkers, which make it hard for you to see what other people, especially Pigou, are at.[1]

Correspondence with Hawtrey about the drafting of the *General Theory* did not start until March 1935.[2] From then on it was voluminous. Many of Hawtrey's criticisms were based on misunderstanding on his part and of his thinking on entirely different lines. Some of them were helpful and resulted in important amendments.

But in a letter to me dated 29 July, Keynes wrote:

Hawtrey's comments indicate that he hasn't the faintest idea what I'm driving at.[3]

(The letter began: 'I am in the stage of not liking my book very much. It all seems very angry and much ado about a matter much simpler than I make it appear.')

In the course of a letter dated 8 November Keynes wrote to Hawtrey: 'If this correspondence does not fatigue you, there is nothing that I like better.'[4]

My own view was that – apart from sentiment over discussion with an old friend – Keynes was wasting time. Keynes submitted the correspondence to Joan Robinson for an opinion. In the course of her reply she wrote: 'I certainly don't think an archangel could have taken more trouble to be fair and to be clear.'[5]

The correspondence with Hawtrey continued after the final page-proof had gone to the printer – indeed until May 1937. From 31 August 1936 it dealt with a draft of some of the chapters of Hawtrey's *Capital and Employment*. In the course of a letter written on that day Keynes wrote:

---

1. *Letter* from Dennis H. Robertson, *29 December 1936*; published *ibid.*, pp. 95-100 (the quotation on p. 95).

2. Exchange of letters between Ralph G. Hawtrey and John Maynard Keynes from 12 March 1935 to 6 January 1936; published in KEYNES, vol. XIII, pp. 565-633.

3. From a *Letter* to Richard F. Kahn, *29 July 1935*; excerpt published *ibid.*, p. 634.

4. *Letter* to Ralph G. Hawtrey, *8 November 1935*; published *ibid.*, pp. 600-4 (the quotation on p. 600)

5. *Letter* from Joan Robinson, *2 December 1935*; published *ibid.*, p. 612.

Although still disagreeing with a great deal of it, I like this document of yours enormously better than any of its predecessors. I feel that the trouble we have had in our correspondence has not been wasted.[1]

Keynes did not send the proofs to Roy Harrod until 5 June 1935. From then on the correspondence was continuous.[2]

Both sides took great trouble and some important – as well as many less important – amendments resulted. Unlike Robertson and Hawtrey, Harrod was an enthusiastic backer of Keynes.

Towards the end of my next Lecture, in Section 10, I deal with the complaint that Keynes was unnecessarily provocative in discussing the 'classical economists'. Here I regard Harrod's role – in persuading Keynes to be somewhat more suave – as harmful. But many take a different view.[3] Otherwise Harrod was extremely helpful. This is illustrated in an odd way by a letter from Keynes to me dated 27 August 1935:

I have been going in more detail into Roy's comments and have now written him an enormous letter. It is quite clear that he has not grasped what my theory of the rate of interest is, and I fancy that those chapters written a long time ago are a long way from being as clear as they might be. So I am having to face a complete re-doing.[4]

The writing of the *General Theory* was an enterprise the immensity of which is demonstrated by that part of the documents which has survived. In my next Lecture I discuss the finished product.

1. *Letter* to Ralph G. Hawtrey, *31 August 1936*; published in KEYNES, vol. XIV, pp. 46-9 (the quotation on p. 46).

2. Exchange of letters between Roy F. Harrod and John Maynard Keynes from 5 June 1935 to 10 October 1935; published in KEYNES, vol. XIII, pp. 526-65.

3. See MURRAY MILGATE, 'Keynes on the "classical" theory of interest', *Cambridge Journal of Economics*, March 1977, pp. 307-15.

4. From a *Letter* to Richard F. Kahn, *27 August 1935*; excerpt published in KEYNES, vol. XIII, p. 634.

FIFTH LECTURE
'The General Theory of Employment, Interest and Money'

1. *Introduction.* – 2. *The word 'general'.* – 3. *The character of the achievement.* – 4. *The money-wage.* – 5. *The propensity to consume.* – 6. *Liquidity preference.* – 7. *The inducement to invest: foreword.* – 8. *The inducement to invest: Keynes' basic chapter.* – 9. *Keynes' chapter on investment in real life.* – 10. *Limitations of the 'General Theory'.* – 11. *The post 'General Theory' Keynes on 'finance'.*

1. Introduction

The Preface to the *General Theory* ends with the words:

> The composition of this book has been for the author a long struggle of escape, and so must the reading of it be for most readers if the author's assault upon them is to be successful, – a struggle of escape from habitual modes of thought and expression. The ideas which are here expressed so laboriously are extremely simple and should be obvious. The difficulty lies, not in the new ideas, but in escaping from the old ones, which ramify, for those brought up as most of us have been, into every corner of our minds.[1]

The Preface opens with the words:

> This book is chiefly addressed to my fellow economists. I hope that it will be intelligible to others. But its main purpose is to deal with difficult questions of theory, and only in the second place with the applications of this theory to practice.[2]

---

1. KEYNES, vol. VII, p. xxiii.
2. *Ibid.*, p. xxi.

2. The word 'general'

The book opens as follows:

I have called this book the *General Theory of Employment, Interest and Money*, placing the emphasis on the prefix *general*. The object of such a title is to contrast the character of my arguments and conclusions with those of the *classical* theory of the subject, upon which I was brought up and which dominates the economic thought, both practical and theoretical, of the governing and academic classes of this generation, as it has for a hundred years past. I shall argue that the postulates of the classical theory are applicable to a special case only and not to the general case, the situation which it assumes being a limiting point of the possible positions of equilibrium. Moreover, the characteristics of the special case assumed by the classical theory happen not to be those of the economic society in which we actually live, with the result that its teaching is misleading and disastrous if we attempt to apply it to the facts of experience.[1]

In Chapter 2 Keynes discussed the *Postulates of the Classical Economics* in unnecessarily complex fashion, as Keynes admitted in his article in the *Quarterly Journal of Economics* of February 1937.[2] The relevant postulate is in effect that there is no 'involuntary unemployment'. Keynes regarded the classical position of the economy as the limiting position of 'full employment'.

Keynes' Preface to the French edition was signed on 20

1. KEYNES, vol. VII, p. 3.
2. KEYNES, 'The General Theory of Employment', *Quarterly Journal of Economics*, February 1937, pp. 209-23; reprinted in KEYNES, vol. XIV, pp. 209-23. See in particular on p. 110 the opening of Keynes' reply to JACOB VINER's article 'Mr. Keynes on the Causes of Unemployment. A Review', *Quarterly Journal of Economics*, November 1936, pp. 147-67.
In a contribution to a Conference organised by the Royal Economic Society held at Durham in March 1974, referring to Keynes' complicated definition of *'involuntary' unemployment* of the *General Theory* (KEYNES, vol. VII, p. 15), I said:
'I am today unable to see why it was necessary to be so complicated [. . .] there is involuntary unemployment to the extent that, at the current money-wage and with the current price-level, the number of men desiring to work exceeds the number of men for whose labour there is a demand ('Unemployment as seen by the Keynesians', in GEORGE DAVID N. WORSWICK (ed.), *The Concept and Measurement of Involuntary Unemployment*. London: George Allen and Unwin; Boulder, Colorado: Westview Press, 1976, p. 21).

February 1939 – more then three years after the signature of the Preface to the English edition. The following is a long extract:

my readers will sometimes wonder what I am talking about when I speak, with what some of my English critics consider a misuse of language, of the 'classical' school of thought and 'classical' economists. It may, therefore, be helpful to my French readers if I attempt to indicate very briefly what I regard as the main *differentiae* of my approach.

I have called my theory a *general* theory. I mean by this that I am chiefly concerned with the behaviour of the economic system as a whole [. . .].

I argue that important mistakes have been made through extending to the system as a whole conclusions which have been correctly arrived at in respect of a part of it taken in isolation.

Let me give examples of what I mean. My contention that for the system as a whole the amount of income which is saved, in the sense that it is not spent on current consumption, is and must necessarily be exactly equal to the amount of net new investment has been considered a paradox and has been the occasion of widespread controversy. The explanation of this is undoubtedly to be found in the fact that this relationship of equality between saving and investment, which necessarily holds good for the system as a whole, does not hold good at all for a particular individual.[1]

This is a far more fruitful exposition of the meaning of the word 'general' – the result of three years of discussion and thought.

---

1. KEYNES, vol. VII, pp. xxxii.

3. The character of the achievement

A good account of the character, in Keynes' own mind, of the achievement of the *General Theory* is provided by an extract from a letter written to Roy Harrod on 30 August 1936, in commenting on a draft article by Harrod. It is reproduced by the Royal Economic Society Edition Editors in their own Introduction to Vol. VII of Keynes' *Collected Writings* (*The General Theory*):[1]

You don't mention *effective demand* or, more precisely, the demand schedule for output as a whole, except in so far as it is implicit in the multiplier. To me the most extraordinary thing, regarded historically, is the complete disappearance of the theory of demand and supply for output as a whole, *i. e.* the theory of employment, *after* it had been for a quarter of a century the most discussed thing in economics. One of the most important transitions for me, after my *Treatise on Money* had been published, was suddenly realising this. It only came after I had enunciated to myself the psychological law that, when income increases, the gap between income and consumption will increase, – a conclusion of vast importance to my own thinking but not apparently, expressed just like that, to anyone else's. Then, appreciably later, came the notion of interest being the measure of liquidity preference, which became quite clear in my mind the moment I thought of it. And last of all, after an immense amount of muddling and many drafts, the proper definition of the marginal efficiency of capital linked up one thing with another.[2]

The *General Theory* is short-period in the Marshallian sense:

We take as given the existing skill and quantity of available labour, the existing quality and quantity of available equipment, the existing technique, the degree of competition, the tastes and habits of the consumer, the disutility of different intensities of labour and of the activities of supervision and organisation, as well as the social structure including the forces, other than our variables set forth below, which determine the distribution of the national income. This does not mean that we assume these factors to be constant; but merely that,

---

1. It is a part of an encouraging letter to Roy F. Harrod about a draft of his article on 'Mr. Keynes and Traditional Theory' (*Econometrica*, January 1937, pp. 74-86).

2. KEYNES, vol. VII, p. xv. This letter appears in full in vol. XIV, pp. 84-6.

in this place and context, we are not considering or taking into account the effects and consequences of changes in them.[1]

Most of the exposition is based on the assumption of given stocks of equipment at a moment of time and given technical knowledge. The subject of investigation is the degree of utilisation of the equipment and the labour supply.

There is little study of the effects of accumulation with the passage of time as the result of investment.

However, this subject does enter in a fundamental sense into the very important chapters on 'The Marginal Efficiency of Capital', 'The State of Long Term Expectations', 'Sundry Observations on the Nature of Capital' and 'Concluding Notes on the Social Philosophy to which the General Theory might Lead'.

Keynes set out, and then elaborated, those factors knowledge of which is sufficient, and of which knowledge is necessary, to determine the position of an economy. Under the term 'position' is to be included not only such physical entities as rates of investment, consumption, output, and employment, but also rates of interest, and in addition the price-level of consumption-goods in terms of money-wage units (the real wage) and the prices of capital-assets.

The chapters on 'The Principle of Effective Demand' and 'Expectation as Determining Output and Employment', 'The Marginal Efficiency of Capital' and 'The State of Long-Term Expectations', 'The General Theory of the Rate of Interest' together with 'The Psychological and Business Incentives to Liquidity', and the three chapters on the 'Propensity to Consume', constitute the real kernel of the book (amounting to 117 pages out of the total of 382), together with the discussions of the influence of the money-wage and the behaviour of money-wages and prices. In these chapters the factors causatively responsible for the state of the economy are elaborated.

There is no separate compartment labelled 'monetary theory'. The Quantity Theory of Money had finally been abandoned.

1. KEYNES, vol. VII, p. 245.

But, as the full title of the book indicates, money plays a vital role, and the behaviour of the system is influenced by the behaviour of the quantity of money.

Although Keynes was not interested in the actual process of movement from one position to another, he did in fact devote three pages to the lag in the response of the output of consumption-goods to an unforeseen increase in the output of capital-goods. He emphasised that this did not detract from 'the logical theory of the multiplier, which holds good continuously, without time-lag, at all moments of time'.[1]

He wrote:

The fact that an unforeseen change only exercises its full effect on employment over a period of time is important in certain contexts; – in particular it plays a part in the analysis of the trade cycle (on lines such as I followed in my *Treatise on Money*). But it does not in any way affect the significance of the theory of the multiplier as set forth in this chapter; nor render it inapplicable as an indicator of the total benefit to employment to be expected from an expansion in the capital goods industries. Moreover, except in conditions where the consumption industries are already working almost at capacity so that an expansion of output requires an expansion of plant and not merely the more intensive employment of the existing plant, there is no reason to suppose that more than a brief interval of time need elapse before employment in the consumption industries is advancing *pari passu* with employment in the capital-good industries with the multiplier operating near its normal figure.[2]

In Section 1 of my last Lecture I quoted from an article published by Keynes in 1933 in which, using my figures, he demonstrated how short the income-expenditure time lag is: 'seven-eighths of the total effects [of a change] come from the primary expenditure and the first two repercussions',[3] so that if between the payment and expenditure of wages the average time-lag is a week, seven-eighths of the full effect of a change in payments are experienced in three weeks.

1. KEYNES, vol. VII, p. 122.
2. *Ibid.*, pp. 124-5.
3. KEYNES, vol. IX, p. 343.

As late as February 1935 Dennis Robertson was still pleading for recognition of the time element,[1] a tribute to Robertson's persistence and to Keynes' patience. Had Keynes given way he would have had largely to rewrite the book, which was in fact completed nine months later. Lack of interest by Keynes in time-lags accounted in part for Robertson's failure to accept Keynes' methods.

Pigou devoted the final passage of his partial renunciation of his bitter and sarcastic review-article[2] on the *General Theory* to an account – for the most part highly acceptable to Keynesians – of the same fundamental factors which I am identifying as determining the position of the economy.

Keynes' method could then tell us, not merely what employment, investment and so on tend to be at the two dates, but what they actually will be. But it could not tell us what happens to employment, investment and so on while the system is in *course of movement* from one of these equilibrium positions to the other; what they will be on the intervening days or months or years of this disequilibrium. Thus even in the most favourable circumstances that analysis is a staccato one, adapted to provide, not a moving picture, but only a succession of stills.

These are very serious limitations – limitations of which it is special-ly proper to remind ourselves when attempts are made to apply Keynes' apparatus directly to the solution of practical problems. This is in no sense to 'attack' Keynes or to decry his achievement. When a man has devised a new way of tackling an unclimbed moun-tain, we may, indeed, regret that this way has not led him to the top. But for the effort which has advanced him *towards* the top nothing is due but praise.[3]

Pigou was a great mountaineer, like, but better than, so many economists.

1. *Letter* from Dennis H. Robertson, *3 February 1935*; published in KEYNES, vol. XIII, pp. 496-506.

2. ARTHUR C. PIGOU, 'Mr. J. M. Keynes' General Theory of Employment, Interest and Money', *Economica*, May 1936, pp. 115-32.

3. ARTHUR C. PIGOU, *Keynes's General Theory*. London: Macmillan, 1950, pp. 64-5.

4. The money-wage

Of the factors on which in the *General Theory* the position of the whole structure depends I begin with the money-wage. It is the fulcrum which supports the price-structure – all prices, incomes of every kind, and all money values. A lower level of money-wages means that everything expressed in terms of money is lower in the same proportion. The one important exception is the quantity of money. If it is held constant, its real value rises, and a lower money-wage means that in real value – in terms of its purchasing power over labour and goods – the quantity of money is higher. The important influence on the real state of the economy of a lower money-wage takes the form of the lower rates of interest, and the general relaxation of credit, which result from an increase in the value of the quantity of money expressed in real terms.

In addition, all incomes and debts fixed contractually in terms of money are larger in real value as a result of the money-wage being lower.

For the present-day reader it is ridiculous to write of lower, and falling money-wages. But I am lecturing about Keynes and, until shortly before the outbreak of the Second World War, the questions were why wages did not fall and whether employment would not be increased if they were cut. This was the great issue dividing Keynes from Pigou, Robertson and many other of the leading economists of the day.

The implications of rising money-wages can be presented by simply reversing the sign. But when money-wages rise as fast as in recent years, the mechanism is thrown out by time-lags and the character of expectations.

The basis of the fundamental role of the money-wage in determining all prices, money-incomes, and money-values is that money-wages not only form part of costs of production but, because they are to a large extent spent, they form part of total purchasing power expressed in terms of money. The costs resulting from a higher level of money-wages are met by the resultant raising of demand in terms of money; even if in real terms demand is unaltered.

Of course this theorem applies only in the aggregate. If money-wages rose more than the average in one part of the economy, real wages are there raised, and are lowered everywhere else, so that the aggregate real wage is unchanged.

This statement about the role of the money-wage is not to be regarded as absolutely watertight. It implies that no change in the distribution of income results from a reduction in money-wages. But I have already admitted a redistribution to those whose incomes are contractually fixed in terms of money.

If we abstract from the possible effect of a higher level of effective demand, the assumption that the distribution of income is unchanged when money-wages are lower is consistent with the findings of Kenneth Coutts, Wynne Godley and William Nord-haus over that part of the economy which they have studied.[1] The *normal price hypothesis* which they confirm by econometric methods is that

the firm calculates the level of costs at a normal level of output, and sets prices as a mark up on normal costs without reference to temporary variations in demand.[2]

(The proportional amount of the mark-up has been found to fall over time.)

Although this provides econometric confirmation of Keynes' view for a particular level of effective demand, it is inconsistent with Keynes' view and the view of many present-day economists, including myself, of the relation between the real wage and the level of effective demand when demand is so high as to bring output sharply against the constraint of limited physical capacity.

In the *Treatise*, Keynes had switched from the Quantity Theory of Money to the flow of money-income. The important role played by the money-wage in the *General Theory* arises from

1. Chemical and allied industries, mechanical engineering, electrical engineering, textiles, clothing and footwear.

2. KENNETH COUTTS, WYNNE GODLEY and WILLIAM NORDHAUS, *Industrial Pricing in the United Kingdom*. Cambridge: Cambridge University Press, 1978, pp. 1-2.

its determining the money-value of everything else – profits, and other income, and prices. By this I do not of course mean that the magnitude of the money-wage determines real values. That would be absurd. But it takes the place of the Quantity Theory.

The fact that the quantity of money is an exception is, of course, the basis of discussion of monetary influences.

The 'wage-theorem', as Professor Sir John Hicks has conveniently called it, is to be regarded as somewhat rough-and-ready in character. At a time of rapid changes, values in terms of money-wages will display temporary variations, partly determined by expectations of the behaviour of money-wages. Of considerable significance is the recent experience of advanced industrial countries of the small movements in real-wages in the face of high, and rapidly changing, rates of wage-inflation in the years since 1973. (I do not apply the same doctrine to cases of high rates of demand inflation.)

I was surprised by Hicks' statement that:

All expositors of Keynes (including myself) have found this procedure [working in terms of wage-units] a difficulty [. . .] We had to find some way of breaking the circle. The obvious way of doing so was to begin by setting out the rest (multiplier, liquidity preference and so on) on the assumptions of *fixed* money wages.[1]

The result, as Hicks points out, is the false impression that Keynes assumed wages to be constant at any level of employment short of full employment.

Hicks' procedure is completely unnecessary. Keynes, in many contexts, emphasised the 'stickiness' of wages. But that was not the reason for the use of the money-wage as a unit. There is not a word in Chapter 4 (on 'The Choice of Units') to suggest that it was.

I have, however, little doubt that Keynes' concern, over a great part of his working life, with the behaviour of wages in practice, did lead him on to his choice of unit.

1. JOHN R. HICKS, *The Crisis in Keynesian Economics*. Yriö Jahnsson Lectures. Oxford: Basil Blackwell, 1974, p. 60.

Already in 1925 in the *Economic Consequences of Mr Churchill* (the return of sterling to the pre-war parity in April 1925), Keynes emphasised the unwillingness of wages to fall under the pressure of heavy unemployment. To avoid subjecting the unsheltered industries to an intolerable reduction in real wages, money-wages would have to be pushed down in the sheltered industries as well. This would necessitate the extension of heavy unemployment to the sheltered industries, involving an extremely large total of unemployment, to avoid grossly increasing inequalities of wages between the sheltered and unsheltered industries.[1]

On the Macmillan Committee (which reported in June 1931) a reduction of money-wages was discussed as a means of improving the country's competitive position.[2] Keynes' influence is clear. In the main Report itself it was recognised that, if it was to be relevant, 'a substantial general change, amounting, to (say) 10 per cent. or more, in the level of money costs and incomes', would be called for, that as a matter of equity such a reduction 'should apply to every category of income alike, including those protected by contract'; and that such a 'great social change' would require 'general consent'. It could not, therefore, 'be left to natural economic forces'.[3]

Furthermore, for 'country after country to feel compelled to resort to competition in wage-cutting' would be a counsel of despair: it would help nobody. But if 'the downward race' began (later on called a 'beggar-my-neighbour' method), 'no one can afford to lag far behind under penalty of losing all his trade'.[4]

In the important Addendum to the Macmillan Report, Keynes' influence is shown in a short passage in which the effect on employment of a reduction of wages is discussed quite apart from any consequent improvement in the country's competitive position.

1. KEYNES, vol. IX, p. 215.
2. MACMILLAN COMMITTEE ON FINANCE AND INDUSTRY, *Report*. Presented to Parliament by the Financial Secretary to the Treasury, June 1931. Cmd 3897. London: His Majesty's Stationery Office, 1931, pp. 196-9. (The Committee was appointed on 5 November 1929.)
3. *Ibid.*, pp. 198-9.
4. *Ibid.*, pp. 196-7.

It is impossible to calculate in advance what increase of employment could be expected from a given average reduction of wages. But the relation of the one to the other might disappoint the expectations of many people, inasmuch as a false analogy is often drawn from the obvious great advantages to an individual employer of a reduction of the wages which he has to pay. For each employer perceives quite clearly the advantages he would gain if the wages which he himself pays were to be reduced, but not so clearly the disadvantages he will suffer if the money-incomes of his customers are reduced. Just as it is to the advantage of each producer that every product should be cheap except his own, similarly it is to his advantage that all costs and wages should be high except those which he himself incurs – since the demand for his product comes from the incomes which are paid out as costs by other producers.[1]

In the *General Theory*, Keynes dealt with the 'crude conclusion' that a reduction in money-wages would increase employment by two different methods.

The simplest method is adopted late in the book. Let us

follow up the course of events on the hypothesis most favourable to this view, namely that at the outset entrepreneurs *expect* the reduction in money-wages to have this effect. It is indeed not unlikely that the individual entrepreneur, seeing his own costs reduced, will overlook at the outset the repercussions on the demand for his product and will act on the assumption that he will be able to sell at a profit a larger output than before. If, then, entrepreneurs generally act on this expectation, will they in fact succeed in increasing their profits? Only if the community's marginal propensity to consume is equal to unity, so that there is no gap between the increment of income and the increment of consumption [...] [otherwise] the proceeds realised from the increased output will disappoint the entrepreneurs and employment will fall back again to its previous figure.[2]

Very early in the book Keynes disputed

the assumption that the general level of real wages is directly determined by the character of the wage bargain. In assuming that the wage bargain determines the real wage the classical school have slipt in an illicit assumption [...] There may exist no expedient by

1. MACMILLAN COMMITTEE ON FINANCE AND INDUSTRY, *Report*, p. 194; reprinted in KEYNES, vol. xx, p. 289.
2. KEYNES, vol. vii, p. 261.

which labour as a whole can reduce its *real* wage to a given figure by making revised *money* bargains with the entrepreneurs. This will be our contention. We shall endeavour to show that primarily it is certain other forces which determine the general level of real wages.[1]

Keynes of course agreed that

any individual or group of individuals, who consent to a reduction of money-wages relatively to others, will suffer a *relative* reduction in real wages, which is a sufficient justification for them to resist it [. . .].

In other words, the struggle about money-wages primarily affects the *distribution* of the aggregate real wage between different labour-groups, and not its average amount per unit of employment, which depends, as we shall see, on a different set of forces. The effect of combination on the part of a group of workers is to protect their *relative* real wage. The *general* level of real wages depends on the other forces of the economic system.[2]

If for the words 'consent to a reduction of money-wages' are substituted the words 'agree to accept a wage increase which will prove to be less than the average for the country as a whole', these words of Keynes present a very important element in the present-day problem of trying to resist wage-inflation. A patriotic response to an appeal from the Government, and perhaps the Trades Union Congress, confined to limited sectors of the labour force, penalises them. In an extreme case it is possible that, not merely do real wages lag behind, but actually suffer an absolute fall.

Keynes did not have to assume that individual unemployed workers did not on occasion secure jobs by slightly under-cutting the money-wage. The Keynesian contention is that no additional net employment would result. Workers hitherto employed would be dismissed, so that the total number employed remained constant.

In discussing the various effects of falling wages, Keynes stressed the influence of expectations.

1. *Ibid.*, p. 13.
2. *Ibid.*, p. 14.

If the reduction of money-wages is expected to be a *reduction relatively to money-wages in the future*, the change will be favourable to investment, because [. . .] it will increase the marginal efficiency of capital [expected money profits in relation to the current costs of capital assets]; whilst for the same reason it may be favourable to consumption. If, on the other hand, the reduction leads to the expectation, or even to the serious possibility, of a further wage-reduction in prospect, it will have precisely the opposite effect. For it will diminish the marginal efficiency of capital and will lead to the postponement both of investment and of consumption.

[. . .] the depressing influence on entrepreneurs of their greater burden of debt may partly offset any cheerful reactions from the reduction of wages. Indeed if the fall of wages and prices goes far, the embarrassment of those entrepreneurs who are heavily indebted may soon reach the point of insolvency, – with severely adverse effects on investment. Moreover the effect of the lower price-level on the real burden of the national debt and hence on taxation is likely to prove very adverse to business confidence.[1]

About the time when Keynes started work on the *General Theory*, a very severe fall in prices had resulted in a series of banking crises – starting in Austria and Germany in July 1931.

To quote Keynes:

all this nervousness, and hysteria and panic, which is making a farce of our currency arrangements and bringing the world's financial machine to a standstill, is only superficially traceable, though it has all happened suddenly, to quite recent events. It has its roots in the slow and steady sapping of the real resources of the banks as a result of the progressive collapse of money values over the past two years.

This is a quotation from the article which this critical state of affairs had led Keynes to write, entitled *The Consequences to the Banks of the Collapse of Money Values*. It was published originally in an American popular monthly magazine (*Vanity Fair*) in August 1931 (revised version in October).[2]

After setting out the facts he concluded:

Fortunately our own domestic British banks are probably at present

1. KEYNES, vol. VII, pp. 263-4.
2. Reprinted in KEYNES, vol. IX, pp. 150-8. The passage quoted is on p. 151.

– for various reasons – among the strongest. But there is a degree of deflation which no bank can stand. And over a great part of the world, and not least in the United States, the position of the banks, though partly concealed from the public eye, may be in fact the weakest element in the whole situation. It is obvious that the present trend of events cannot go much further without something breaking. If nothing is done, it will be amongst the world's banks that the really critical breakages will occur.

Modern capitalism is faced, in my belief, with the choice between finding some way to increase money values towards their former figure, or seeing widespread insolvencies and defaults and the collapse of a large part of the financial structure.[1]

He added that 'The present signs suggest that the bankers of the world are bent on suicide'.[2]

Keynes was prophetic. In February 1933 all the American banks had to close for a short period. I remember this well because I was just about to travel by train from Harvard to New York, and therefore armed myself with an ample supply of bank notes. The result was that all the way from Boston to New York I was the only occupant of a whole Pullman coach: nobody else possessed enough cash to buy a ticket.

1. *Ibid.*, p. 157.
2. *Ibid.*

133

5. The propensity to consume

In essence the 'propensity to consume' is a simple concept and I do not need to say much about it. It has of course been developed tremendously – both conceptually and econometrically. Professor Duesenberry wrote in 1949:

By now [. . .] Hicks and others have shown that the Keynesian consumption function is a special case of the general theory of consumer behavior and can be deduced from it by making certain assumptions.[1]

Keynes attempted only a superficial treatment. He pointed to the fundamental psychological law that at higher levels of income the rate of saving was also higher (but not necessarily the ratio of saving to income).[2] In other words the marginal propensity to consume is less than unity. This Keynes regarded as the 'key to our practical problem', in his basic chapter on 'The Principle of Effective Demand'. It meant that, with a given propensity to consume, employment cannot increase except as a result of an increase in the rate of investment.[3] The treatment suffers from the defect that no distinction is drawn between saving out of profits and out of wages.

Being a psychological 'law' of behaviour, Keynes recognised that its quantitative operation depended on the character of the change under review, and the length of time which had elapsed since it occurred.

The extent to which a man will adjust his standard of life to a rise in his income depends on the length of time which has elapsed since the rise has occurred and the confidence with which it can be felt that it will not be reversed.

Keynes was concerned with the behaviour of the economy as a whole: mainly with the relation between income and saving as income reacted to a change in a given short-period situation. But in the concluding chapter there is some discussion of the longer-term future.

1. JAMES S. DUESENBERRY, *Income, Saving, and the Theory of Consumer Behavior*. First published as Harvard Economic Study, Number 87. Cambridge, Mass.: Harvard University Press, 1949, p. 1.
2. KEYNES, vol. VII, p. 96.
3. *Ibid.*, pp. 29-30.

Keynes did not in any systematic way consider the effect of wealth per head on the propensity to consume. A clue is provided in a short and unsatisfactory passage on *windfall changes in capital values*.

These are of much more importance in modifying the propensity to consume, since they will bear no stable or regular relationship to the amount of income.[1]

Don Patinkin has pointed out that Keynes was here thinking purely of the *temporary* effects on consumption of windfall gains or losses.[2] Keynes left the effects of income on consumption to proxy for the effect of wealth on consumption – not a satisfactory treatment.

Don Patinkin has pointed to one exceptional passage – in Keynes' profound Chapter 16 on 'Sundry Observations on the Nature of Capital'. Here Keynes contemplated

an amount of wealth sufficiently great to satiate to the full the aggregate desire on the part of the public to make provision for the future, even with full employment, in circumstances where no bonus is obtainable in the form of interest.[3]

In Chapter 19, on 'Changes in Money-Wages', which appears late in the *General Theory* and from which I have already quoted, Keynes does not mention the Real Balance Effect. Mention of it would have served to reinforce arguments which are already very strong.

Keynes mentioned several favourable influences of falling money-wages although the unfavourable ones are overwhelming.

One exception is the case in which 'money-wages are believed to have touched bottom, so that further changes are expected to be in the upward direction'.[4]

Keynes had on the previous page mentioned the rise in the real burden of the National Debt and taxation. This was in addition

1. *Ibid.*, p. 92.
2. DON PATINKIN, *Keynes' Monetary Thought. A Study of its Development.* Durham, North Carolina: Duke University Press, 1976, p. 111.
3. KEYNES, vol. VII, p. 218. Patinkin refers to this passage on p. 110 of his book.
4. *Ibid.*, p. 265.

sense but was prepared to include such instruments as three-month treasury bills. Towards the end of my treatment of 'The Inducement to Invest', I shall be suggesting a much more extensive generalisation – covering, e.g., overdraft facilities and prospective marketability of a firm's equities and bonds.

Apart from the *transactions motive* for holding money, Keynes dealt with

the precautionary-motive, i.e. the desire for security as to the future cash equivalent of a certain proportion of total resources; and [. . .] the speculative-motive, i.e. the object of securing profit from knowing better than the market what the future will bring forth.[1]

The distinction between these two motives is not entirely watertight. This will become very clear when, in Section 11, I bring in to the discussion the concept of 'finance', introduced by Keynes in the course of the immediately post-*General Theory* controversies in the *Economic Journal*. A firm may cover its prospective investment programme – at least in part – by holding cash or short-term securities; this Keynes called finance. This is 'precautionary'. The question is why it does not hold a portfolio of fixed-interest securities maturing at the dates on which payments for the investment will become due, and meanwhile secure higher rates of interest. This is 'speculative'. The firm holds cash to the extent that it is afraid that interest-rates may rise, in which case the prices of the longer-term securities would fall.

In a published article I have tried to deal with the difficulties of distinguishing between the precautionary and speculative motives, the distinction between which is very blurred:

in principle the precautionary motive can be said to operate in so far as some persons think that the rate of interest is likely to move; the speculative motive in so far as some persons think that on balance it is likely to move one way rather than the other.[2]

---

1. KEYNES, vol. VII, p. 170.
2. RICHARD KAHN, 'Some Notes on Liquidity Preference', *Manchester School of Economic and Social Studies*, September 1954, p. 239; reprinted in *Selected Essays on Employment and Growth*. Cambridge: Cambridge University Press, 1972, p. 81.

Under the influence of the precautionary motive the firm makes provision for financing its investment programme; but only in the form of cash unless the influence of the so-called speculative motive operates.

Keynes gives the impression, when he discusses the speculative motive, that he is thinking mainly of the management of portfolios by financiers, ranging from private individuals to large investment trusts and insurance companies. But industrial companies also play an important part.

In so far as the precautionary and speculative motives can be distinguished Keynes pointed out that the quantity of cash held under the influence of the precautionary motive 'is not very sensitive to changes in the rate of interest'.[1]

The elasticity of response of the rate of interest to the excess of the total quantity of money over that absorbed by the transactions motive is largely derived from the speculative motive.

The magnitude of this elasticity varies greatly between one time and one situation and another. It is not an easy subject to elucidate. In the same published article I tried to show that the elasticity is greater, the greater the density of the population around the margin between 'bulls' and 'bears' of long-term bonds. (There is not only an extensive margin. There is also an intensive margin inside the head of any individual who is doubtful – who is not a completely convinced bull or bear.)

As Keynes put it, 'Public opinion can be fairly rapidly accustomed to a modest fall in the rate of interest and the conventional expectation of the future may be modified accordingly'.[2] A few pages earlier Keynes wrote:

It is evident, then, that the rate of interest is a highly psychological phenomenon.[3]

And:

It might be more accurate, perhaps, to say that the rate of interest is a highly conventional, rather than a highly psychological, phenom-

---

1. KEYNES, vol. VII, p. 171.
2. *Ibid.*, p. 204.
3. *Ibid.*, p. 202.

enon. For its actual value is largely governed by the prevailing view as to what its value is expected to be. *Any* level of interest which is accepted with sufficient conviction as *likely* to be durable *will* be durable.[1]

Exclusion of assets other than fixed-interest securities

It is strange that in the first passage from the *General Theory* quoted in this section Keynes contemplated no liquid forms of wealth other than cash and fixed-interest securities. There is an appreciable elasticity of substitution between money and equities; and also between money and houses, and between money and commodities which are dealt with in organised produce markets. And of course there are elasticities of substitution between every pair of these assets. It is not only the price-level of fixed-interest securities which is related to the excess of the quantity of money over that absorbed by the transactions-motive. There is an infinite number of combinations of the prices of these various assets each of which is compatible with any particular such excess of the quantity of money.

In fact what Keynes needed was a simple form of portfolio analysis. After the publication of the *General Theory* he ventured into this field, with rather unsatisfactory results.[2]

In the *Treatise on Money*, Keynes presented a primitive form of liquidity preference theory.[3] The securities which Keynes had in mind were equities. But the ambiguity of the word 'investment' caused considerable confusion. Before long the price of an equity becomes the price of the underlying capital-good. For example:

> The price level of investments as a whole, *and hence of new investments*, is that price level at which the desire of the public to hold savings deposits is equal to the amount of savings deposits which the banking system is willing and able to create.[4] [My italics.]

1. KEYNES, vol. VII, p. 203.
2. JOHN MAYNARD KEYNES, 'The Theory of the Rate of Interest', in ARTHUR D. GAYER (ed.), *The Lessons of Monetary Experience. Essays in Honor of Irving Fisher*. London: George Allen and Unwin, 1937, pp. 145-52; reprinted in KEYNES, vol. XIV, pp. 101-8.
3. KEYNES, vol. V, pp. 127-31.
4. *Ibid.*, p. 129.

Keynes, in the *General Theory*, recalled his treatment in the *Treatise*. He objected to it because 'bearishness' (the *Treatise* equivalent of liquidity preference) was there defined as the relationship

not between the rate of interest (or price of debts [i.e. fixed-interest securities]) and the quantity of money, but between the price of assets and debts, taken together, and the quantity of money. This treatment, however, involved a confusion between results due to a change in the rate of interest and those due to a change in the schedule of the marginal efficiency of capital [the inducement to invest], which I hope I have here avoided.[1]

1. KEYNES, vol. VII, pp. 173-4.

7. The inducement to invest: foreword

The determination of the rate of investment is the subject to which, for obvious reasons, the bulk of the *General Theory* is devoted. It presents far greater difficulties of abstraction – and therefore of exposition – than the propensity to consume, which basically is a matter of common-sense. The major achievement of the *General Theory* is twofold. First, there is the conception of Effective Demand which, given the conditions of supply, determines the level of output and employment. Second, there is the determination of the rate of investment. While lower than the rate of consumption, this is the constituent of Effective Demand which is mainly responsible for fluctuations, and also for demand being often chronically unduly low – as well as, on occasion, unduly high.

In the causal processes involved in the determination of investment, expectations play a dominating part. If it is conceded to Keynes that in the world as we know it expectations are subject to a high degree of risk and of uncertainty, the case for a revolution of thought is overwhelming.

I shall find it convenient to bring within the orbit of discussion of the *General Theory* two contributions made by Keynes after its publication. One is the reply to Professor Viner in the *Quarterly Journal of Economics* of February 1937.[1] The other, to which I shall be referring later, is a series of articles which appeared in the *Economic Journal* from June 1937 to June 1938 and included important additions to his thought, made in the course of controversy, on the subject of 'finance'.

In the course of his reply to Viner, Keynes explained the character of his innovation on the subject of expectations subject to risk. I quote a few passages:

these more recent writers [Edgeworth, Pigou and other later and contemporary writers] like their predecessors were still dealing with

---

1. JOHN MAYNARD KEYNES, 'The General Theory of Employment', *Quarterly Journal of Economics*, February 1937 pp. 209-23. See footnote 2 on p. 120, of this Lecture, for references to Viner's article and Keynes' reply; and also KEYNES, vol. XIV, pp. 109-123.

a system in which the amount of the factors employed was given and the other relevant facts were known more or less for certain. This does not mean that they were dealing with a system in which change was ruled out, or even one in which the disappointment of expectation was ruled out. But at any given time facts and expectations were assumed to be given in a definite and calculable form; and risks, of which, though admitted, not much notice was taken, were supposed to be capable of an exact actuarial computation. The calculus of probability, though mention of it was kept in the background, was supposed to be capable of reducing uncertainty to the same calculable status as that of certainty itself.

[. . .] the fact that our knowledge of the future is fluctuating, vague and uncertain, renders wealth a peculiarly unsuitable subject for the methods of the classical economic theory [. . .] [The theory], requires, I suggest, considerable amendment if it is to be applied to a world in which the accumulation of wealth for an indefinitely postponed future is an important factor; and the greater the proportionate part played by such wealth accumulation the more essential does such amendment become.

By 'uncertain' knowledge, let me explain, I do not mean merely to distinguish what is known for certain from what is only probable. The game of roulette is not subject, in this sense, to uncertainty; nor is the prospect of a Victory bond being drawn. Or, again, the expectation of life is only slightly uncertain. Even the weather is only moderately uncertain. The sense in which I am using the term is that in which the prospect of a European war is uncertain, or the price of copper and the rate of interest twenty years hence, or the obsolescence of a new invention, or the position of private wealth owners in the social system in 1970. About these matters there is no scientific basis on which to form any calculable probability whatever. We simply do not know. Nevertheless, the necessity for action and for decision compels us as practical men to do our best to overlook this awkward fact and to behave exactly as we should if we had behind us a good Benthamite calculation of a series of prospective advantages and disadvantages, each multiplied by its appropriate probability, waiting to be summed.

How do we manage in such circumstances to behave in a manner which saves our faces as rational economic men? We have devised for the purpose a variety of techniques [. . .].

Now a practical theory of the future based on these [techniques] has certain marked characteristics. In particular, being based on so flimsy a foundation, it is subject to sudden and violent changes. The practice of calmness and immobility, of certainty and security, suddenly breaks down. New fears and hopes will, without warning, take charge of human conduct. The forces of disillusion may suddenly impose a new conventional basis of valuation. All these pretty, polite techniques, made for a well-panelled board room and a nicely regulated market, are liable to collapse. At all times the vague panic fears and equally vague and unreasoned hopes are not really lulled, and lie but a little way below the surface.[1]

1. Keynes, vol. xiv, pp. 112-15.

8. The inducement to invest: Keynes' basic chapter

Introduction

Keynes' basic chapter on the determination of the rate of investment is Chapter 11 on 'The Marginal Efficiency of Capital'.[1] The subject is the most important one in the *General Theory*. But this chapter is one of the most confused.

The chapter opens:

> When a man buys an investment or capital-asset, he purchases the right to the series of prospective returns, which he expects to obtain from selling its output, after deducting the running expenses of obtaining that output, during the life of the asset [. . .].
> I define the marginal efficiency of capital as being equal to that rate of discount which would make the present value of the series of annuities given by the returns expected from the capital-asset during its life just equal to its supply price. This gives us the marginal *efficiencies* of particular types of capital-assets. The greatest of these marginal efficiencies can then be regarded as the marginal efficiency of capital in general [. . .].
> Now it is obvious that the actual rate of current investment will be pushed to the point where there is no longer any class of capital-asset of which the marginal efficiency exceeds the current rate of interest. In other words, the rate of investment will be pushed to the point on the investment demand-schedule where the marginal efficiency of capital in general is equal to the market rate of interest.[2]

One clear statement is that the rate of investment 'will be pushed to the point where there is no longer any class of capital-asset of which the marginal efficiency exceeds the current rate of interest'.

Keynes proceeded to express this in a short algebraic passage:

> If Q_r is the prospective yield from an asset at time r, and d_r is the present value of £1 deferred r years *at the current rate of interest*, $\Sigma Q_r d_r$ is the demand price of the investment; and investment will be carried to the point where $\Sigma Q_r d_r$ becomes equal to the supply price of the investment as defined above.[3]

1. KEYNES, vol. VII, pp. 135-46.
2. *Ibid.*, pp. 135-7.
3. *Ibid.*, p. 137.

145

It is clear that by *rate of interest* Keynes meant the risk-free rate of interest.

Keynes emphasised that he was basing his treatment on the *prospective* yield of capital and not on its *current* yield. Even to-day the confusion to which Keynes referred between three meanings of the terms 'profit' and 'rate of profit' prevails.

(i) *Prospective*. Except in the absence of uncertainty, this is subjective, and varies between different individuals. Even for one individual it is not, at any particular date, in the future, one definite amount, and, with the normal association of uncertainty with risk, cannot even be represented by a probability distribution.

(ii) *Current*. This is the sense in which the terms are used in theories of the determination of profit and the rate of profit.

(iii) *Past*. This is objective and a matter of history, but attempts at theoretical explanation are legitimate.

Risk and uncertainty

Keynes identified his 'marginal efficiency of capital' with Irving Fisher's 'rate of return over cost', defined in his *Theory of Interest* as

that rate which, employed in computing the present worth of all the costs and the present worth of all the returns, will make these two equal.[1]

This to-day is the familiar concept of the internal rate of return. To induce new investment Fisher wrote that *'the rate of return over cost must exceed the rate of interest'*.[2]

Keynes wrote in 1937 that the concept implied by his 'marginal efficiency of capital'

was first introduced into economic theory by Irving Fisher in his *Theory of Interest* (1930), under the designation 'the rate of return over

---

1. IRVING FISHER, *The Theory of Interest*. New York: Macmillan, 1930 (First Edition), p. 168; quoted in KEYNES, vol. VII, p. 140.
2. *Ibid.*, p. 159; quoted in KEYNES, vol. VII, pp. 140-1.

cost'. This conception of his is, I think, the most important and fruitful of his recent original suggestions.[1]

The important fact that Keynes failed to mention is that in 106 pages[2] Fisher completely ruled out risk and uncertainty. When Keynes wrote that investment is

pushed to the point where there is no longer any class of capital-asset of which the marginal efficiency exceeds the current rate of interest[3]

he was emphatically not assuming the absence of risk and uncertainty – only the rate of interest was risk-free.

With the prevalence of risk and uncertainty, a prospective rate of return as low as the risk-free rate of interest would be entirely unacceptable. And it is impossible to calculate a substitute for the rate of interest which takes account of risk and uncertainty. The return for risk and uncertainty can be imputed only from the excess of the prospective rate of return which is sufficiently high to encourage the investment over the risk-free rate of interest. Keynes' treatment involves circular argument.

Later in the same chapter, Keynes did discuss the excess, on account of risk, over the rate of interest, 'to give the minimum prospective yield which will induce the investment'[4] but he was of course unable to suggest how it could be computed otherwise than by empirical observations.

On the previous page two types of risk are discussed as affecting the volume of investment: 'entrepreneur's or borrower's risk' and, 'where a system of borrowing and lending exists', the risk to the lender of voluntary or involuntary default by the borrowers. The 'first type of risk [unlike the second] is, in a sense, a real social cost, though susceptible to diminution by averaging.'[5]

Some idea of the order of magnitude which Keynes had in mind is provided by a discussion of the difficulty of 'bringing the effective rate of interest below a certain figure [. . .] in an era of

1. JOHN MAYNARD KEYNES, 'The Theory of the Rate of Interest', in ARTHUR D. GAYER, *The Lessons of Monetary Experience. Essays in Honor of Irving Fisher*; reprinted in KEYNES, vol. XIV, p. 101, note 2.

2. IRVING FISHER, *The Theory of Interest*, pp. 99-205.

3. KEYNES, vol. VII, p. 136.

4. *Ibid.*, p. 145.

5. *Ibid.*, p. 144.

low interest rates'.[1] He had taken the view that 'a long-term rate of interest of (say) 2 per cent leaves more to fear [by way of a future rise] than to hope' [by way of a further fall].[2]

This passage suggests a very low allowance for risk, especially as Keynes had lender's risk in mind.

The *General Theory* was published early in 1936. It is curious that in a 1934 draft of the third page of what was to be Chapter 11 (on 'The Marginal Efficiency of Capital'), the phrases 'after allowance for risk', 'with equal risk', and 'with an allowance for risk' all appear.[3] Why these phrases came to be dropped is completely obscure.

Keynes can be justifiably criticised for exaggerating the importance – compared with other factors – of the risk-free rate of interest as an influence on the rate of investment. Among the other factors are risk and uncertainty, depreciation and obsolescence. In the following Section I cite Keynes as a very strong advocate against the predominance of the rate of interest, compared with other factors, the most important of which can be covered by the portmanteau phrase 'state of finance'.[4]

At the same time, as of course Keynes was well aware, a considerable proportion of a country's investment is in durable assets such as dwellings, public utilities, roads and railways. Here there is usually little risk and annual depreciation is low. The rate of interest is an important influence.

This is why the level of rates of interest has some bearing on the activity of the economy as a whole, investment in durable undertakings being an important part of effective demand.

Of course, as the quotation from his reply to Viner indicates,

1. KEYNES, vol. VII, p. 208.
2. *Ibid.*, p. 202.
3. KEYNES, vol. XIII, p. 452.
4. Among the many investigations conducted in this field by questioning industrialists may be mentioned the relevant sections of *Oxford Studies in the Price Mechanism* (edited by TOM WILSON and P. W. S. ANDREWS. Oxford: Clarendon Press, 1951, pp. 1-74). HUBERT HENDERSON (pp. 16-27) supported the view put forward in my text. Some of the Oxford economists were surprised by the replies which they received. (I reviewed the book in the *Economic Journal*, March 1952, pp. 119-30).

Keynes' thinking was dominated by the prevalence of risk –
especially when combined with uncertainty. This makes it difficult to refer to the prospect of a definite rate of return which
will just induce investment by a firm in a particular class of
capital-goods at a specified rate. But the symbol Q_r was clearly
intended by Keynes to serve as a proxy for the state of mind of
entrepreneurs as to the prospects of profits on a particular line
of investment at time r. The legitimacy of this simplifying procedure becomes less with an increase in the degree of uncertainty
attaching to the risk.

9. Keynes' chapter on investment in real life

Introduction

Having ridden on a tight rein in Chapter 11 on 'The Marginal Efficiency of Capital', Keynes seems to have become bored – perhaps dissatisfied – and in Chapter 12 on 'The State of Long-Term Expectations' allows himself the pleasure of a full gallop. The contrast is astonishing. There is little similarity to the scholastic treatment of Chapter 11.

The role of equity prices

Both in the *Treatise* and in the *General Theory* the treatment of equities, as opposed to fixed-interest securities, is limited in scope and hesitant as to the importance of the behaviour of equities as an influence on real investment. Keynes attached more importance to the influence on consumption. There was no lack of familiarity with the subject – as First Bursar of his College, a Director of two Investment Trusts, and on his own personal account, he took a lively and practical interest in equity markets. It does not, of course, follow that he believed that the behaviour of equity markets constituted a real influence on the economy. Some of the passages which I quote from Chapter 12 suggest that he did believe that it was. But there is considerable ambivalence.

Ambivalence on this issue has prevailed among economists up to the present day. In the following section I venture to give an indication of my own views.

Considerable confusion is caused – Keynes was not immune to this confusion – by the ambiguity of the word 'investment', which is used to mean both real investment and the purchase of Stock Exchange securities.

This is one of the occasions on which the French vocabulary is richer than the English. For over twenty years Joan Robinson, acting on a hint from Hicks, has avoided the confusion by borrowing from France the word *placement* to mean the purchase of securities.[1]

---

1. JOAN ROBINSON, *The Accumulation of Capital*. London: Macmillan, 1956, p. 8.

In the *Treatise*, equities play an important role as constituents of portfolios and they are discussed at a number of points in the text. Their price-levels are rarely, however, mentioned as an influence on the rate of investment. In one exceptional passage Keynes alluded to the fact that in the United States boom of 1928-29 high short-term money rates deliberately imposed by the Federal Reserve Bank were proving rather unsuccessful in achieving the desired effect of 'retarding investment and so bringing the period of business prosperity to an earlier conclusion'. Keynes' explanation was that

the very high prices of common shares, relatively to their dividend yields, offered joint stock enterprises an exceptionally cheap method of financing themselves. Thus, whilst short-money rates were very high and bond rates somewhat high, it was cheaper than at any previous period to finance new investment by the issue of common stocks [equities]. By the spring of 1929 this was becoming the predominant method of finance. Thus easy terms were maintained for certain types of investment, in spite of the appearance of very dear short-money.[1]

By the time he came to the *General Theory*, Keynes did not accept this form of explanation. This seems very odd. Referring back to this passage in a footnote, he stated that his interpretation would now be that 'a high quotation for existing equities involves an increase in the marginal efficiency of the corresponding type of capital'.[2]

This footnote appears in the very chapter which I am now discussing, in which the behaviour of the prices of equities, in some passages but not in others, has an important influence on real investment. It has to be regarded as an aberration.

Extracts from Chapter 12 which do not suggest influences on real investment

I have tried, in quoting some extracts from the chapter, to pick out, in the first place, those which do *not* suggest that the

1. KEYNES, vol. VI, pp. 174-5.
2. KEYNES, vol. VII, p. 151, note 1.

behaviour of equity markets is an influence on the level of activity of the economy.

A conventional valuation which is established as the outcome of the mass psychology of a large number of ignorant individuals is liable to change violently as the result of a sudden fluctuation of opinion due to factors which do not really make much difference to the prospective yield; since there will be no strong roots of conviction to hold it steady.

[. . .] It might have been supposed that competition between expert professionals, possessing judgment and knowledge beyond that of the average private investor, would correct the vagaries of the ignorant individual left to himself. It happens, however, that the energies and skill of the professional investor and speculator are mainly occupied otherwise. For most of these persons are, in fact, largely concerned, not with making superior long-term forecasts of the probable yield of an investment over its whole life, but with foreseeing changes in the conventional basis of valuation a short time ahead of the general public. They are concerned, not with what an investment is really worth to a man who buys it 'for keeps', but with what the market will value it at, under the influence of mass psychology, three months or a year hence. Moreover, this behaviour is not the outcome of a wrong-headed propensity. It is an inevitable result of an investment market organised along the lines described. For it is not sensible to pay 25 for an investment of which you believe the prospective yield to justify a value of 30, if you also believe that the market will value it at 20 three months hence.

Thus the professional investor is forced to concern himself with the anticipation of impending changes, in the news or in the atmosphere, of the kind by which experience shows that the mass psychology of the market is most influenced. [. . .] The social object of skilled investment should be to defeat the dark forces of time and ignorance which envelop our future. The actual, private object of the most skilled investment to-day is 'to beat the gun', as the Americans so well express it, to outwit the crowd, and to pass the bad, or depreciating, half-crown to the other fellow.

This battle of wits to anticipate the basis of conventional valuation a few months hence, rather than the prospective yield of an investment over a long term of years, does not even require gulls amongst the public to feed the maws of the professional; – it can be played by professionals amongst themselves. Nor is it necessary that anyone should keep his simple faith in the conventional basis of valuation having any genuine long-term validity. For it is, so to speak, a game of Snap, of Old Maid, of Musical Chairs – a pastime in which he is victor who says *Snap* neither too soon nor too late, who passed the Old Maid to his neighbour before the game is over, who secures a chair for himself when the music stops. [. . .] Or, to change the metaphor slightly, professional investment may be likened to those newspaper competitions in which the competitors have to pick out the six prettiest faces from a hundred photographs, the prize being awarded to the competitor whose choice most nearly corresponds to the average preferences of the competitors as a whole; so that each competitor has to pick, not those faces which he himself finds prettiest, but those which he thinks likeliest to catch the fancy of the other competitors, all of whom are looking at the problem from the same point of view [. . .] We have reached the third degree where we devote our intelligences to anticipating what average opinion expects the average opinion to be. And there are some, I believe, who practise the fourth, fifth and higher degrees.[1]

Extracts from Chapter 12 which do suggest influences on real investment

The outstanding fact is the extreme precariousness of the basis of knowledge on which our estimates of prospective yield have to be made. Our knowledge of the factors which will govern the yield of an investment some years hence is usually very slight and often negligible.[2]

[. . .] Business men play a mixed game of skill and chance, the average results of which to the players are not known by those who take a hand. If human nature felt no temptation to take a chance, no satisfaction (profit apart) in constructing a factory, a railway, a mine or a farm, there might not be much investment merely as a result of cold calculation.

Decisions to invest in private business of the old-fashioned type were, however, decisions largely irrevocable, not only for the community as a whole, but also for the individual. With the separation between ownership and management which prevails to-day and with the development of organised investment markets, a new factor of great importance has entered in, which sometimes facilitates investment but sometimes adds greatly to the instability of the system. In the

---

1. KEYNES, vol. VII, pp. 154-6.
2. *Ibid.*, p. 149.

absence of security markets, there is no object in frequently attempting to revalue an investment to which we are committed.

[. . .] the daily revaluations of the Stock Exchange, though they are primarily made to facilitate transfers of old investments between one individual and another, inevitably exert a decisive influence on the rate of current investment. For there is no sense in building up a new enterprise at a cost greater than that at which a similar existing enterprise can be purchased: whilst there is an inducement to spend on a new project what may seem an extravagant sum, if it can be floated off on the Stock Exchange at an immediate profit. Thus certain classes of investment are governed by the average expectation of those who deal on the Stock Exchange as revealed in the price of shares, rather than by the genuine expectations of the professional entrepreneur.[1] How then are these highly significant daily, even hourly revaluations of existing investments carried out in practice?[2]

[. . .] if there exist organised investment markets and if we can rely on the maintenance of the convention, an investor can legitimately encourage himself with the idea that the only risk he runs is that of a genuine change in the news *over the near future*, as to the likelihood of which he can attempt to form his own judgment, and which is unlikely to be very large. For, assuming that the convention holds good, it is only these changes which can affect the value of his investment, and he need not lose his sleep merely because he has not any notion what his investment will be worth ten years hence. Thus investment becomes reasonably 'safe' for the individual investor over short periods, and hence over a succession of short periods however many, if he can fairly rely on there being no breakdown in the convention and on his therefore having an opportunity to revise his judgment and change his investment, before there has been time for much to happen. Investments which are 'fixed' for the community are thus made 'liquid' for the individual.

It has been, I am sure, on the basis of some such procedure as this that our leading investment markets have been developed. But it is not surprising that a convention, in an absolute view of things so arbitrary, should have its weak points. It is its precariousness which

---

1. This does not apply, of course, to classes of enterprise which are not readily marketable or to which no negotiable instrument closely corresponds. The categories falling within this exception were formerly extensive. But measured as a proportion of the total value of new investment they are rapidly declining in importance.

2. KEYNES, vol. VII, pp. 150-1.

creates no small part of our contemporary problem of securing sufficient investment.[1]

[. . .] Investment based on genuine long-term expectation is so difficult to-day as to be scarcely practicable. He who attempts it must surely lead much more laborious days and run greater risks than he who tries to guess better than the crowd how the crowd will behave; and, given equal intelligence, he may make more disastrous mistakes. There is no clear evidence from experience that the investment policy which is socially advantageous coincides with that which is most profitable. It needs *more* intelligence to defeat the forces of time and our ignorance of the future than to beat the gun.

[. . .] it is the long-term investor, he who most promotes the public interest, who will in practice come in for most criticism, wherever investment funds are managed by committees or boards or banks. For it is in the essence of his behaviour that he should be eccentric, unconventional and rash in the eyes of average opinion. If he is successful, that will only confirm the general belief in his rashness; and if in the short run he is unsuccessful, which is very likely, he will not receive much mercy. Worldly wisdom teaches that it is better for reputation to fail conventionally than to succeed unconventionally [. . .].

A collapse in the price of equities, which has had disastrous reactions on the marginal efficiency of capital, may have been due to the weakening either of speculative confidence or of the state of credit. But whereas the weakening of either is enough to cause a collapse, recovery requires the revival of *both*. For whilst the weakening of credit is sufficient to bring about a collapse, its strengthening, though a necessary condition of recovery, is not a sufficient condition.

These considerations should not lie beyond the purview of the economist. But they must be relegated to their right perspective. If I may be allowed to appropriate the term *speculation* for the activity of forecasting the psychology of the market, and the term *enterprise* for the activity of forecasting the prospective yield of assets over their whole life, it is by no means always the case that speculation predominates over enterprise. As the organisation of investment markets improves the risk of the predominance of speculation does, however, increase. In one of the greatest investment markets in the world, namely, New York, the influence of speculation (in the above sense)

---

1. *Ibid.*, pp. 152-3.

is enormous. [. . .] Speculators may do no harm as bubbles on a steady stream of enterprise. But the position is serious when enterprise becomes the bubble on a whirlpool of speculation. When the capital development of a country becomes a by-product of the activities of a casino, the job is likely to be ill-done. The measure of success attained by Wall Street, regarded as an institution of which the proper social purpose is to direct new investment into the most profitable channels in terms of future yield, cannot be claimed as one of the outstanding triumphs of *laissez-faire* capitalism – which is not surprising, if I am right in thinking that the best brains of Wall Street have been in fact directed towards a different object [. . .][1]

Even apart from the instability due to speculation, there is the instability due to the characteristic of human nature that a large proportion of our positive activities depend on spontaneous optimism rather than on a mathematical expectation, whether moral or hedonistic or economic. Most, probably, of our decisions to do something positive, the full consequences of which will be drawn out over many days to come, can only be taken as a result of animal spirits – of a spontaneous urge to action rather than inaction, and not as the outcome of a weighted average of quantitative benefits multiplied by quantitative probabilities. Enterprise only pretends to itself to be mainly actuated by the statements in its own prospectus, however candid and sincere. Only a little more than an expedition to the South Pole, is it based on an exact calculation of benefits to come. Thus if the animal spirits are dimmed and the spontaneous optimism falters, leaving us to depend on nothing but a mathematical expectation, enterprise will fade and die; – though fears of loss may have a basis no more reasonable than hopes of profit had before.[2]

[. . .] it is our innate urge to activity which makes the wheels go round, our rational selves choosing between the alternatives as best we are able, calculating where we can, but often falling back for our motive on whim or sentiment or chance [. . .][3]

For my own part I am now somewhat sceptical of the success of a merely monetary policy directed towards influencing the rate of interest. I expect to see the State, which is in a position to calculate the marginal efficiency of capital-goods on long views and on the basis

1. KEYNES, vol. VII, pp. 157-9.
2. *Ibid.*, pp. 161-2.
3. *Ibid.*, p. 163.

of the general social advantage, taking an ever greater responsibility for directly organising investment; since it seems likely that the fluctuations in the market estimation of the marginal efficiency of different types of capital, calculated on the principles I have described above, will be too great to be offset by any practicable changes in the rate of interest.[1]

1. *Ibid.*, p. 164.

10. Limitations of the 'General Theory'

Misconceptions about the General Theory

Keynes made it clear in his Preface that the book's 'main purpose is to deal with difficult questions of theory, and only in the second place with the applications of this theory to practice'.[1] This is often overlooked. For example:

1) The book contains almost no references to international trade and the problem of reconciling an acceptable balance of payments with a high level of activity. And yet in Keynes' more practical writings this problem was uppermost in his mind. Very often it took the form of regarding excessive overseas lending as part of the cause of the country's troubles, both because, if in excess of the current account balance of payments, it resulted in a loss of monetary reserves, and because, to avoid this, the necessary rise in rates of interest had a discouraging effect on domestic investment and so caused unemployment.

Keynes did develop this theme in 'Notes on Mercantilism', his penultimate chapter on a number of historical topics.[2] At the very end of the book he wrote that 'if nations can learn to provide themselves with full employment by their domestic policy [. . .] there need be no important economic forces calculated to set the interest of one country against that of its neighbours',[3] each country's exports benefiting from the other countries' high level of activity.

The world still has to accept this simple lesson taught by Keynes.

2) Only in one passage did Keynes advocate the policy with which his name still is so closely associated – largely as a result of *Can Lloyd George Do It?* – 'loan expenditure' by public authorities as a means of sustaining employment if other means fail.

'wasteful' loan expenditure may [. . .] enrich the community on balance. Pyramid-building, earthquakes, even wars may serve to

---

1. KEYNES, vol. VII, p. xxi.
2. *Ibid.*, Chapter 23: 'Notes on Mercantilism, The Usury Laws, Stamped Money and Theories of Under-Consumption', pp. 333-71.
3. *Ibid.*, p. 382.

increase wealth, if the education of our statesmen on the principles of the classical economics stands in the way of anything better.[1]

3) Many of the passages in the book are not easy to read, and some of the chapters are profound, and therefore especially difficult – namely Chapter 16 on 'Sundry Observations on the Nature of Capital', Chapter 17 on 'The Essential Properties of Interest and Money', and the final Chapter 24 on 'Concluding Notes on the Social Philosophy'. Nevertheless, it was Keynes' object, in presenting his basic propositions, to avoid the qualifications and complications which were called for by a comprehensive treatment. In his burning anxiety to convince, he did enormously over-simplify.

This statement will be ill-received by those who find the book difficult and believe that the essence of it can be presented by some simple geometry or algebra.

That is the great tragedy. The behaviour of the economy is an immensely complicated subject. The diagrams and bits of algebra in the text-books up to the present day have often led to the difficulties being submerged, and incidentally to Keynes being discredited.

For example, both in his exposition of the liquidity preference theory of the rate of interest and in his exposition of the inducement to invest, Keynes made use of schedules – simple relationships between two parameters, one the rate of interest in both cases – which could be represented by a curve or by a piece of algebra of the type $y = f(x)$. And yet Keynes' insistence on the overwhelming importance of expectations, highly subject to risk and uncertainty, was one of his biggest contributions. This completely undermines the prevalent idea – for which Keynes' attempt at simplification is responsible – that such schedules can be regarded as stable relationships handed down from heaven.

Keynes' letter of 31 March 1937 to John R. Hicks about Hicks' article on 'Mr Keynes and the Classics' (1937)[2] is friendly in tone but contains one criticism:

1. *Ibid.*, pp. 128-9.
2. JOHN R. HICKS, 'Mr. Keynes and the "Classics": A Suggested Interpretation', *Econometrica*, April 1937, pp. 147-59; reproduced in JOHN R. HICKS, *Critical Essays in Monetary Theory*. Oxford: Clarendon Press, 1967, pp. 126-42.

At one time I tried the equations, as you have done, with *I* [income] in all of them. The objection to this is that it over-empha-sises current income. In the case of the inducement to invest, expected income for the period of the investment is the relevant variable. This I have attempted to take account of in the definition of the marginal efficiency of capital [. . .] whilst it may be true that entrepreneurs are over-influenced by present income, far too much stress is laid on this psychological influence, if present income is brought into such prominence.[1]

Keynes' rebuke was too mild. It left Hicks unrepentant. In the course of his reply of 9 April, he wrote:

Of course I agree that it is expected income that logically matters; but the influence of current events on expectations (admittedly a loose and unreliable connection) seems to me potentially so important, that I feel much happier if it is put in and marked unreliable.[2]

The result has been that the elementary teaching of Keynesian economics has been the victim of *IS-LM* and related diagrams and algebra. It is tragic that Keynes made no public protest when they began to appear.

As Joan Robinson has recently put it:

modern teaching has been confused by J. R. Hicks' attempt to reduce the General Theory to a version of static equilibrium with the for-mula IS/LM. Hicks has now repented and changed his name from J. R. to John, but it will take a long time for the effects of his teaching to wear off.[3]

As recently as 1977 Hicks wasstill insisting about his *IS-LM* diagram:

There is indeed much more in the *General Theory* of Keynes than this formal model [. . .] I am nevertheless convinced that those later writers (so many later writers!) who have taken their Keynes from the *ISLM* diagram have indeed taken over what is one of the ele-ments in what Keynes said.[4]

---

1. *Letter* to John R. Hicks, *31 March 1937*; published in Keynes, vol. xiv, pp. 79-81.

2. *Letter* from John R. Hicks, *9 April 1937*; published *ibid.*, pp. 81-3.

3. Joan Robinson, *Contributions to Modern Economics*. Oxford: Basil Blackwell, 1978, p. xiv.

4. John R. Hicks, *Economic Perspectives*. Oxford: Clarendon Press, 1977, p. viii.

It is comforting to read in an article included in the same book, but published four years earlier, that

the *General Theory* [. . .] provides a model on which academic economists can comfortably perform their accustomed tricks. Haven't they just? With *ISLM* I myself fell into the trap.[1]

Keynes' provocative tone

It is widely held that Keynes was mistaken in adopting a provocative tone in his comments on the classical economists, especially on his friend and colleague, Pigou.

About the drafts of Chapter 14 on 'The Classical Theory of the Rate of Interest', Harrod remonstrated with Keynes for being unduly provocative.[2] A short extract from a reply from Keynes will suffice:

I expect a great deal of what I write to be water off a duck's back. I am certain that it will be water off a duck's back unless I am sufficiently strong in my criticism to force the classicals to make rejoinders. I *want*, so to speak, to raise a dust; because it is only out of the controversy that will arise that what I am saying will get understood.[3]

In his Preface Keynes wrote:

Those, who are strongly wedded to what I shall call 'the classical theory', will fluctuate, I expect, between a belief that I am quite wrong and a belief that I am saying nothing new [. . .] My controversial passages are aimed at providing some material for an answer.[4]

Sir Austin Robinson touched on this issue in his Biography:

Keynes had meant to shock. An ordinary book, wooing with sweet reason, would not have fulfilled his purpose. The ideas that happened to be congenial might have been accepted, the others discarded according to taste.[5]

---

1. *Ibid.*, pp. 147-8, reprinted from JOHN R. HICKS, 'Recollections and Documents', *Economica*, February 1973, p. 11.

2. *Letter* from Ralph F. Harrod, *21 August 1935*; published in KEYNES, vol. XIII, pp. 544-6.

3. *Ibid.*, p. 548.

4. KEYNES, vol. VII, p. xxi.

5. AUSTIN ROBINSON, 'John Maynard Keynes, 1883-1946', *Economic Journal*, March 1947, p. 40.

Keynes and finance

Keynes' thinking developed after the publication of the *General Theory*. Every number of the *Economic Journal* from March 1937 to June 1938 devoted at least one article or note to discussions and controversy with Professor Bertil Ohlin, the Swedish economist, Dennis Robertson and Ralph Hawtrey. These are outside the scope of this book.

But Keynes' exposition of the concept of 'finance' is an important qualification of the *General Theory* exposition of the determination of the rate of investment. It is discussed in the June 1937, December 1937 and June 1938 issues of the *Journal*.

It is a factor in the determination of the rate of investment additional to expectations of future profitability, the physical capacity of the industries producing the capital goods in question, and 'animal spirits'. It provides an answer to all those who are doubtful about the strength of the risk-free rate of interest when set off against expectations of profits, highly subject to risk and uncertainty.

Keynes now brought in the availability of funds as a more important restraint, irrespective of the rate of interest.

It is not necessary to regard Keynes' treatment as entirely satisfactory, to appreciate the great importance of the concept.

Keynes' basic statement was

the fact (which may deserve more emphasis than I have given it previously) that an investment *decision* [. . .] may sometimes involve a temporary demand for money before it is carried out, quite distinct from the demand for active balances which will arise as a result of the investment activity whilst it is going on.

[. . .] There has, therefore, to be a technique to bridge this gap [. . .].

This service may be provided either by the new issue market or by the banks; – which it is, makes no difference.[1]

Either there will be increased pressure on the limited facilities which the market is prepared to provide (the new issue market or

---

1. JOHN MAYNARD KEYNES, 'Alternative Theories of the Rate of Interest', *Economic Journal*, June 1937, p. 246; reprinted in KEYNES, vol. XIV, pp. 207-8.

the banks) or the entrepreneurs will accumulate extra cash balances. Finance Keynes 'regarded as lying half-way, so to speak, between the active and the inactive balances'.

If investment is proceeding at a steady rate, the finance (or the commitments to finance) required can be supplied from a revolving fund of a more or less constant amount, one entrepreneur having his finance replenished [. . .] as another exhausts his [. . .] But if decisions to invest are (e. g.) increasing, the extra finance involved will constitute an additional demand for money.[1]

(Keynes should have added 'or overdraft facilities or new issue market facilities'.)

[. . .] lack of finance may prove an important obstacle to more than a certain amount of investment decisions being on the tapis at the same time.[2]

In a footnote to the first page of his following article in the December 1937 issue of the *Economic Journal* – which I am coming on to – Keynes conceded:

In what follows I use the term 'finance' to mean the credit required in the interval between planning and execution.[3]

Nevertheless, I do not feel that I am being captious in taking exception to Keynes' contention that 'It is, so to speak, as though a particular piece of saving had to be earmarked against a particular piece of investment before either has occurred'.[4] (But in the December 1937 issue of the *Economic Journal* Keynes conceded that the two are not necessarily equal.[5]) The basic concept was:

a heavy demand for investment can exhaust the market and be held up by lack of financial facilities on reasonable terms.[6]

---

1. *Ibid.*, p. 247; reprinted in KEYNES, vol. xiv, p. 209.

2. *Ibid.*

3. JOHN MAYNARD KEYNES, 'The "Ex-Ante" Theory of the Rate of Interest', *Economic Journal*, December 1937, p. 663, note 2; reprinted in KEYNES, vol. xiv, p. 216, note 1.

4. JOHN MAYNARD KEYNES, 'Alternative Theories of the Rate of Interest', p. 246; reprinted in KEYNES, vol. xiv, p. 207-8.

5. JOHN MAYNARD KEYNES, 'The "Ex-Ante" Theory of the Rate of Interest', pp. 663-4; reprinted in KEYNES, vol. xiv, p. 216.

6. JOHN MAYNARD KEYNES, 'Alternative Theories of the Rate of Interest', p. 248; reprinted in KEYNES, vol. xiv, p. 210.

Part of the trouble is that the character of the funds required for the finance of investment does not match the character of the saving which flows with the investment. The economy would operate far more smoothly if the only form of investment was house-building financed by building societies and the only possible home for saving was deposits with building societies.

Later in the same article in the December 1937 issue of the *Economic Journal*:

the banks hold the key position in the transition from a lower to a higher scale of activity. If they refuse to relax, the growing congestion of the short-term loan market or of the new issue market, as the case may be, will inhibit the improvement [. . .] On the other hand, there will always be *exactly* enough ex-post saving to take up the ex-post investment.[1]

The crowding-out effect in some quarters to-day

In some quarters this 'growing congestion' has been regarded as evidence that Keynes, late in his life, had come in effect to accept the 'crowding-out' effect believed in by many economists and financiers at the present day. It is a question of degree. The 'crowding-out' effect is absolute: any increase in the rate of investment in one field – at any rate if it is public investment financed by the banking system – is said to involve an equal reduction in some other field. It is our old friend 'the Treasury view'. Keynes' 'growing congestion' means that the rate of total investment will rise, in response to improving prospects of the future, but only to a limited extent unless the provision of 'finance' improves. The word 'finance' is a portmanteau word, incapable of quantitative definition, indicating the degree of confidence of entrepreneurs about the ease – in terms both of sacrifice and availability – with which funds will be made available for paying for the investment as it takes place.

Keynes pointed out, incidentally, that there was no reason for confining the restrictive influence of shortage of finance to the

[1]. JOHN MAYNARD KEYNES, 'The "Ex-Ante" Theory of the Rate of Interest', pp. 668-9; reprinted in KEYNES, vol. XIV, p. 222.

production of capital goods: it applied equally to the much narrower case of that of production of consumption-goods, which has to be planned ahead.[1]

The inducement to invest in real life

Keynes' concept of finance brings his theory of the inducement to invest into much closer line with modern practice – especially of large firms providing a wide range of products.

The period into the future for which the management plans depends on the character of the products and of the markets in which they are sold. They usually operate on the basis of a moving horizon.

They estimate the funds which might be made available over the period – from the firm's own liquid assets, from its undistributed profits, from banks, and from new issues, so far as they can be estimated.

The management try to obtain estimates of the prospective internal rates of return on capital invested to be derived from the various projects brought to their notice. Such estimates are notoriously unreliable, partly as a result of uncertainty, and partly as a result of the Napoleonic instincts of the experts in each particular field. Some pruning of the estimates is usual.

It then becomes a delicate and difficult problem of distributing the available finance between the various projects. Account is taken of the estimated internal rates of return, their reliability, of the amount of surplus capacity in each line of production, of the speed with which this capacity could be expanded, of technical innovations – actual and prospective – of the probable policies of competitors, and of the availability of labour – especially of the labour endowed with the particular skills required.

The estimate of the funds prospectively available is flexible. At a time when the profitability of the relevant future looks especially hopeful the various sources will be stretched; when it looks gloomy, funds – actual and borrowing powers – will be conserved for better times.

---

1. *Ibid.*, p. 667; reprinted in KEYNES, vol. XIV, pp. 220-1.

There is usually a minimum qualifying cut-off rate of the estimated internal rates of return – again dependent on the state of confidence about the future.

The part played by the equity varies enormously between countries. I write only about the United Kingdom. Even here it is the subject of controversy.

A very vague but diverse relationship exists between the state of confidence about the future on the Stock Exchange and the state of confidence about future profitability entertained by industrialists. It is a two-way relationship and neither state of mind can be described as horse rather than cart. Some of my cynical quotations from Keynes' Chapter 12, presented in Section 9 of this Lecture, bear on this issue.

I turn to less vague issues. Many of my economist colleagues argue that in our country aggregate retained profits are so great and, as a result of various Government concessions, Corporation Tax so low, that the industrial and commercial sector, taken as a whole, is self-financing.

But those who argue on this line overlook the wide polarisation between companies, at one extreme, which rely heavily on new issues of equities and those, at the other extreme, which accumulate financial assets and make successful take-over bids for other companies. The financial position would be much eased if the companies at the latter extreme bought the shares of the companies at the former extreme. But – apart from take-over bids – they do not.

However, my argument does not rest mainly on the quantitative importance of new issues of equities. It raises the much-debated question of the extent to which the management of a company is influenced by a sense of loyalty to its shareholders and how it is expressed.

Except in the cases in which some of the directors own personally, and on behalf of members of their families, considerable holdings of their shares, I accept the general view that the strong motive is to grow, under the influence of Keynes' 'animal spirits', and to finance growth as far as possible from retained profits.

It very well suits wealthy shareholders, subject to high marginal rates of tax on unearned income (as especially in the United Kingdom), to obtain their return in the form of a rising price of the shares rather than dividends.

But frequently the large shareholders are institutions – pension funds, insurance companies and investment trusts – whose clients are not wealthy and want income. There is always hanging over the management of a company the threat of a group of dissident institutions ganging up together and threatening gradually to change the composition of the Board of Directors if a higher proportion of profits is not distributed.

Another very real danger to the management arises if the price of the share is seriously below the value per share of the real underlying assets. The danger is that of a successful take-over bid, which may result in the directors being displaced.

Another factor is the pride of the management in presenting an annual report which is well received.

Finally, the value placed on a share by the Stock Exchange is partly determined by its earnings yield (more than by its dividend yield). The rate of capital appreciation depends on the rate of increase of earnings per share.

For these various reasons the management are subject to strong pressure to avoid growing so fast as seriously to prejudice the rate of growth of earnings and the price of the shares.

The result is that, indirectly if not directly, pressure is exercised on them to take account of their shareholders' interests. The prospective earnings yield per share, both on the real assets of the company (the internal rate of return) and on its shares, must not fall below the rate generally prevailing in the country. This factor acts as a restraint on the rate of growth of the company rather than Keynes' rate of interest. This is why the price of a company's shares matters to its management even if there is no question of making an issue of shares.

We have come quite a long way in this Lecture from Section 7 – the first section on the inducement to investment – to this final subsection dealing with real life. The long intervening discussion has not radically undermined Keynes' theory. I am not, of course, suggesting that the behaviour of entrepreneurs –

as opposed to that of all those who try to manage economies – is influenced by Keynes' teaching. What I am saying is that Keynes was a great pioneer – in the sense that he evolved the theory of how things happen in real life which no economist before him had succeeded in evolving.

SIXTH LECTURE
Personal relations with Keynes

1. Introduction. – 2. My own first contact. – 3. Keynes' impression on the Fellows of his College. – 4. Working with Keynes. – 5. My part in the 'General Theory'. – 6. Keynes' relations with Lionel Robbins. – 7. Keynes' relations with Dennis H. Robertson. – 8. Keynes' relations with Arthur C. Pigou.

1. Introduction

Keynes was 44 years old when I first came into contact with him in October 1928. The Keynes whom I came to know had had his life and character transformed by his marriage on 4 August 1925 to Lydia Lopokova, the great Russian ballerina: 'the best thing that Maynard ever did', Alfred Marshall's widow once remarked to Roy Harrod.[1] Although Keynes continued to live at 46 Gordon Square, in Bloomsbury, – in fact she more than he – and there was no breach, Keynes became far less a member of the Bloomsbury intelligentsia, and far more devoted to serious creative work. As Harrod puts it: 'In the ten years to come the basic pattern was to be different. They were to be years, not primarily of criticism, but of creation'.[2]

---

1. ROY F. HARROD, *The Life of John Maynard Keynes.* London: Macmillan, 1951, p. 365.
2. *Ibid.,* p. 367.

2. My own first contact

I took my First Degree in June 1927 at Cambridge in Mathematics (very elementary) and Physics. My father was an amateur economist. My father had a feeling, to which I responded, that I would enjoy economics as an academic subject of study.

I got a second-class degree in Physics and saw no prospects in the scientific field. I returned to my College for a fourth year to take the third-year undergraduate course in Economics, sitting for the examination in June 1928. I was placed in the First Class.

Some years later Schumpeter paid us a short visit. As the youngest economist on the staff, I was put in charge of his activities. It was explained to him how I had become an economist. His comment was that 'many a failed race-horse makes quite a good hack'.

I was taught by Gerald Shove, of whom I spoke in Section 5 of my first Lecture. Once a fortnight, together with three other privileged King's College undergraduates, I was supervised by Keynes.

For Shove and Keynes we each wrote two essays. Thus in alternate weeks I wrote two and four essays. On top of lectures and reading, and discussion among ourselves, it was hard work. But we not only learnt economics, we learnt to write English prose. The main reading had to be kept for the Christmas and Easter vacations.

I had worked hard during the previous Long Vacation of 1928 – from the end of June until the beginning of October. I found parts of Marshall's *Principles* difficult to understand, particularly Book v, Chapter xii, on increasing returns, and Book vi, Chapters vi, vii and viii on interest, profits and capital. When I came to attend Piero Sraffa's stimulating lectures my doubts were reinforced. The section on the short period in Book v, Chapter iii, appealed to me most: it was going to influence my intellectual life, and also Keynes'. To-day I am surprised to find how short this section is.

My antipathy to the Quantity Theory of Money dated from

boyhood as I explained in Section 8 of my second Lecture. Keynes' *Tract* was therefore a great worry to me.

Keynes had given up his University Lectureship and delivered only eight Lectures a year (not always that). The course which I first attended was entitled *The Pure Theory of Money*. He was a marvellous lecturer: one could not guess that he was lecturing from galley proof – at that time of an early draft of the *Treatise* – but I found his lectures extremely puzzling, based, as they were, on the Quantity Theory. (The great change occurred in the Summer Term of 1932.)

Robertson's *Banking Policy and the Price Level* I found completely unintelligible.

I actually trembled as I was about to enter Keynes' rooms in College for my first supervision (informal College teaching). I had heard so much of his fame, and had been moved by his *Economic Consequences of the Peace*. But as soon as the three other students and I had settled down round the open fire, we found talking to us – and encouraging us to talk – a man who was friendly and genial, and anxious to build up our confidence.

Keynes usually spent part of Saturday afternoon in the company of Piero Sraffa, looking at old books in Cambridge second-hand bookshops, including stalls in the Market Place. He was a great collector of rare books published in the seventeenth and eighteenth centuries, especially on economics and philosophy.

Sunday was free for work. (Lunch he took with his parents at Harvey Road.) Keynes drafted rapidly in pencil, reclining in an armchair. The pencil draft he sent straight to the printers. They supplied him with a considerable number of galley proofs, which he would then distribute to his advisers and critics for comment and amendment. As he published on his own account, Macmillan & Co, the 'publishers' (in reality they were distributors), could not object to the expense of Keynes' method of operating. They came out of Keynes' profit (Macmillan & Co merely received a commission). Keynes' object was to simplify the process of circulating drafts; and eventually to secure good sales by fixing the retail price lower than would Macmillan & Co.

More work on Monday morning, disturbed only by telephone

calls from stockbrokers. Monday afternoon was partly spent in the Bursary.

On each alternate Monday evening at 8.30 p.m. he presided over his Political Economy Club (the 'Keynes Club'), held in his own room. It was founded by him in 1909.[1]

During this long week-end Keynes was approached by Fellows of our own College, members of our Faculty and others who wanted his advice. Anybody who came to see Keynes with a reasonable purpose got the impression that he was a man of leisure, with nothing else to attend to. He very rarely gave any impression of operating under pressure.

On Monday afternoons or Tuesday mornings, Keynes returned to London to join his wife at 46 Gordon Square. Between then and Friday he conducted his busy life of affairs, including talks to the editor of the *Nation*, Hubert Henderson – from 1931 to Kingsley Martin, editor of the *New Statesman and Nation*.[2] Keynes took a lively interest in the editorial policy of the weekly, which he supported financially.

Part of each vacation he and his wife spent at Tilton, at the northern foot of the South Downs – a lovely region which the Bloomsbury group had captured. It was only then that he could concentrate properly on the book which he was writing – the *Treatise* when I first knew him, and then the *General Theory*. In the long summer Vacation he usually spent several months at Tilton. I will speak of life at Tilton when I began to go there myself to work with Keynes.

---

1. See ROY F. HARROD, *The Life of John Maynard Keynes*, pp. 149-52 and pp. 327-30. Also LORIE TARSHIS, 'Keynes as Seen by his Students in the 1930s', in DON PATINKIN and J. CLARK LEITH (eds.), *Keynes, Cambridge and the General Theory*, Proceedings of a conference held at the University of Western Ontario. London: Macmillan, 1977, pp. 50-1; and AUSTIN ROBINSON, 'A personal view', in MILO KEYNES (ed.), *Essays on John Maynard Keynes*. Cambridge: Cambridge University Press, 1975, pp. 10-11.

2. See ROY F. HARROD, *The Life of John Maynard Keynes*, p. 397.

3. Keynes' impression on the Fellows of his College

The impression which Keynes made on the Fellows of King's College in the thirties is best described by the following contribution made to the College Obituary pamphlet by my predecessor as Second Bursar of the College (Hugh Durnford), a simple man and in no sense an intellectual.

King's was for Maynard Keynes the inner citadel within his beloved native town, and on it he lavished his special affection [. . .] This avoidance of Cambridge out of Term was not, I think, due solely to the domestic claims [of his wife] of his London [or his country] house or, later, of his Sussex farm. It seemed as if he needed the pulse and movement of the College working in all its arteries to keep him happy: that he shunned a depleted Hall, a skeleton High Table, and courts emptied of undergraduates [. . .]

But with Fellows it was quite otherwise. With them there was no need for sought physical contact. He sat amongst them in his hour of relaxation in the Combination Room after dinner, playing patience and accessible to all [. . .]

This is not the place for a recapitulation of what was done, and done so quickly, to enrich the College materially and equip it for its further progress in other spheres. Again and again reviewing those changes, one is forced back to the conclusion that it could not have been carried through by anyone else – or perhaps in any other College. It was one of those rare combinations of time and men and place which make minor history. It was certainly the greatest epoch in the annals of King's [. . .]

If there was then this mellowing to be noticed in him – as to which I voice only my own opinion – about that time, then the last chink in his super-armoury was closed up, and there was nothing on which he could be faulted. It was interesting to speculate – when it appeared as if he might just go on more or less indefinitely as he was, the publicist in his academic fastness, the supreme scholar – Maecenas – whether there was indeed anything which he would not do perfectly if he put his hand to it; to visualise him as a staff officer, a playwright, a viceroy, a barrister or a bridge-builder. That was fancy. The last thing that could be foreseen was that he would actually die within ten years in the role of a plenipotentiary.[1]

1. Hugh G. Durnford, 'The Bursar', in *John Maynard Keynes, 1883-1946. Fellow and Bursar. A Memoir*. Cambridge: King's College, 1949, pp. 15-20. Harrod in his *Life* reproduces extracts from Durnford's contribution.

After I had taken the examination in June 1928, Keynes was anxious that I should write a Dissertation and compete for a College Research Fellowship. He did not at that stage engross any of my time on his own work, because a Fellowship Dissertation, to be successful, had to be original and show strong signs of promise, not only to those Electors who were economists (Keynes and Pigou) but to a high majority of the other Electors as well, all of whom read each candidate's Dissertation, each to the best of his ability.

Nonetheless, Keynes felt that he could kill two birds with one stone by securing for me, as a basis for my Dissertation, access to the statistics of the Midland Bank through the Chairman, his friend Reginald McKenna. My attitude of scepticism as to the usefulness of the Quantity Theory of Money being what it was, I had not the slightest idea what I would be intended to do with these statistics. I felt it difficult to decline. I put my hope in a *deus ex machina*. My hope was realised.

Keynes took me along to meet McKenna. The Head of the Intelligence Department was present. McKenna was completely acquiescent. Then the Head of the Intelligence Department took me along to his own room. He bluntly informed me that if anybody was going to make use of his statistics, it would be he and not I. I tremble to think what my life would have been like had he taken a conciliatory line.

It was an escape from disaster. Keynes then left me to choose my own subject. I chose the Economics of the Short Period, under the influence of Marshall.

I did not realise when I made my choice – nor did Keynes when he approved it – that my work would turn out relevant in the radical restructuring of the shape of Keynes' own work.

I completed my Dissertation in December 1929. Keynes then felt reasonably confident about my career and free to invite me to help him with the *Treatise on Money*. Any lingering doubt in his mind was dismissed by my election to a College Fellowship in March 1930. Of course I was delighted by this suggestion that I might help Keynes, without having any idea how far it would lead.

I came on the scene in January 1930. The final proof copy of the *Treatise* was passed in September 1930. The book had been started in 1924. It had been heavily rewritten in 1929, most of the changes being in the fundamental theoretical chapters.

I had done no work of my own on the subject. I had been completely unable to understand Robertson's *Banking Policy and the Price Level* (published in 1926) and was disturbed by the knowledge that Keynes had collaborated closely with Robertson.

I was completely bewildered and uninventive at that stage. For Keynes' acknowledgment to me in the *Preface*, the emphasis should clearly be on 'the avoidance of errors, and the compilation of the Index'.

It was in the course of the year 1930 that I began to spend part of most vacations staying with Keynes and Lydia at Tilton. The main object was to help Keynes with his work but also to enable me to carry on work of my own.

Life at Tilton was an enormous pleasure. Keynes and I both derived enjoyment from walking on the South Downs. Keynes delighted in simple pleasures.

After a few years he started keeping pigs on a domestic scale. We had great fun on Sunday mornings catching each one and weighing it in a home-made form of scales, devised by Keynes, to ascertain whether it was yet ripe for the bacon market.

Early in 1937 Keynes rented the farm of which Tilton House had originally been the farmhouse. The College owned a large estate in Lincolnshire, half of which we farmed ourselves. Keynes took a lively amateur interest in farming. As Bursar he kept a watchful eye on our activities in Lincolnshire. He was delighted to farm on his own account, with the help of a manager.

During the morning we usually worked together in his study. There were two interruptions. One was a telephone call from at least one stockbroker. The other was to pick the vegetables for lunch and dinner.

Part of the evening after dinner was spent by Keynes in doing

175

what he called 'non-work'. Apart from the newspapers there were numerous economic journals to be glanced through, and the *Corn Trade News* and the *Metal Bulletin*. Here I must interpolate that the magnitude of Keynes' operations on organised produce markets is often exaggerated. They were really a hobby calculated to illustrate the economic principles involved.

Above all to be dealt with after dinner there were the contributions to the *Economic Journal*, of which Keynes was the editor who dealt with articles (his co-editor, Austin Robinson, dealt with reviews and everything else). Of course the number of articles submitted was minute compared with the present time. Only very rarely did Keynes reject an article without a letter explaining his reason, and he rarely accepted an article without suggesting some improvements.

5. My part in the 'General Theory'

The final pages of Lecture IV are devoted to an attempt to diagnose why it took over four years to write the *General Theory*. After all progress from the *Treatise* to the *General Theory* was far less than from the *Tract* to the *Treatise*. The *Treatise* took six years to write, but towards the end of this period Keynes had to give up a considerable amount of time to *Can Lloyd George Do It?*, the Macmillan Committee, the Economic Advisory Council[1] and its Committee of Economists.[2]

I drew attention to the great volume of correspondence with Dennis Robertson, but I regarded that as unavoidable – for reasons of sentiment if no other.

It is only a few years ago that I began to reflect on those four years. What was the character of the help that I was able to give to Keynes? What did pass between us in the course of those many mornings which I spent, in that period, at Tilton?

The publication of Volumes XIII and XXIX of Keynes' *Collected Writings* has added to the mystery. When I read my own letters to Keynes I was taken aback to find that so many of them were far from helpful in any constructive sense. And no signs of drafts or memoranda written by me.

The traditional explanation – which I believe to be valid – is that my written – as opposed to oral – contributions were made in the margins of galley proofs which have not survived. Such a note would take the form either of minor redrafting; or of an indication that Keynes and I should discuss the passage indicated, or of the correction of a misprint.

The scope of such notes in the margins of galley proofs is limited.

The explanation is, I think, to be found at the end of Keynes' Preface to the *General Theory*:

The writer of a book such as this, treading along unfamiliar paths, is extremely dependent on criticism and *conversation* if he is to avoid

1. See Section 2 of Lecture III.
2. See Section 1 of Lecture IV.

177

an undue proportion of mistakes. It is astonishing what foolish things one can temporarily believe if one thinks too long *alone*, particularly in economics (along with the other moral sciences), where it is often impossible to bring one's ideas to a conclusive test either formal or experimental.[1]

I have put the words *conversation* and *alone* in italics. I relieved the solitude and provided, by being on the spot, a more rapid method of discussion than correspondence by post. And I looked out for the errors.

Schumpeter's suggestion that my

share in the historic achievement cannot have fallen very far short of co-authorship[2]

is clearly absurd. Perhaps it was inspired by unconscious hostility to Keynes.

It has to be remembered that the book from which this quotation is taken was written in the last nine years of Schumpeter's life. He was always, when we met, very friendly to me. His friendship with Keynes – in spite of his own remarkable output of books – was towards the end tainted by a trace of jealousy. Keynes had found a solution to the basic problem for which Schumpeter had, for a great part of his life, searched in vain. Schumpeter used to say to his friends:

When I was young I had three ambitions: to become a great lover, a great horseman, and a great economist. I realised only two.

---

1. KEYNES, vol. VII, p. xxiii.
2. JOSEPH A. SCHUMPETER, *History of Economic Analysis*. New York: Oxford University Press; London: George Allen and Unwin, 1954, p. 1172.

6. Keynes' relations with Lionel Robbins

Keynes first made the acquaintance of Professor Lionel Robbins in September 1930 on the Committee of Economists which I referred to at the end of Section 1 of Lecture IV. He was thirty-two years old. A year earlier he had been brought from Oxford to London as a Professor at the London School of Economics – the youngest Professor in the country.

Robbins was in fundamental disagreement with the rest of the Committee, being more classical in his economic thought even than Pigou.

In his *Autobiography* Robbins recalls:

The two matters on which this sharp difference took place were the desirability of increased public expenditure during the slump and the policy of free imports. On the first of these I now believe that I was wrong. On the second I am not at all ashamed of the record.[1]

The most serious issue arose over protection. A strong case was made by Keynes, Henderson and Stamp for tariffs on iron and steel, and, after serious examination, possibly on pigs and poultry.[2] Pigou accepted the view that the existence of heavy unemployment invalidated the classical case for free trade, but put forward a number of reasons of a political character against protection. One of them was that once a tariff is imposed it is politically extremely difficult to remove it.[3]

Robbins wrote his own minority Report. It included a section in which a strong case was made against tariffs.[4]

I agree with Susan Howson and Donald Winch that Keynes 'hoped to be able to secure a high degree of consensus on remedies' as well as diagnosis.[5] And indeed, as they put it:

---

1. LIONEL ROBBINS, *Autobiography of an Economist*. London: Macmillan, 1971, p. 152.

2. SUSAN HOWSON and DONALD WINCH, *The Economic Advisory Council 1930-1939. A Study in Economic Advice during Depression and Recovery*. Cambridge: Cambridge University Press, 1977, pp. 202-11.

3. *Ibid.*, pp. 225-6.

4. *Ibid.*, pp. 229-31.

5. *Ibid.*, pp. 46-7.

The older members of the committee were more concerned with consensus [. . .] In order not to damage the chances of useful economic policies being adopted, they were prepared to minimise their disagreements over matter of economic theory.[1]

A rift developed with Robbins. Keynes believed, supported by the Secretary of the Cabinet, that there was no 'precedent for a minority report by a single member. By this time feelings were running high on both sides [. . .] Hemming [my co-Secretary] and Henderson managed to persuade Keynes and Robbins to accept the inclusion of a statement by Robbins at the end of the report.'[2] (This 'statement' was printed as *Report by Professor L. Robbins*.)

Having capitulated, Keynes, according to Robbins' account, 'read aloud to the committee a letter to the Secretary commenting very adversely on my emotional state [. . .] It was intimated [. . .] that my presence was no longer desired at the final meeting of the committee.'[3]

Robbins continues:

All this was unspeakably painful and anxious while it lasted. But it did not last long [. . .] it was not many weeks before Keynes and I were meeting again at the executive committees of the London and Cambridge Economic Service as if there were nothing but intellectual differences between us [. . .] I never felt that he was other than a great man and one whose stature was such that idiosyncrasies of personal behaviour, such as those of which I had been the victim, sank into unimportance in the general perspective of his quality and his character.[4]

Robbins assures me that, as he makes clear in his *Autobiography*, this episode, so far as he personally was concerned, was not the cause of the 'breach' which at that time developed, as it seemed to us in Cambridge, between the London School and our Cambridge Faculty. Robbins is, of course, right in describing as 'highly misleading' the

1. SUSAN HOWSON and DONALD WINCH, *The Economic Advisory Council 1930-1939. A Study of Economic Advice during Depression and Recovery*, p. 63.
2. *Ibid.*
3. LIONEL ROBBINS, *Autobiography of an Economist*, p. 152.
4. *Ibid.*

picture often presented suggesting a state of acute enmity and mutual distrust, with the leading personalities barely on speaking terms and professional relations non-existent [. . .] Nevertheless, on the general policy of financial expansion to counter the depression, which I should hesitate to involve all my London colleagues in what I now believe to be a mistaken outlook, I think there was enough manifestation of opposition to policies which were widely supported in Cambridge to provide sufficient substance for the allegation of group conflict. I would not wish to minimize the public significance of this particular episode and I have no doubt that, at the time, it may have been the occasion for some ill feeling on both sides.[1]

The 'breach' was the result of Friedrich von Hayek being brought from Vienna in 1931 to become Tooke Professor at the L.S.E. Hayek preached doctrines which were in direct opposition to Keynes'. Possibly wrongly but in Cambridge we had the impression that the intention was to set Hayek up as an idol to serve as an antidote to Keynes (a function which he still fulfils as an antidote to the post-Keynesian anti-monetarists). Robbins did not initiate the appointment. He describes it as having been suggested by William Beveridge (Director of the L.S.E.), 'much to Robbins' surprise'. 'To the delight of all concerned', Hayek accepted a unanimous offer.[2]

Before he was appointed to the Chair, Hayek was tried out by being invited to deliver some lectures. In January 1931 he delivered the four lectures which were published as his *Prices and Production*.[3] Robbins gives a description:

In the event the lectures were a sensation, partly for their revelations of an aspect of classical monetary theory which for many years had been forgotten.[4]

It was just the opposite in Cambridge. We invited Hayek, before delivering the four lectures in London, to talk to the Marshall Society. He had a large audience of students, and also of leading members of the Faculty. (It was on a Thursday even-

---

1. *Ibid.*, pp. 133-4.
2. *Ibid.*, p. 127.
3. FRIEDRICH A. HAYEK, *Prices and Production*. London: George Routledge & Sons, 1931; Second Edition 1935.
4. LIONEL ROBBINS, *Autobiography of an Economist*, p. 127.

ing, so that Keynes was in London.) It is only fair to Hayek to mention that he had to condense the four lectures into one, and that they were written when he had a high temperature.

The members of the audience – to a man – were completely bewildered. Usually a Marshall Society talk is followed by a lively and protracted barrage of discussions and questions. On this occasion there was complete silence. I felt that I had to break the ice. So I got up and asked:

Is it your view that if I went out tomorrow and bought a new overcoat, that would increase unemployment?

'Yes', said Hayek. 'But', pointing to his triangles on the board, 'it would take a very long mathematical argument to explain why.'[1]

Hayek reviewed Keynes' *Treatise* in *Economica*, August 1931 and February 1932. In the course of his reply Keynes wrote:

The reader will perceive that I have been drifting into a review of Dr. Hayek's *Prices and Production* [. . .] The book, as it stands, seems to me to be one of the most frightful muddles I have ever read, with scarcely a sound proposition in it beginning with page 45, and yet it remains a book of some interest, which is likely to leave its mark on the mind of the reader. It is an extraordinary example of how, starting with a mistake, a remorseless logician can end up in Bedlam. Yet Dr. Hayek has seen a vision, and though when he woke up he has made nonsense of his story by giving the wrong names to the objects which occur in it, his Khubla Khan is not without inspiration and must set the reader thinking with the germs of an idea in his head.[2]

So far as the young were concerned the so-called breach did not last long. Joan Robinson has recently described how the *Review of Economic Studies* 'was founded as a forum for discussion' between Cambridge and the younger graduate students at the L.S.E. after 'a delegation led by Abba Lerner (then a graduate student at LSE) came to Cambridge to suggest that the young generation on each side should get together and settle the debate

1. JOAN ROBINSON, *Contributions to Modern Economics*. Oxford: Basil Blackwell, 1978, pp. 2-3.
2. JOHN MAYNARD KEYNES, 'The Pure Theory of Money. A Reply to Dr. Hayek', *Economica*, November 1931, p. 394; reprinted in KEYNES, vol. XIII, p. 252.

amongst themselves'.[1] The first number of the *Review* was published in October 1933.

In August 1933 a week-end meeting was held at an inn in Newport (symbolically regarded as half-way between London and Cambridge but actually much closer to Cambridge). Cambridge was represented by Joan and Austin Robinson, James Meade, of Oxford (who had spent the academic year 1930-31 with us in Cambridge), and myself; the L.S.E. by Abba Lerner and three others.

Joan Robinson writes an amusing account of the progress of the week-end. She continues:

Abba came to spend a term in Cambridge. He had been used to being the intellectual leader of his group and he very candidly admitted that he had been distressed to meet an argument that he could not answer. After passing the term in mental agony, he found out that saving is necessarily equal to investment and became for some time an only too fanatical supporter of Keynes.[2]

The oubreak of the Second World War led to the evacuation of the London School of Economics to Cambridge. Keynes and Hayek had a common interest in rare books, and they became quite close friends.

In the spring of 1940 Robbins joined the Economic Section of the War Cabinet Office and he soon became Director of the Section. Keynes and Robbins in the early years of the War collaborated and became real friends – but not very closely. In the course of the various negotiations with the Americans and of the Conferences in the United States they worked closely together, and each appreciated the other. Robbins wrote of Keynes at that time:

In all the activity, both creative and diplomatic [. . .] the dominating figure was that of John Maynard Keynes [. . .] It goes without saying that Keynes was one of the foremost economists of his age [. . .] there were other economists [. . .] There was, however, only one Keynes [. . .] when he came into a room we all cheered up [. . .] all in

1. JOAN ROBINSON, *Contributions to Modern Economics*, p. xv.
2. *Ibid.*

all, I would certainly regard Keynes as the most remarkable man I have ever met.[1]

In the course of a speech in the House of Lords on 28 July 1966 Robbins said:

In the inter-war period when mass unemployment actually prevailed, I was on the wrong side: I opposed measures of reflation which I now think might have eased the situation.[2]

I was present. It was a moving occasion.

Robbins has developed the theme at greater length in his *Autobiography*.[3]

I shall always regard this aspect of my dispute with Keynes as the greatest mistake of my professional career.[4]

1. LIONEL ROBBINS, *Autobiography of an Economist*, pp. 192-3.
2. HOUSE OF LORDS, *Official Report*. Third volume of Session 1966-1967, Session of 28 July 1966, col. 953.
3. LIONEL ROBBINS, *Autobiography of an Economist*, pp. 152-5.
4. *Ibid.*, p. 154.

7. Keynes' relations with Dennis H. Robertson

There is little that need be added to what I have already said about Keynes' relations with Robertson. I began in Section 3 of Lecture 1 over Robertson's *A Study of Industrial Fluctuation*, written before the First World War and published in 1915. In 1910, Keynes was made Director of Studies in Economics at Trinity College, Cambridge, and Robertson was one of his first pupils. From then on they became close friends and collaborated in one another's work. I described how before that War it was Robetson who was the pioneer. In Section 1 of my third Lecture I touched on their discussions over Robertson's *Banking Policy and the Price Level*, published in 1926. Although Keynes in letters to Robertson expressed himself as unhappy about the publication of this curious book, their collaboration continued throughout the writing of Keynes' *Treatise*. It is difficult to choose, for strength of feeling, between the tributes paid by each to the other in the Prefaces to the two books.

In Section 3 of my fourth Lecture I touched on the growing breach between them during the writing of the *General Theory* – Keynes desperately anxious to get Robertson to understand, Robertson desperately anxious to save Keynes from error. It was not until 11 March 1935, only nine months before publication, that it was agreed between them that discussion of the proofs cease. In the course of a friendly letter dated 10 October Keynes offered to send Robertson the page proofs, without imposing on Robertson 'any obligation' to comment.[1] In the course of a friendly reply Robertson wrote that he would prefer now to wait until the book was published.[2] In the end Keynes came to the sad decision to make no reference to Robertson in the Preface – in my view a mistake.

I then referred to a renewal of friendly relations, revealed in a good-humoured exchange of letters towards the end of 1936, including Keynes' remark:

1. *Letter* to Dennis H. Robertson, *10 October 1935*; published in KEYNES, vol. XIII, pp. 523-4.
2. *Letter* from Dennis H. Robertson, *11 October 1935*; published in KEYNES, vol. XIII, p. 524.

I certainly date all my emancipation from the discussions between us which preceded your *Banking Policy and the Price Level*.[1]

In 1938 Robertson took the opportunity of leaving Cambridge provided by an offer of a Professorship at the London School of Economics. It was an agonising wrench. But, to quote his obituarist, John Hicks: 'Cambridge, in the full tide of "Keynesian Revolution", he decided (after what agony one can imagine) was no place for him.'[2]

He did not stay long at the London School of Economics. Soon after the outbreak of War he became a Treasury official (he was called an 'adviser'). I remember Keynes remarking to me at the time that potentially he could become a powerful influence in the Treasury but that he could not bring himself to exploit his position. Harrod describes how

he threw himself into the routine of his daily duties, and overtaxed himself – in expiation as it were. He was assigned the task of keeping track of the British balance of payments, and this he did without staff, in his own fair hand.[3]

Keynes began to work in the Treasury in June 1940, first of all as a member of a Consultative Council: a little later he was given a room, and was allowed a roving commission. His appearance livened up Robertson's activities and extended his field of operation. Usually there was close co-operation between them. Unlike Hubert Henderson, Robertson was a great help to Keynes rather than a thorn in his flesh. Occasional disagreement was conducted on a playful basis.

How to Pay for the War was published in February 1940.[4] Robertson wrote to Keynes calling it 'your best work since

1. *Letter* to Dennis H. Robertson, *13 December 1936*; published in KEYNES, vol. XIV, pp. 89-95 (the quotation on p. 94).

2. JOHN R. HICKS, Obituary of 'Dennis Holmes Robertson, 1890-1963', *Proceedings of the British Academy*, vol. L, 1964, p. 312.

3. ROY F. HARROD, *The Life of John Maynard Keynes*, p. 530.

4. JOHN MAYNARD KEYNES, *How to Pay for the War*. London: Macmillan, 1940; reprinted in KEYNES, vol. IX, pp. 367-439. An early version was published in the form of articles in *The Times* on 14 and 15 November 1939; reprinted in KEYNES, vol. XXII, pp. 41-51.

E.C.P.'[1] [*Economic Consequence of the Peace*, published in 1919]. This remark might be regarded as spiteful. I regard it as playful.

There was a friendly controversy in April 1941 about 'An Analysis of the Sources of War Finance',[2] which led to the first Budget White Paper. Keynes conducted it in the form of a 'conundrum'. Eventually – after Robertson had failed to solve it – Keynes produced the solution.

Strictly speaking, in place of 'requiring domestic finance', the passage should read 'requiring to be financed out of taxation and primary saving, if inflation is to be avoided, on the assumption of no change in the propensity to spend'.[3]

I mention these trivial incidents because Hicks, in his Obituary, writes that while

superficially there was a reconciliation [. . .]
Yet it was only in [the] particular field [of the establishment of International Monetary Institutions] that there was a reunion; elsewhere they were wide apart. Even the temporary reconciliation was not easy.[4]

I completely disagree with Hicks. Although my own work in the Treasury lay in different fields, I saw much of Keynes and on occasion worked with Robertson. The Treasury was a fairly small Department, and, at the senior level, everybody knew everybody else. I neither saw nor heard anything to justify Hicks' view.

Robertson's really great opportunity came with the discussions which ultimately led up to the Bretton Woods Agreement and the International Monetary Fund.

On receiving in November 1941 Keynes' second draft of his proposals for an International Currency Union, Robertson wrote to Keynes on 27 November 1941:

I sat up last night reading your revised 'proposals' with great excitement, – and a growing hope that the spirit of Burke and Adam

1. KEYNES, vol. XXII, p. 106.
2. *Ibid.*, pp. 338-47.
3. *Ibid.*, p. 342.
4. JOHN R. HICKS, Obituary of 'Dennis Holmes Robertson, 1890-1963', p. 313.

Smith is on earth again to prevent the affairs of a Great Empire from being settled by the little minds of a gang of bank-clerks who have tasted blood (yes, I know this is unfair!).

And then also a growing hope that we shall choose the right things and not the wrong ones to have such rows with the Americans about [. . .].[1]

Robertson was fully involved in the lengthy process of re-drafting and negotiation which culminated finally in the Conference at Bretton Woods, which opened on 1 July 1944. Relations with Keynes became especially warm during the Conference. In the course of a letter to Richard Hopkins, Permanent Secretary of the Treasury, on the last day of the Conference, Keynes wrote:

Everyone in our team has played together splendidly. If anyone is picked out, I think it would have to be Dennis, whose help has been absolutely indispensable. He alone had the intellectual subtlety and patience of mind and tenacity of character to grasp and hold on to all details and fight them through Bernstein [the number two in the U.S. Treasury team], so that I, frequently occupied otherwise, could feel completely happy about the situation.[2]

Robbins made a note in his journal at the time about the seriousness of the drafting difficulties which arose during the Conference and referred to the yeoman services of Dennis Robertson.

Three days after the end of the Conference Keynes wrote to his mother: 'Dennis Robertson is perhaps the most useful of all – absolutely first-class brains do help!'[3]

Hicks has not read this remark to Keynes' mother – and presumably also Keynes' letter to Hopkins – *au pied de la lettre*. 'Keynes was condescending, Robertson was easily hurt.'[4] It is very difficult to accept Hicks' view.

---

1. *Letter* from Dennis H. Robertson, *27 November 1941*; published in KEYNES, vol. XXV, p. 67; in slightly abbreviated form in ROY F. HARROD, *The Life of John Maynard Keynes*, p. 531.

2. ROY F. HARROD, *The Life of John Maynard Keynes*, pp. 578-9.

3. *Ibid.*, p. 578.

4. JOHN R. HICKS, Obituary of 'Dennis Holmes Robertson 1890-1963', p. 313.

8. Keynes' relations with Arthur C. Pigou

Pigou was six years older than Keynes. Throughout his long life, of 82 years, he took an interest in the young. Pigou, who had just been elected a Fellow of King's College in March 1902, soon spotted the brilliance of Keynes, who entered King's College as an undergraduate in October of the same year. They became friends, and remained friends, for the whole of Keynes' life.

After Keynes took the final examination in mathematics in June 1905, he decided to work for the Civil Service examination. His interest in economics developed, only partly because it was one of the subjects which he was to take in that examination. Marshall, whom he had known as a family friend, tried hard to persuade him to become a professional economist. Harrod writes: 'Pigou [Marshall's pious disciple] had him to breakfast once a week and gave him coaching in the subject.'[1]

Keynes spent less than two years in the India Office. He devoted part of that time to writing his Fellowship Dissertation on *Probability*,[2] and was elected a Fellow in March 1909.

But already a year earlier he accepted an offer from Marshall of a Lectureship in Economics with a salary of £100 a year paid out of Marshall's own pocket. When a few months later Pigou succeeded Marshall, he continued the payment for a number of years.

Relations between Pigou and Keynes then became established on a basis of common interests. The fact that they were both Fellowship Electors alone brought them close together – particularly as they were both outstandingly good Electors. Pigou acknowledged Keynes' help in his Preface to his *Wealth and Welfare*.[3]

They were both widely cultured. Pigou first read History and then obtained his degree in the Moral Sciences Tripos, taking

1. Roy F. Harrod, *The Life of John Maynard Keynes*, p. 107.
2. Publication was held up by the First World War. It was eventually published in 1921 entitled *A Treatise on Probability* (Keynes, vol. VIII).
3. Published in 1912. London: Macmillan.

Ethics and Political Philosophy (with special distinction in Advanced Political Economy: the Economics Tripos was established three years later). Keynes as a boy knew as family friends the great Cambridge philosophers and as an undergraduate came strongly under the influence of two of the greatest of them all – George E. Moore and Bertrand Russell. Pigou as a young man won a University Prize for an essay on Robert Browning as a religious teacher.

Their friendship was so firmly based that it survived disagreement from time to time – sometimes intense – on economic issues.

Pigou consented to serve on the Cunliffe Committee of 1918-19[1] and on the Chamberlain–Bradbury Committee of 1924-25,[2] the Reports of which were directed, by limiting the note issue, towards the imposition of a deflationary influence – and preparing the way for the eventual restoration of the pre-War sterling dollar parity.

Although Keynes' name is so closely associated with opposition to the policy, he made up his mind definitely rather late in the day. In his *Tract on Monetary Reform*, published in 1923, he included Great Britain in the group of countries for which an argument could be made in favour of such restoration.[3] However, a few pages earlier in the same book he expressed some doubt,[4] and he was very critical of the recommendations of the Cunliffe Committee.[5]

In his 'Speeches of the Bank Chairmen' of February 1924,[6] Keynes made it clear that he was opposed to a return to the pre-War parity in the near future. A few months later he presented this view emphatically in evidence to the Chamberlain-Bradbury Committee, while expressing the hope that in the longer

---

1. See DONALD MOGGRIDGE, *British Monetary Policy 1924-1931. The Norman Conquest of $4.86*. Cambridge: Cambridge University Press, 1972, pp. 19-20. See also ARTHUR C. PIGOU, 'The Problem of the Currency', *Contemporary Review*, February 1920, pp. 169-76.

2. DONALD E. MOGGRIDGE, *British Monetary Policy 1924-1931*, pp. 48-9.

3. KEYNES, vol. IV, p. 122.

4. *Ibid.*, pp. 116-17.

5. *Ibid.*, pp. 145, 152-3.

6. KEYNES, vol. IX, pp. 188-92.

term the pre-War parity would be restored as a result of a rise in United States prices.[1] He repeated this view again in February 1925 in his second article on 'Speeches of the Bank Chairmen',[2] and finally in his 'Economic Consequences of Mr Churchill',[3] from which I have quoted in Section 4 of Lecture V. This was preceded by a note by Keynes in the *Economic Journal* of June 1925,[4] ending with the words:

one would expect an historic document [. . .] at any rate an armoury of up-to-date arguments in favour of old-fashioned expedients. But we find instead a few pages, indolent and jejune.[5]

In the course of his pungent criticisms of the Cunliffe and Chamberlain–Bradbury Committees, Keynes refrained from mentioning that Pigou was a member of both.

Although Pigou's economics was so different from Keynes', they shared a desire to direct their teaching and writing to – and now I quote from Pigou's Preface to his *Economics of Welfare* –

the bettering of human life. The misery and squalor that surround us [. . .] the injurious luxury of some wealthy families, *the terrible uncertainty overshadowing many families of the poor* – these are evils too plain to be ignored [. . .] Out of the darkness light![6]

The basic motive for the study of economics was the same. But it is the words which I have italicised that most strongly suggest common ground between Pigou and Keynes.

Unemployment of the type which concerned Keynes is not discussed. But it was not discussed by Keynes until *Can Lloyd George Do It?* (1929). The following sentence appears at the opening of Part II, Chapter 1, of *Economics of Welfare*.

Throughout this discussion, except when the contrary is expressly stated, the fact that some resources are generally unemployed against

---

1. DONALD E. MOGGRIDGE, *British Monetary Policy 1924-1931*. Cambridge: Cambridge University Press, 1972, pp. 42-3.

2. KEYNES, vol. IX, pp. 192-200.

3. Originally published in July 1925; reprinted in KEYNES, vol. IX, pp. 207-30

4. JOHN MAYNARD KEYNES, 'The Committee on the Currency', *Economic Journal*, June 1925, pp. 299-304; KEYNES, vol. XIX, Part I, pp. 371-8.

5. *Ibid.*, p. 304; reprinted in KEYNES, vol. XIX, Part I, p. 378.

6. ARTHUR C. PIGOU, *The Economics of Welfare*. London: Macmillan, 1920, p. vii.

the will of the owners is ignored. This does not affect the substance of the argument, while it simplifies its exposition.[1]

Later in the book involuntary unemployment is referred to only in the chapters on 'Employment Exchanges', 'Unemployment *versus* Short Time', 'The Practicability of Interference to Raise Wages' above the 'natural rate' which would prevail in the absence of interference, and 'Methods of Engaging Labour'.

The Preface to *Wealth and Welfare* (1912), from which the *Economics of Welfare* originated, opens with the words:

Several years ago I began to study the causes of unemployment. It soon became apparent, however, that these causes are so closely interwoven with the general body of economic activity that an isolated treatment of them is scarcely practicable.[2]

(The Preface concludes by acknowledging the help of Keynes in 'avoiding error and ambiguity'.)

The phrase 'natural rate' of wages appears in the text of the *Economics of Welfare*, but almost entirely in relation to attempts to raise low wages. There are several chapters about variability of income, but they deal with the importance for economic welfare of spreading a given amount of aggregate consumption evenly over time, rather than with unemployment.

A year later, in 1913, Pigou published a little popular book entitled *Unemployment*. From the fact that there is no copy in the King's College Library, I infer that Pigou was ashamed of it (Fellows of the College invariably present copies of their works to their Library). Here Pigou really did deal with unemployment – indeed with 'involuntary unemployment':[3] possibly he invented

1. ARTHUR C. PIGOU, *The Economics of Welfare*; see 1920 Edition, p. 111, 1924 Edition, p. 113, 1929 Edition, p. 129, 1932 Edition, p. 127. In the 1920 Edition, but not in the later ones, there follow the words: 'This reservation will need to be withdrawn in the later Parts.' Pigou was referring to the final part of the 1920 Edition on 'The Variability of the National Income'. This was not included in the later editions, because Pigou hoped 'in the next year or two, to be able to complete a study of industrial fluctuations' (Preface to 1924 Edition). His *Industrial Fluctuations* was published in 1927.

2. ARTHUR C. PIGOU, *Wealth and Welfare*. London: Macmillan, 1912, p. vii.

3. For the confusion between the uses of the words 'voluntary' and 'involuntary' unemployment see my contribution ('Unemployment as Seen by the Keynesians') to DAVID N. WORSWICK (ed.), *The Concept and Measurement of Involuntary Unemployment*. London: George Allen and Unwin; Boulder, Colorado: Westview Press, 1976, pp. 19-25.

the phrase. There is 'involuntary unemployment' if at the ruling wage workers would be willing to provide more work than is available.[1] But it is caused 'by maladjustment between wage-rates and demand'.[2]

Pigou's first serious book on unemployment was not published until 1933.[3] (His *Industrial Fluctuations*, published in 1927, dealt rather casually with unemployment.)

The Appendix to Chapter 19 of the *General Theory* was devoted to a heavy attack on this book, though expressed in reasonably polite language. Pigou's review article of the *General Theory* was expressed in extremely vigorous language.

How is it that an author, whose powers of exposition enabled him to write on the philosophy of Probability in a way that amateurs could follow – not to say one whose vividness of phrase has made him a valued contributor to the *Daily Mail*, when he comes to the subject to which he has devoted most attention, is barely intelligible to many – for I am not alone in this – of his own professional colleagues?[4]

The final sections of the review were designed to mollify:

even those parts of his discussion which least command agreement are a strong stimulus to thought. We have watched an artist firing arrows at the moon. Whatever be thought of his marksmanship, we can all admire his virtuosity.[5]

Keynes did not publish any rejoinder. In a letter to Robertson dated 20 September 1936 Keynes wrote:

I was distressed by the Prof's review and even more so that you should think it worthy of him [. . .] I thought [it] profoundly frivolous in substance.[6]

And yet Pigou on many occasions in the thirties gave public support, during the slump, to State action designed to stimulate

1. ARTHUR C. PIGOU, *Unemployment*. New York: Henry Holt and Co.; London: Williams and Norgate, 1913, pp. 14-16.
2. *Ibid.*, p. 51.
3. ARTHUR C. PIGOU, *The Theory of Unemployment*. London: Macmillan, 1933.
4. ARTHUR C. PIGOU, 'Mr. J. M. Keynes' General Theory of Employment, Interest and Money', *Economica*, May 1936, p. 119.
5. *Ibid.*, p. 132.
6. From a *Letter* to Dennis H. Robertson, *20 September 1936*; excerpt published in KEYNES, vol. XIV, pp. 87-8.

employment. I gave one good example towards the end of Section 2 of my Third Lecture. He wrote a number of similar letters to *The Times*.

The difference between Pigou and Keynes in those days of heavy unemployment was not over the question whether expansionist action taken by the State and Central Bank would fail to reduce unemployment. The difference was over the mechanism. Pigou believed it was because prices were raised and real wages reduced. This made it profitable to bring plant into operation on which otherwise a loss would be incurred. Without denying that real wages might be reduced, Keynes thought in commonsense terms of the effect of raising demand.

Before the Macmillan Committee on 29 May 1930 Pigou attributed a 'large part of the present unemployment [. . .] to the rate of wages being out of adjustment to the general conditions of demand'.[1]

But in the course of a Note presented to the Committee after he had completed his evidence Pigou wrote:

The government should put in hand and should encourage local authorities and public utility companies to put in hand enterprises of a useful character, even though they are likely to yield a return substantially below current rates, and even though guarantees of interest involving a cost to the Treasury are necessary.[2]

Pigou took the same line on the Committee of Economists.

Pigou published several little semi-popular books. One of them, *Socialism versus Capitalism*, was published in 1937.[3] Passages in the chapter on 'Unemployment' suggest that Keynes was beginning to have some influence on Pigou:

There is general agreement that absolute movements of industrial activity on a large scale are usually centred in changes of attitude towards investment on the part of persons interested in the manufacture of capital goods [. . .] in the modern world, especially in this country, money rates of wages are considerably 'sticky' [. . .]

---

1. Macmillan Committee on Finance and Industry, *Minutes of Evidence*, vol. ii, 29 May 1930. London: His Majesty's Stationery Office, 1931, p. 78, question no. 6432.
2. Note by Hopkins, *ibid.*, p. 93.
3. Arthur C. Pigou, *Socialism versus Capitalism*. London: Macmillan, 1937.

Hence the swings in money demand affect the volume of employment [. . .] It is a fact and a paradox that, in periods when the quantity of labour engaged in making capital goods is increasing, the extra labour wanted there is not obtained, even in part, by transfers from industries making consumption goods, but the quantity of labour engaged in those industries also is increased.[1]

I sent the book to Keynes. He replied on 20 October 1937:

As in the case of Dennis [Robertson], when it comes to practice, there is really extremely little between us. Why do they insist on maintaining theories from which their own practical conclusions cannot possibly follow? It is a sort of Society for the Preservation of Ancient Monuments.[2]

It was just at that time that a difficult situation was created by the submission by Pigou for publication in the *Economic Journal* of an article on 'Real and Money Wage Rates in Relation to Unemployment'.[3] Keynes, the editor of the *Economic Journal*, was convalescing from his first heart attack at Ruthin Castle in Wales. The co-editor, Austin Robinson, was in charge. Keynes wrote to Robinson on 7 August:

Unless my heart has had a worse effect on my mind than his on his, Dennis [Robertson] has committed an unforgivable crime in passing [Pigou's article] for publication.[4]

(Pigou suffered from a chronic bad heart.)

Donald Moggridge, as editor of Volume XIV of Keynes' *Collected Writings*, wrote that:

[Keynes] first attempted to hold the article up, largely to protect Pigou [. . .] from embarrassment, and to prevent an economist of Pigou's standing from looking foolish, as he feared he might, in the eyes of the world.[5]

Austin Robinson wrote to Keynes: 'I find an almost insuper-

---

1. *Ibid.*, pp. 52-3.
2. *Letter* to Richard F. Kahn, *20 October 1937*; published in KEYNES, vol. XIV, p. 259.
3. ARTHUR C. PIGOU, 'Real and Money Wage Rates in Relation to Unemployment', *Economic Journal*, September 1937, pp. 405-22; see Keynes, vol. XIV, pp. 235-68.
4. From a *Letter* to Austin Robinson, *7 August 1937*; excerpt published *ibid.*, p. 234.
5. KEYNES, vol. XIV, p. 234.

able difficulty in balancing one's affection for Pigou against one's love of truth.'[1]

In the end the article was published.[2] Gerald Shove, a tolerant man, another Fellow of King's College, told me 'that without exception this is the worst article he has ever read'.[3]

Keynes' reply appeared as a Note in the December 1937 issue of the *Economic Journal*,[4] together with a Note on the same subject by Nicholas Kaldor[5] (not yet a Fellow of King's College).

Pigou drafted a 10,000 word rejoinder. We put on to Pigou David Champernowne – a young Fellow of King's College, a mathematical economist for whom Pigou had a high regard. He discovered two fallacies in the draft.

The result was that the 10,000 words were reduced to $4\frac{1}{2}$ pages.[6] In effect it was a complete and frank withdrawal of Pigou's previous argument. But, as submitted, it was confined to Kaldor's Note. Pigou wrote to Keynes on 23 December 1937:

I have said nothing about your note because, to tell the truth, I don't understand it and also I'm sure that you ought not to be dragged into economic discussions while you're unfit.[7]

In a letter to me six days later, Keynes wrote: 'It would not, however, have upset my health too seriously to be informed that he now accepts all my criticisms in toto!'[8]

It spontaneously occurred to Pigou

that to say nothing about [Keynes'] note, while discussing Kaldor's,

---

1. KEYNES, vol XIV, p. 239.

2. ARTHUR C. PIGOU, 'Real and Money Wage Rates in Relation to Unemployment', *Economic Journal*, September 1937, pp. 405-22.

3. *Letter* from Richard F. Kahn, *18 October 1937*; published in KEYNES, vol. XIV, p. 258.

4. JOHN MAYNARD KEYNES, 'Prof. Pigou on Money Wages in Relation to Unemployment', *Economic Journal*, December 1937, pp. 743-5; reprinted in KEYNES, vol. XIV, pp. 262-5.

5. NICHOLAS KALDOR, 'Prof. Pigou on Money Wages in Relation to Unemployment', *Economic Journal*, December 1937, pp. 745-53.

6. ARTHUR C. PIGOU, 'Money Wages in Relation to Unemployment', *Economic Journal*, March 1938, pp. 134-8.

7. From a *Letter* from Arthur C. Pigou, *23 December 1937*; excerpt published in KEYNES, vol. XIV, p. 266.

8. From a *Letter* to R. F. Kahn, *29 December 1937*; excerpt published *ibid.*

might look offensive to outsiders, though of course it wasn't meant to be.[1]

The result was the addition of a short footnote. Pigou stated that he had been unable to understand Keynes' note but that he had now moved much closer to Keynes' general view.

It must be extremely difficult, in the light of what I have written, for anybody who was not living in Cambridge – indeed in King's College – in the thirties to believe in the friendship between Pigou and Keynes which I emphasised near the outset of this section. Each, in a different way, admired the other. Pigou recognised that Keynes was breaking valuable new ground. He wished that he would clarify his exposition – Pigou himself often failed to follow it – and forgo destructive criticism, especially of Marshall, whom they both revered, and of Pigou himself. Keynes was sad that Pigou, whom as a man he admired, found it so difficult to appreciate new modes of thought.

Pigou was on the whole averse to oral discussion of economics. He knew that it was safe to sit next to Keynes at Hall Dinner. The merits of a Fellowship candidate or some problem facing the Faculty would be seriously discussed. Pigou was Chairman of our Faculty Board, and Keynes, Robertson and Austin Robinson the most active members.

Austin Robinson knew them well. In the course of his official Biography of Pigou he writes:

Pigou and Keynes had a great mutual regard and affection for each other, and their personal friendship was never seriously jeopardized by their intellectual differences.[2]

Already in his Preface to his *Employment and Equilibrium*, dated July 1940, Pigou wrote:

Whatever may be thought of the value of Keynes' criticisms upon other people, or of the solutions which he has himself offered, the author of *The General Theory of Employment, Interest, and Money* has

---

1. *Ibid.*, p. 268.
2. AUSTIN ROBINSON, Obituary of 'Pigou Arthur Cecil, 1877-1959'. *Dictionary of National Biography. 1951-1960.* London: Oxford University Press, 1971, p. 817.

rendered a very great service to economics by asking important questions. When once that has been done, the task of answering the questions is often a relatively pedestrian one. In this field, therefore, Mr. Keynes is a true pioneer.[1]

Pigou in the course of his contribution to the Memoir published by King's College after Keynes' death wrote of him:

Keynes could disagree violently with particular bits of an author's work without weakening in his admiration for the whole; just as he could write scathingly in controversy without a touch of malice or personal ill-feeling [. . .]
After Marshall's main work was finished [. . .] we were pedestrians, perhaps a little complacent. Keynes' *Treatise on Money* and later his *General Theory* broke resoundly that dogmatic slumber [. . .]
The period of tranquillity was ended.[2]

And:

When the Memoir appeared Lydia Keynes kissed Pigou: the only woman known to have done so since his childhood. After that it happened quite often and the Prof. seemed to like it.[3]

I conclude with the two lectures on 'Keynes's *General Theory*'[4] delivered in Cambridge in November 1949 before an audience of students and members of the Faculty of Economics. It was another moving occasion, Pigou was 72 years of age. Pigou began by referring to his *Economica* review article of May 1936. Now, thirteen years later, Pigou made

an appraisement, as objective as I can make it, of what [. . .] the book accomplished constructively.[5]

Pigou took his stand on Keynes' 'fundamental conception', in which Keynes summarised in one paragraph the ultimate

---

1. ARTHUR C. PIGOU, *Employment and Equilibrium*. London: Macmillan, 1941. Second Edition, 1949.

2. ARTHUR C. PIGOU, 'The Economist', in *John Maynard Keynes, 1883-1946. Fellow and Bursar. A Memoir*, pp. 21-2. See also 'John Maynard Keynes. 1883-1946', *Proceedings of the British Academy*, vol. XXXII (1946), pp. 395-414.

3. JOHN SALTMARSH and PATRICK WILKINSON, *Arthur Cecil Pigou, 1877-1959*. Cambridge: King's College, 1960, pp. 13-14.

4. ARTHUR C. PIGOU, *Keynes's 'General Theory', A Retrospective View*. London: Macmillan, 1950.

5. *Ibid.*, p. 1.

'independent variables [. . .] [which] determine the national income [. . .] and the quantity of employment'.[1] Referring to this 'kernel of Keynes' contribution', Pigou said:

Whatever imperfection there may be in his working out of the fundamental conception embodied there, the conception itself is an extremely fruitful germinal idea. In my original review-article on the *General Theory* I failed to grasp its significance and did not assign to Keynes the credit due for it. Nobody before him, so far as I know, had brought all the relevant factors, real and monetary at once, together in a single formal scheme, through which their interplay could be coherently investigated.[2]

As a renunciation it was only partial, but, as Austin Robinson has put it:

It was the very noble act of a man who put truth beyond vanity and another's reputation beyond his own.[3]

---

1. *Ibid.*, p. 20. Pigou quoted this paragraph in full from the *General Theory* (KEYNES, vol. VII, pp. 246-7).
2. ARTHUR C. PIGOU, *Keynes's 'General Theory'*, p. 65.
3. AUSTIN ROBINSON, 'Obituary of Pigou', p. 816.

DISCUSSION

JOAN ROBINSON: The great trouble with Keynes was that he was an idealist. He thought that when people could understand his theory, could understand how the capitalistic system actually works, they would then behave in a reasonable manner and operate the system in such a way as to produce favourable results, to produce in particular a high and stable level of employment.

Now, it happened that for twenty years after the war there was a rather satisfactory operation of the capitalistic system. There was continuous growth interrupted only by shallow depressions: each time there was a depression there was a recovery very quickly so that over the whole period there was continuous growth in the industrial world and there was a fairly high level of employment, a rather low level of unemployment, in all the western countries; and there was what is now realised was a very moderate rate of inflation, and so it appeared that the problems had been solved.

During this period the understanding which Keynes had supplied of how a market economy operates was smothered. In the United States the great development of the economy took the centre of gravity away from Europe in economic power and in the teaching of economic theory. The economic theory which was developed in America was a return to pre-Keynesian doctrines; – that there is a natural tendency to equilibrium in the market economy; – that unemployment, if it does occur, is only due to wages being too high. The understanding which Keynes had provided of the economic system was lost in this return to *laissez faire* and equilibrium theory.

The doctrines in the United States were derived from the stream of thought elaborated by Robert Clower, taken up by Axel Leijonhufvud, which tried to derive Keynes from the general equilibrium theory of Walras, considered to be the foundation of economics. Clower tried to show that Keynes was not inconsistent with this, that Keynes' theory was merely that unemployment arises from a failure of the generation of equilibrium according to the doctrine of *laissez faire*, that is of the operation of a market system through movements of prices; so that all the old doctrines were reestablished.

Paul Samuelson, who was the leading influence on teaching in the United States, produced the Neo-Classical Synthesis, which reduced Keynes once more to a version of equilibrium theory.

After this period of capitalistic prosperity the world has now fallen again into a slump, but the teaching which Keynes had established has been lost, the theory has been lost and the practice has been lost. Why should it happen that a very unconvincing and quite empty theory, like that of the Monetarists or the theory of Walrasian equilibrium, should prevail over a very intelligent theory such as that offered by Keynes? Keynes was very innocent, he thought that an intelligent theory would prevail over a stupid one. But of course in real life the influence on policy does not come from an intelligent understanding of the economy but from the play of vested interests and from the desire to defend capitalism against the currents of radical thought which have been emerging during this period.

So there is no use really arguing on merits. On merits, hardly anybody could possibly prefer Milton Friedman to Keynes or to Kalecki, but this does not mean that the influence of Keynes will prevail over the influence of Milton Friedman.

There is a particular problem at the present time which needs to be introduced into the discussion, because it is a very clear example of how understanding a problem does not provide a solution for it. This is the problem at the present time of the indebtedness of the third world countries. Here there is a perfectly ridiculous situation in the world. In the industrial countries there is unemployment and underutilisation of plant, and, in particular, extreme overcapacity for the production of steel. So there is unemployment and low profits in the industrial world for lack of demand. There is the third world which is supposed to be developing: development needs investment and investment needs steel. Here is an enormous real demand and an enormous real oversupply.

They cannot be brought together. Why?

They cannot be brought together because of the lack of finance. The third world countries are already deeply indebted. A great part of their exports have to be used to service the debt they have already incurred. So they are not able to carry forward a development plan for lack of finance and the developed countries are unable to produce the steel and the machinery which these peoples need because they have no purchasing power. This is a prime example of what Keynes called the humbug of finance. The whole world has tied itself up in this totally unreal tangle and why? The reason is that during the great inflationary boom, particularly in 1972 and 1973, a number of respectable banks were lending to the third world countries, and part of the debt which they now have to service, is debt to the western banking system, so that any reasonable solution, any way of reducing the amount of debt and starting demand again, would threaten the very basis of the financial system of the western world. And so the system is immobilised, unable to solve the real problem because of the financial problem. Now this can be understood perfectly well; the problem is quite well understood, but it is impossible to do anything about it. This was the weakness in Keynes' position: he showed how to understand the problems but he did not understand how to solve them.

GIACOMO BECATTINI[1] dealt with some of the questions raised by Professor Kahn in his first Lecture, that is to say the relationship between the thinking of Alfred Marshall and that of Keynes. Professor Kahn spoke of Keynes' view – without however explicitly endorsing it – that the successors of John Stuart Mill eliminated the problem of general overproduction from the economic *corpus* not by solving it, but by ignoring it.

Apart from the Marxist statement of Say's Law, ignored by most British economists of the nineteenth century, this problem remained dormant, according to Keynes, until the appearance in 1889 of Hobson and Mummery's *Physiology of Industry*.

To these assertions of Keynes it might perhaps be objected that the problem actually remained open, though without further theoretical developments, in the official teaching of economics at Cambridge since it was dealt with in the manual by Henry Fawcett. Fawcett, drawing on Mill, distinguished between two

1. Professor of Economics, Università degli Studi, Firenze.

types of overproduction – goods produced in quantities such that they cannot be sold at remunerative prices and goods produced in quantities such as to exceed people's wants, admitting quite definitely the first type of overproduction. True, this state of overproduction is, in Fawcett, a mysterious anomaly of the working of the market, whose causes are unspecified and for which no remedies are prescribed. The treatment of this problem, as Professor Kahn has rightly noted, takes a qualitative leap with Marshall's analysis.

The first point to stress in this connection is that this 'qualitative' leap in the problem of overproduction is no mere accident in Marshall's intellectual development, but is the significant and necessary result of the converging of different lines of his progress as a theorist.

One of the first lines of progress concerns monetary theory: here the young Marshall went beyond 'quantitative' theory and formulated the famous Cambridge equation. It is not quite certain when Marshall arrived at this new formulation, but there are good reasons to suppose it was in the early 1870s. In this formulation, money takes on the explicit role of a bridge between the present and the future: the proportion of his assets that an individual holds in liquid form reflects his hopes and fears for the future. Contemporary with this formulation of monetary theory is the reformulation of the theory of relative prices, distinguished by the systematic introduction of adjustment delays and by the expression of the phenomena of irreversibility, instability and multiplicity of the equilibrium points. Compared with a dry, abstract classical theory, which allowed no bridge between invisible natural prices and observable market prices, this reformulation is distinguished by the attempt to integrate concrete market phenomenology with economic analysis. The key idea behind both of these *theoretical outlines* is the integration of time in economic theory, with its inherent delays and irreversibilities and with the forecasting it demands.

Another line of progress in Marshall's thinking, although it appears to be a distant one, is in fact of relevance to the problem under discussion. Marshall takes very seriously the contrast between the market economy and a socialist or communist-type economic regime. He was one of the very few British economists to read and study Marx and Lassalle around 1870. While he regards the labour theory of value as clearly wrong, he is much struck by their castigation of the anarchy of the capitalistic market and by the link which is thus presented with the problem of economic fluctuations. At one point in his *Theory of Foreign Trade*, written when he was a young man and then thrown aside in 1877, when nearly finished, for the rats to critically devour, Alfred Marshall writes, speaking of Ferdinand Lassalle:

> He observed rightly that the evils of such periods are much aggravated by the fact that in them each branch of industry, afraid that it will not meet with an adequate market for its own wares, refuses to purchase the wares of others; and thus helps to cause the stagnation which it fears.[1]

In the light of this explicit link with Lassalle's philosophy, in other words with German socialist thinking, even the passage from *The Economics of Industry* quoted by Professor Kahn takes on a different flavour. The cumulative mechanisms of depression and recovery no longer seem mere superficial descriptions for the external shapes of the business cycle, but indicate a certain degree of adherence to Lassalle's diagnosis of the anarchy in the capitalistic market. With regard to Mill and to Fawcett, the step forward is remarkable because it brings to light the fact that in *normal* market conditions there is a tendency to cumulative developments both upwards or downwards. Where Marshall does not go along with socialist thinking is in the indication of the deep causes of disequilibria where socialists say these lie in the unavoidable contrast between productive forces and production relations, Marshall maintains they may be of various kinds, either general or particular, but never unavoidable, never incurable. For Marshall, the market is not a perfect mechanism which automatically absorbs every shock, nor is it a mechanism which inevitably produces increasingly deep crises until it finally collapses. All the young Marshall's lines of thinking, both ideo-

---

1. JOHN K. WHITAKER, *The Early Economic Writings of Alfred Marshall, 1867-1890.* London: Royal Economic Society, 1975, vol. II, p. 38, note 4.

logical and analytical, converge on this concept of the market. From the ideological point of view, Marshall learned enough from socialist thinking and the historical school, to see in the market and in capitalism just *one* form of social organisation, not the final, finished form. And from the analytical point of view he already had his tools – monetary theory and price theory – allowing him to take into account the infinite folds and twists, resistances and discontinuities of actual economic movement, and yet avoid vagueness and fragmentation.

In short, Dennis H. Robertson was surely right in his argument with Keynes, when he said that his youth – i.e. his studies under Pigou and in the glow of Marshall's philosophy – had not been afflicted by overweening respect for Say's Law.

If this is true – it seems to be – the following problem arises: if there is so little difference between Keynes' and Marshall's basic diagnosis of the nature and functioning of the market, how is it that the therapy suggested by Keynes is so different from that suggested by Marshall? All the more does the question arise in view of the fact that Marshall was certainly neither less aware of, nor less sensitive to, the negative social effects of unemployment than Keynes; and it should be noted that the unemployment or underemployment that Marshall had in mind stood to what Keynes had in mind, much as Victorian England stood to the England of the 1930s. As Professor Kahn explained in the face of the confidence trick implicit in the exposition of Marshall's *The Economics of Industry*, Keynesians hold that direct and fundamental State intervention is a more reliable way of restoring normal conditions. So why, having identified the potential for destabilisation hidden in normal market functioning, does Marshall stop at a Platonic reference to the confidence trick? It is fairly clear that, when involved in actual Royal Commissions of inquiry, or in the more general context of economic policy questions, for instance in *Industry and Trade*, Marshall never relies mechanically on the principles of *laissez faire*, and does not find it difficult to propose very incisive public intervention. He is, however, rather reluctant about counter-cyclical intervention. I believe that this dislike for counter-cyclical policies can be explained by his personal view of the world.

Briefly, Alfred Marshall's view of the world is founded on two premises: for the first of these, the basic aim of the social process, that which makes it progressive, which in other words makes it an approximation to an ideal state and not a mere alternation of generations is a transformation of the character of mankind, reinforcing what Victorian society considered the most noble motives for human action (social conscience, responsibilities to future generations, etc.) in such a way as gradually to make these motives (and not those others, less lofty but more powerful ones such as the pursuit of one's own or one's group interests, which have hitherto made the fortune of the market economy) the driving forces of material development. This, according to Marshall, is the course of history that it is to expect and wish for. The second premise is that the character of man, the formation of which we have now seen to constitute, for Marshall, the basic aim of the social process (final consumption being only a subordinate target) depends less on the formal education he receives than on the way in which he earns his living and the social relationships thus generated. From these two premises stems the basic yardstick that Marshall uses to measure every concrete public intervention, which he conceives as always indissolubly acting at all economic and moral levels of the human character.

The ultimate yardstick is the lasting effect produced, presumably, by the planned intervention on the character of the people directly or indirectly concerned. If, besides its direct and immediately observable effect, the public intervention promises to arouse constructive energies and hopes in individuals and to reinforce in them the sense of social awareness and of responsibility to their neighbours and to their descendants Marshall is in favour of it. Where he is perplexed, and perhaps even contrary, is when public intervention, after a first wave of positive economic effects, reveals glimpses of further waves of effects presumably regressive on the human character. He has a liking for the 'constructive' spirit of Lassalle's proposals (while he condemns Marx's vision as purely destructive) without adopting them himself lest the 'secret sources of human action' be harmed. For Marshall, the basic problem is to provide a sufficient stimulus for that superior morality which is needed, if there is to be any hope of overcoming the individualistic solution to the human economic problem.

Analysis of this point would require an investigation in depth in order to make it at least plausible to those accustomed to seeing Marshall as an old hypocrite, who disguises a defence of capitalism behind sentences oozing with Victorian morality! To round off with a brief comparison between the basic policies of Marshall and those of Keynes on the problems of social reform, subject to any – welcome – comments from Professor Kahn or Joan Robinson, the conclusion would seem to be as follows: whilst in Marshall it is the strategic prospect of perfecting human nature, allowing the transition to another kind of society, that dominates any practical measure eliminating many kinds of counter-cyclical intervention, in Keynes, and perhaps for the entire post-Victorian generation, it is the tactical dimension that prevails. How far Keynes was tormented by the problem of moulding human nature is for expert witnesses to say. But the impression one gains is that Keynes was not overburdened by this problem when he was devising an effective policy for full employment. Struck by the dramatic economic and social conditions of the 1930s, Keynes seemed to resign himself to taking man as he found him . . . declining to compound his problem with restrictions based on a concern – incidentally typically Victorian – for the improvement of human nature. Thus new solutions, inconceivable earlier, became possible. To draw an image from greyhound racing: where Marshall concerns himself with altering the personality of the greyhound, Keynes accepts the dog for what it is, and tries to make it run faster by manipulating the hare.

GIANGIACOMO NARDOZZI:[1] During the first series of Raffaele Mattioli Lectures Professor Modigliani repeated and amplified the message of his Presidential Address to the American Economic Association. The message was 'we are all monetarists now', by which he meant that Keynesians and monetarists are in broad agreement as to the theoretical framework underlying the work-

1. Professor of Economics, Università degli Studi, Firenze.

ings of the economy (and as to the importance of money) and that the area of disagreement is confined to the lines of economic policy.

This conciliatory position may be seen as the end-result of the IS–LM scheme, which is sufficiently general to encompass different views and so constitute the terrain for what may be regarded as the prevailing orthodoxy.

Lord Kahn's message in these lectures was certainly not conciliatory. He argued strongly on several grounds that the Keynesian approach of Cambridge cannot be reduced to current orthodoxy. The controversy between the Cambridge Keynesians and the prevailing way of thinking is one of those cases in which, as Lord Kahn recalled, on the one hand there is a handful of people maintaining that they have a theory of their own and on the other the majority that maintains that everyone is really saying the same thing. What Joan Robinson called the mindless majority claims to include the minority that considers itself intelligent.

The principal differences between Cambridge Keynesian thinking and the prevailing trend which Lord Kahn identified in his lectures are broadly:
– regarding investment as exogenous when determining the level of income;
– dealing with inflation *before* introducing money.

This approach conflicts not only with monetarist thinking, on which Lord Kahn concentrated his criticism, but also with the usual IS–LM schemes.

It may therefore be assumed that what characterises the Cambridge school is not so much the insistence on one aspect rather than another within a scheme of macroeconomic equilibrium used by everyone but a different approach to the problems of macroeconomics. To take the question of investment, the assumption that investment is governed by 'animal spirits' is not equivalent to proposing the inclusion of some variables rather than others into the investment function. Nor is it to be taken as a flight from the problem of analysing the determinants of investment towards non-economic ground. This assumption depends on the conviction that, in order to explain the mechanism whereby national income is determined one must *not* explain what determines capital accumulation (this does not mean that investment decisions are not important, quite the contrary). In other words, this approach to analysis derives from an important point of method: if one wants to explain everything (as with an all-inclusive scheme like IS–LM) one ends by explaining nothing. But this is exactly the type of problem that current theory shies away from. It is thus important to discuss it. The difficulty in accepting the Cambridge approach (a difficulty that accounts for its limited acceptance) may be summed up in the following question: Why should a theory that fails to account for some things (investment) and disregards some others (money) be thought better than another theory that accounts for and considers these aspects?

FRANCO BRUNI[1] raised one of the subjects Professor Kahn said he had no time to analyse adequately and that could be dealt with during the discussion: the Swedes. The specific question: how Keynesian was Knut Wicksell?

When looking at the relationship between Wicksell and Keynes one might concentrate on the later Wicksell (the second volume of the *Lectures*)[2] and the earlier Keynes (up to the *Treatise*). But in this case, in spite of some contemporaneity, the relationship, while probably very close, is less interesting and more difficult to discuss. But there is a somewhat neater comparison namely between the pure, perhaps 'crude', nineteenth-century Wicksellian monetary theory, as expounded in *Interest and Prices*, and the mature Keynes of the *General Theory*.

By taking this earlier Wicksell nothing essential is lost of his contribution to monetary theory: as Ohlin states in his splendid introduction to the English edition of *Interest and Prices*,[3] trans-

1. Associate Professor of International Monetary Theory and Policy, Università Commerciale Luigi Bocconi, Milano.

2. J. G. KNUT WICKSELL, *Föreläsningar i Nationalekonomi*. Lund, 1901-1908. Translation from the Swedish by E. Cassen: *Lectures on Political Economy*. Vol. I, *General Theory*; vol. II, *Money*. With an introduction by Lionel Robbins. London: G. Rotledge & Sons, 1934, 1935.

3. J. G. KNUT WICKSELL, *Geldezins und Güterpreise. Eine Studie über die den Tauschwert des Geldes bestimmenden Ursachen*. Jena: Gustav Fischer, 1898. Translation from the German by Richard Kahn: *Interest and Prices. A Study of the Causes regulating the Value*

lated by Professor Kahn, Wicksell did not change his ideas about monetary theory very much during the twentieth century. The way he expounds his model in the *Lectures*, compared with the *Interest and Prices* style, is simply a bit more sophisticated and precise analytically but perhaps weaker and less enthusiastic.

On the other hand, to consider the later Keynes means looking at a man who had brought to solution some of his own problems and even Wicksell's.

Wicksell and Keynes: the first thing to do is to deemphasise an obvious difference: *Interest and Prices* is a full-employment model while the core of the *General Theory* is non-full-employment equilibrium. The difference is surely important. But, besides the fact that the Keynesian model can be used also as a theory of inflation, much of the analytical content of Wicksellian macroeconomics has its duality in a model with fixed prices and variable employment. This is what Hicks has to say in *Capital and Growth*:

There is a remarkable correspondence between the instability of the Harrod-type model, when it is established in this manner, and that of the Wicksell-Lindahl model [. . .]. The Wicksellian 'cumulative process' is a property of a Flexprice model, [The Harrod-type instability] is a property of a Fixprice model; the one disequilibrium is a price disequilibrium, the other is a quantity disequilibrium; these are exactly the relations that one would expect from 'duals', in something like the sense that Linear Programming theory has made familiar. The more one works it out, the clearer it becomes that there is in fact a duality relation between the two theories [. . .].

In the Flexprice model there is cumulative inflation (or deflation) if the expected rate of profit is out of line with actual interest; in the Fixprice model there is cumulative expansion (or contraction) if the expected growth rate is out of line with that which saving makes attainable. The rate of interest in the one theory is dual to the rate of growth in the other.[1]

It is now possible to seek a relationship between *Interest and Prices* and the *General Theory* without fear of dealing with two completely different worlds. The relationship that will here be

of Money. With an introduction by Bertil Ohlin. Published on behalf of the Royal Economic Society, London: Macmillan, 1936.

1. JOHN R. HICKS, *Capital and Growth*. Oxford: Clarendon Press, 1965, pp. 121-2.

stressed rests on a traditional reading of Keynes and is therefore different from the one which has been recently established by Laidler[1] on the basis of a Clower – Leijonhufvud interpretation of the *General Theory*.

What Wicksell and Keynes seem to have in common are some important problems. Schematically these problems can be reduced to the following two: the *instability* of the natural rate of interest, on the real side, and the *elasticity* of the financial market in the other side of the economy.

Both for Wicksell and for Keynes only the former problem usually causes the sorrows of the economy: but these sorrows are allowed to torment the economic system, to bite at it, to stay and not to disappear, by the monetary problem. In the typical Wicksellian example when the natural rate *goes up* inflation develops because the financial system will produce an *excess supply* of credit. In the typical Keynesian case, when the investment schedule *comes down* unemployment develops following an *excess demand* for money at the full employment level of income.

The excess supply of money in Wicksell, exactly as in Keynes' inflationary case, is due to the stickiness of the bank rate. The excess demand for money in Keynes' unemployment case comes from the stickiness of prices and wages *and* from the stickiness of the interest rate (which is totally rigid in the liquidity trap). In both cases the *elasticity* of the money market, which allows the real shock to find its way through the economy, comes from the *rigidity* of the rate of interest which lags behind the changing real conditions. To give a theoretical explanation to this elasticity of the money market (the slope of the LM curve) Keynes looks at the shape of the *demand* for money while Wicksell looks at the *supply* (the shape of the latter, on the other hand, is largely determined by the behaviour of banks' demand for liquidity). But the problems are the same: the instability of the real sector depending on the elasticity of the financial sector.

To match these two problems Wicksell and Keynes have different policies: the Swede wants, and thinks it possible, to neutralise the elasticity of the money market; Keynes wants,

1. DAVID LAIDLER, 'On Wicksell's Theory of Price Level Dynamics', *Manchester School of Economic and Social Studies*, vol. XL, 1972, p. 125.

and thinks it possible, to stabilise (mainly by fiscal policy) the real side of the economy. But even this difference must not be overstated because Keynes certainly did not reject monetary policy.

Wicksell and Keynes were therefore troubled by the same basic problems, to be sure, but only Keynes was able to *solve* them, from an analytical point of view, in a convincing manner. He succeeded because he found a new, potent theoretical apparatus to deal with them. What he did was to analyse the instability of the real sector with the use of the very powerful concept of *marginal efficiency of investment* (while Wicksell remained entangled with the confusing and mechanical idea of the natural rate) and to tackle the problem of explaining the elasticity of the monetary sector with the equally powerful concept of *liquidity preference*. Particularly impressive is the fact that if the Keynesian theory of liquidity preference is applied to banks' demand for reserves, the Wicksellian theory of credit supply becomes terribly modern and readily explains some contemporary monetary developments.

The relation between Wicksell and Keynes can be summed up by saying that they were both worried to a great extent about the same problems and that they both dedicated deep and precious thoughts to them; but only the second eventually found a solution to those problems and only after long years of struggle when his similarity with Wicksell, whose work he did not know very well, was such, to quote a recent book by Fausto Vicarelli, as 'to authorize doubts about his originality'.[1]

This exposition has certainly involved too schematic an approach. A distinction should be made, for instance, between the theory of very short-run fluctuations and the one explaining medium- and long-term cycles. From the point of view of the latter, Wicksell's analysis of cumulative financial disequilibrium contains, to be sure, some theoretical insights that cannot be found in Keynes. Moreover, to quote Leijonhufvud, 'It seems clear that Keynes consciously did his best to dodge the issues raised in the post-Wicksellian debate. In retrospect it is amazing

1. FAUSTO VICARELLI, *Keynes: l'instabilità del capitalismo.* Milano: Etas Libri, 1977, p. 96.

how successful he was [. . .].'[1] In fact modern macroeconomics is in some sense still waiting for a successor to Wicksell's study on 'what goes wrong with relative values'[2] in macroeconomic fluctuations; this investigation, in spite of the important contribution by Lindhal, Myrdal and von Hayek, was 'in short order forgotten'[3] after the appearance of the *General Theory*.

Therefore it seems that, although Keynes succeeded in solving some of Wicksell's problems by using superior analytical tools, there is much in Wicksell which has still to be fully discovered and exploited.

PAOLO SAVONA[4] was grateful to Lord Kahn for recalling the core of Keynes' thinking when he referred to the sentence in the introduction to the *General Theory* in which Keynes stated that classical (or in today's terms neo-classical) theory accounts only for some cases whereas the *General Theory* is capable of envisaging many more, such as those in which full employment cannot be attained by reliance on market forces.

Since then – as Joan Robinson has pointed out – Keynes' proposition that classical theory explains only a few cases has become according to the Keynesians that classical theory was always wrong. The proposition that the market does not guarantee full employment in certain circumstances has become that the market never guarantees full employment.

From these propositions has stemmed a line of economic policy that restricts the operating of the free market instead of removing the conditions that hamper it.

For Italy these propositions have been an excuse for imposing inefficient or corrupt superstructures and for not thinking of mechanisms to ensure that markets work, such as laws on competition to regulate dominant positions. In the public corporation sector, and in that of subsidised firms generally, the dominant positions have often been strengthened, by law or

1. AXEL LEIJONHUFVUD, *On Keynesian Economics and the Economics of Keynes*. New York-London: Oxford University Press, 1968, p. 344.

2. *Ibid.*, p. 343.

3. *Ibid.*, p. 344.

4. Professor of Economic and Financial Policy, Libera Università Internazionale per gli Studi Sociali, Roma.

by administrative decree, with the end-result that the market does not work and full employment is not guaranteed.

Just as it cannot be argued that the neo-classical model is *always* wrong and that the market *never* works, the same goes for monetarism or rather its policy in the oil crisis. The outcome of monetarist therapy, if such it can be called, i.e. the correction of the disequilibria in the oil balances, is leading the western world to a freeze on economic and employment growth. On the other hand, it has also to be admitted that so-called Keynesian therapies, applied to the same disequilibria in the oil balances, are leading, in a system of wages indexation that includes phenomena outside the national economy (e.g. higher oil prices), to the following spiral: alteration of the relative prices between the production factors or between commodities / devaluation / wage rises / inflation / interest rate rises / inflation / devaluation and so on unendingly.

If Keynesians can find no way out of this vicious circle, it is hardly surprising that simplistic ideas like monetarism should get the upper hand. Monetarism appeals to public opinion by starting from the stagflationary results of Keynesian policies but it puts forward a non-solution of its own, to a Keynesian non-solution. The world is at present going ahead, or rather not going ahead, by dint of non-solutions. A situation that breeds simple ideas, which turns out inevitably to be simplistic.

On the subject of Keynesian solutions, one question naturally arises in the presence of Professor Kahn, who did so much to formulate the income multiplier. How is it that in Italy the public deficit has no multiplying effect on income? How is it that, having incurred a higher public deficit than any other industrial country, Italy has such a low growth rate and rising unemployment?

Monetarism thrives on such modest performances. It cannot solve the stagflationary crisis in a system of oligopolies like the oil, labour and capital markets. But one may well be wrong in looking for a solution to the crisis in the context of economics. The crisis goes far beyond the calculations of economists.

Professor Savona went on to say that political and social factors, far-reaching changes in the power relationships within industrial countries and on the international stage combine to stultify the models of reference used in economics. In the present state of knowledge it surely cannot be argued that any one economic model is applicable to all cases everywhere and at all times. There is no such thing as the *General Theory* sought by Keynes. There are historical conditions in this or that country that suggest that economic systems work in a way that Keynes' theory can interpret them, others that suggest responsiveness to the principles of monetarism. The researcher's skill lies in spotting when one or other of the various models fits a given situation and has predictive power in it.

FABIO RANCHETTI,[1] commenting on Lord Kahn's reference to an alliance between Italian and Cambridge economists, felt that some historical remarks regarding the links between Keynes, Kahn, Raffaele Mattioli and the Banca Commerciale Italiana were in order.

In 1922 Raffaele Mattioli, then a young assistant at Bocconi University, published an article by Keynes in the *Rivista Bancaria*,[2] which he edited. It would be gratifying to think that it was Piero Sraffa who advised his friend Mattioli to publish Keynes' article – this supposition being founded on the slender evidence that Sraffa had already visited England and had met Keynes for the first time in 1921.

In the early 1930s the Banca Commerciale Italiana published a review – *Rivista Mensile* – that was very receptive to new economic ideas (it was run by Domenico Boffito, Carlo Boffito's father). Kahn's fundamental article which appeared in the *Economic Journal* in 1931 was quoted in the first issue of this journal in that same year.[3] This was the first time that Kahn's ideas

1. Research Fellow in the Department of Economics, Università degli Studi, Torino.

2. 'La "stabilizzazione" dei cambi europei', *Rivista Bancaria*, May 1922, pp. 251-60. Italian translation of 'The Stabilisation of the European Exchanges: A Plan for Genoa' (see KEYNES, vol. XVII, pp. 355-69).

3. The essay 'Una delle cause del disagio della sterlina. La politica sociale dei sussidi ai disoccupati' (*Rivista Mensile*, September 1931, pp. 1-10) at p. 8 quotes RICHARD F. KAHN, 'The Relation of Home Investment to Unemployment', *Economic Journal*, June 1931, pp. 173-98.

were discussed in an Italian economic journal so soon after their appearance in England.

These two events, now part of the history of economic thought, are recalled because the Banca Commerciale Italiana (and its Research Department) undeniably helped to spread Keynes' ideas in Italy and because there is a special affinity between the thought of Keynes and of Mattioli. There is always an essential link between a 'good' economic theory and sound effective practice, provided in this case by a farsighted bank.[1]

During his lectures Lord Kahn expressed more than once an antipathy for or hostility to that mathematical overformalisation with which some presentday economists dress up their ideas – or, as Lord Kahn put it, their 'nonsense'.

To understand the world and, in particular, economic reality highly complex econometric models are of little use. More often a few fundamental economic concepts will do – the best presumably being those of Keynes and Kahn – but what is absolutely necessary is good logic. As an old French economist once put it, 'Pour être Economiste, il ne s'agit que de ne pas être inconséquent'.[2] Or in the words of Keynes, a little nearer to our time, 'Economics is a branch of logic, a way of thinking [. . .] economics is a science of thinking in terms of models joined to the art of choosing models which are relevant to the contemporary world.'[3]

When Keynes speaks of 'a logical way of thinking', 'a formal structure of thought', one's mind turns at once to mathematics or to theoretical mechanics as models of scientific knowledge. And indeed the application of mathematics to the relationships between economic phenomena seemed to be the means whereby political economy could be made scientific and finally turned into a rigorous science. And yet 'classical theory', which de-

---

1. For an analysis of Raffaele Mattioli's thought, see FABIO RANCHETTI, *Weltanschauung ed Economia Politica nelle Relazioni Comit 1945-1971*. Preliminary draft of a working paper for research on 'The relevance of Economic Theory to the understanding of Economic Practice'. Milano: Fondazione Giangiacomo Feltrinelli, 1977.

2. P. F. LE MERCIER DE LA RIVIÈRE, *Lettre sur les Economistes*, Paris [1787], p. 10.

3. *Letter* to Roy F. Harrod, *4 July 1938*, published in KEYNES, vol. XIV, pp. 295-7. See also the other letter to Harrod, *16 July 1938*, ibid., pp. 299-301.

veloped according to this mathematically-minded approach, has produced results that are not altogether satisfactory for an understanding of the 'economic problems of the real world', as Keynes demonstrated in a masterly fashion.

Thus the question: bearing in mind Lord Kahn's early training in mathematics and physics (Keynes too came to economics via mathematics and logic), what rigour, what peculiar logic should govern economic analysis? Or although this question is still too general, what is the nature of Keynes' economic science and logic? (No one can doubt that political economy should be a rigorous science. As Joan Robinson said: 'when you are doing economics, do not forget your Wittgenstein').[1]

Walras believed that pure political economy was a branch of mathematics and that there was no hope for *scientific* economics outside the mathematical method. Today, reading our contemporary Walrasians – and there are some hardliners at Cambridge too – would Walras himself say the same?

Dr. Ranchetti's second question concerned the future of economics and of economists. This question came to mind when Lord Kahn was analysing Keynes' thinking on capitalism and underlining the importance of the 'variety of life' as 'the most powerful instrument to better the future'.[2]

In his preface to *Essays on Persuasion* Keynes said that 'the economic problem' was only a priority contingent upon the present situation of capitalism and that the time was not far off when the 'pit of want' would belong to the past and that 'our real problems – the problems of life and of human relations, of creation and behaviour and religion'[3] would come into their own. Would Lord Kahn agree with this?

It was not that Dr. Ranchetti was worried about the future of young economists or of a possible reshaping of their profession. But he wanted to know by whom and by what 'dangerous ideas' practical men will be dominated, when they are no longer – as they are today according to Keynes – 'the slaves of some de-

---

1. JOAN ROBINSON, 'A Lecture Delivered at Oxford by a Cambridge Economist', in *Collected Economic Papers*, Oxford: Basil Blackwell, 1973, vol. IV, p. 262.
2. KEYNES, vol. VII, p. 380.
3. KEYNES, vol. IX, p. xviii.

funct economist'.[1] The hope is that they will be guided by their own free convictions and independent values.

PIETRO MANES[2] began by saying how much he agreed with Professor Kahn's remarks on nonsense economics. A large part of what is said and written today in economics is nonsense. This feeling is shared by many, the only trouble being that everyone seems to think that what the others say is nonsense whilst their own view is the shining truth.

The question is: Why is there so much nonsense in economics? Other sciences are also plagued by nonsense but hardly to the same extent as economics. Why is this? Perhaps because no other science is involved so much with money making and therefore no other science is so much under the influence of vested interests. This of course is not the fault of economists.

A second reason is the total lack of precision in the words economists use. And that *is* the fault of economists. There are some fundamental words that should denote well-defined variables, but which in practice have no certain meaning. For instance, Lord Kahn mentioned at one point the ambiguity of the word 'investment' in the *General Theory*. But he said it almost incidentally and the word continues to be used ambiguously. The controversies about savings and investment, with which Lord Kahn dealt in his third lecture, need never have arisen if these two fundamental economic words each had a well-defined meaning. Academic economists should devote a little more time and thought to the task of defining the words they use, for unclear and confused definitions inevitably breed unclear and confused thinking.

Not to mention the use of indefinite concepts in mathematical formulations, which is really scandalous.

Monetarist theories likewise suffer from the lack of distinction between savings and investment, as monetary variables, and from the total lack of analysis of the function of the rate of interest as a creator of money flows.

The strict definition of the basic concepts and the correct and

1. KEYNES, vol. VII, p. 383.
2. Economic Adviser, R. A. S., Riunione Adriatica di Sicurtà, Milano.

consistent use of them are vital to any scientific work. And so long as economists do not come to grips with these problems, do not get themselves a standardised common language, economics will continue to be wide open to contradictions and nonsense.

LUIGI PASINETTI:[1] A series of lectures by Professor Lord Kahn is such an unusual event that it deserves reflexion rather than discussion. In a period of our economic history in which there has been increasing opposition to so called 'Keynesian policies' and at the same time, after the recent publication of the economic writings of J. M. Keynes, increasing interest in and curiosity about what happened in Cambridge between 1926 (the date of publication of Sraffa's famous article) and 1936 (the date of publication of the *General Theory*) the contribution given in these lectures by Professor Lord Kahn is inevitably going to be a very precious one.

Professor Pasinetti then said he would confine himself to one comment and one question.

The comment concerns a comparison between the theory of Keynes as presented by Professor Kahn in these Lectures and the theory of Keynes as it was presented by Professor Modigliani, during the previous series of the 'Mattioli Lectures'.

Kahn has provided a version of Keynes' theory – or rather of the generating process of Keynes' theory – which is very different from the one given by Modigliani. Modigliani – a typical Keynesian who came to Keynes, so to speak, from the outside – presented Keynes' *General Theory* in terms of a few specific contributions (particularly the theory of liquidity preference, in a context of rigid wages) to be inserted into the main stream of traditional economic theory. So strong was this attitude as to lead Modigliani to the striking proposition that, on questions of theoretical principles (though not on questions of emphasis and of practical economic policy implications), there is fundamentally no difference between 'Keynesianism' and 'monetarism'. For Kahn the attitude towards traditional theory is diametrically opposite. Kahn does not even insist on specific

1. Professor of Econometrics, Università Cattolica del Sacro Cuore, Milano.

contributions. He defines what happened in Cambridge in the early 1930s as 'the search for the truth' – a very general term indeed, meant to convey the conviction of having reached a new global vision of the working of the whole economic system. For Kahn it would be inconceivable to try to fit any one of the new contributions into the old stream. For, with the tradition (and in Cambridge, the tradition meant the theory of Marshall and Pigou) there is a sharp break. There can only be opposition, never reconciliation. This attitude has also been confirmed by Professor Joan Robinson, who has joined Kahn in underlining their common concern for the search for what they came to call the 'general theory'.

This led Professor Pasinetti on to his question, namely: What was Kahn's contribution to the *General Theory*? Schumpeter says that Kahn's 'share in the historic achievement cannot have fallen very far short of co-authorship'.[1] Kahn defines this sentence as 'absurd'. Yet it is difficult not to feel some sense of uneasiness and not to find some contradiction in comparing this remark of Kahn's with other remarks made by him in many other places of his Lectures, such as the following: (i) Kahn stated that the laborious process that led to the discovery of 'the truth' in Cambridge took place between the publication of the *Treatise on Money* (1931) and the publication of the *General Theory* (1936); (ii) Kahn said that the 'Circus' used to meet in Cambridge in the early 1930s. The Circus was a group of young economists; a group of bright young men (and a woman), who were discussing very highly relevant theoretical and practical economic problems. Young Kahn, at the time, was the secretary of the group. He was the man who was going back and forth; he was bringing problems to the group from Keynes and was taking back the results of the discussion of the group to Keynes. And this went on for years. This way was quite extraordinary and unprecedented. Keynes knew how to write books. He was a world-famous economist; and yet he was submitting every proposition he was putting forward to the discussion of this group; (iii) Kahn has also said that the crucial change that took place between

1. JOSEPH A. SCHUMPETER, *History of Economic Analysis*. New York: Oxford University Press; London: George Allen and Unwin, 1954, p. 1172.

the *Treatise on Money* and the *General Theory* was in the elaboration of concepts; especially in the change of the concepts of profits, of income, of savings. These changes took place as an effect of long discussion about the generation of savings and of how investments are financed. This started from the publication of Kahn's 1931 article in the *Economic Journal*. There were many contributors to the development of that discussion. Kahn has mentioned James Meade (from Oxford) and Professor Warming (from Copenhagen), but not Keynes. The references to Keynes have been only in the sense that, by adopting the terminology of the *Treatise on Money*, the discussion was rendered more difficult. The *Treatise* seems to have provided obstacles rather than help; (iv) Kahn has also made an interesting side-remark, when he said that he could only talk of Keynes since 1928, i.e. since he came to know him (Kahn was too young to know Keynes before). Kahn added that it was only after 1928 that Keynes became 'a serious economist'. This seems to imply that Keynes was not a 'serious economist' before 1928! If, in 1928, Keynes had been very young, this could be understandable; but Keynes was forty-five, he had practically completed the *Treatise on Money*, i.e. by that time he had already written all his books, except the *General Theory*. It sounds as if Keynes became a 'serious economist' only with the *General Theory*. Bits like these abound in Kahn's Lectures.

The picture of Keynes that emerges from these reminiscences is that of a man whose great merits and abilities appear to be, not so much in the field of creativity, as in that of a great readiness to change his mind and of an extraordinary openness to discussion with the young. This actually makes a very curious contrast with the attitudes of Keynes' colleagues; for example with that of Dennis Robertson, who seemed to be so rigid and stubborn with the earlier ideas. Keynes emerges, on the other hand, from Kahn's accounts, as extremely attentive and ready to listen; actually even rather unsure of himself. But this also amounts to saying that the young people who were around him must have done a lot of work, perhaps a lot of 'collective' work.

If this is not – as Schumpeter puts it – 'almost co-authorship', what is it? Or less straightforwardly: if Keynes, at that time, had not been discussing these problems with that group of bright young economists, would he ever have written the *General Theory*? It may also be interesting to speculate: if Keynes had not written the *General Theory*, who would have written it?

FERDINANDO TARGETTI[1] raised two questions: the first about method and the second about the rate of interest and investment.

On the first point, a similar method of analysis seems to be used by Sraffa and Cambridge Keynesians dealing with different problems. In Sraffa's *Production of Commodities by Means of Commodities* the relative prices and distribution can be defined by taking the techniques of production and level of activity as given and a distributive variable as exogenously given.

This obviously does not mean that parameters such as technical progress and/or level of activity are not influenced by change in the exogenous variable (i.e. the wage rate).

It would appear that Keynes' *General Theory*, as Lord Kahn and his colleagues in Cambridge read it, yields a similar method of analysis for dealing with other problems.

On the theory of output and employment according to which there are several equilibria of underemployment, the multiplier effect on employment of an autonomous expenditure is shown in real terms, that is to say with money wages, and hence price levels, as given. This obviously does not imply that a change in output and employment has no effect on wage dynamics or that wage dynamics have no effect on the propensity to invest and then on output itself, through income redistribution and/or inflation.

In the theory of value, given the techniques of production, an exogenous theory of distribution is required for a definition of relative prices and the theory shows the behaviour of prices due to a change in income distribution. In the theory of output and employment, given the propensity to consume, the levels of output and employment have to be defined and the theory shows how they behave with changes in effective demand.

With a theory of general equilibrium of prices and quantities –

1. Associate Professor of Economics, Libera Università degli Studi, Trento.

and the neoclassical analysis of IS–LM is an aggregate version of such a theory – one cannot arrive at these results, that is to say one cannot have either a theory of prices and distribution or a theory of output and employment. Does Lord Kahn agree on this position?

Professor Targetti's second question concerns the Cambridge Keynesian theory of the rate of interest.

In Marx's *Capital* it is hard to discover a proper theory of interest rates. The rate of interest is the means whereby financial capital gets part of the surplus value, its level being due to an indefinite balance of forces between industrial and financial capital.

In Wicksell's *Lectures* there is a theory of the rate of interest. It is a real theory of the rate of interest. The monetary rate of interest fluctuates, according to banking policies, around the natural rate of interest determined by preferences and scarcity (i.e. marginal productivity of capital).

Keynes' *General Theory* too contains a theory of the rate of interest. It is a monetary theory. The rate of interest is determined by the supply of and demand for money. The demand for money is determined by speculators' expectations regarding the future value of the rate of interest. This explanation is not however very satisfactory from two points of view. From the empirical angle because the explanation probably does not hold in a different institutional context from the Anglo-American one, in the very narrow-based Italian stock exchange market, for example. At a theoretical level, if today's interest rate depends on tomorrow's the theory has to explain the latter. This leaves the door open for a neo-Wicksellian explanation of the rate of interest à la Friedman, according to whom tomorrow's interest rate is the 'natural' one. Furthermore the neo-classical Keynesians à la Hicks–Modigliani hold a similar view. Their interest rate theory is more or less as follows: provided that there are no rigidities in the economic system like rigid money wages or the liquidity trap, an adequate money supply brings the system to an income and interest rate equilibrium of full employment. That rate of interest is Wicksell's 'natural' rate of interest.

Now presumably Cambridge Keynesians reject the 'natural'

interest theory on the basis of Keynes' teaching and the outcome of the debate on capital theory of the 1960s. Thus one seems to be back to Marx's situation: economic theory does not provide a definite theory of the rate of interest. It should be noted that this lack of an interest rate theory affects investment theory as well. If, as Joan Robinson has several times correctly pointed out, Chapter 11 of the *General Theory* must be discarded as one of the weakest in the masterpiece, investment theory is back to square one with a non-explanation of the 'animal spirits' variety. Marx likewise wrote about the forces that make a capitalist accumulate: 'accumulate, accumulate, so the prophets say', which is a sort of non-explanation like Joan Robinson's.

The point is: are interest rates and investment economic facts that defy theory apart from one strictly related to the peculiar historical and institutional context?

ALBERTO DI PIERRO:[1] As a bibliographical follow-up to Professor Becattini's remarks on the young Alfred Marshall's work on Marx, Dr Di Pierro pointed out that there was another 'young man', Thorstein Veblen, in the United States, who was also studying Marx in those years. He wrote two essays in the *Quarterly Journal of Economics* of 1906-1907 under the title 'The Socialist Economics of Karl Marx and his Followers'.[2]

His second point was the similarity between the concept of marginal propensity to save developed by John Maynard Keynes and the concept of the time preference rate developed in mathematical terms by Frank P. Ramsey in 1928.[3] Both concepts appear to be clearly psychological, being determined regardless of the supply of savings/demand for savings mechanism of Irving Fisher.[4] He wondered whether there was an analysis of the implications

1. Senior Economist of the Economic Studies and Researches Department, ENI, Ente Nazionale Idrocarburi, Roma.
2. THORSTEIN VEBLEN, 'The Socialist Economics of Karl Marx and his Followers', Part I: 'The Theories of Karl Marx', *Quarterly Journal of Economics*, August 1906, pp. 575-95; Part II: 'The later Marxism', *Quarterly Journal of Economics*, February 1907, pp. 299-322.
3. FRANK P. RAMSEY, 'A Mathematical Theory of Saving', *Economic Journal*, December 1928, pp. 543-59.
4. IRVING FISHER, *The Rate of Interest, its Nature, Determination and Relation to Economic Phenomena*. New York: Macmillan, 1907. pp. xxii and 442.

of Fisher's model in the rigorous conditions of long-run competitive equilibrium. He felt that such an analysis would lead to the conclusion that one plausible situation within Fisher's model would be one of low investment, low savings and a low interest rate[1] and not one of stagnation coupled with a transfer of cash-flows on behalf of financial capital and against real capital, over and above the profits that the latter may have earned.

Dr Di Pierro went on to ask whether the Keynesian theory of savings, taken to an extreme conclusion, in fact implies that the community will actually operate under a funds rationing constraint, as a result of which investment choices will be made by means of an ex ante comparison among the expected marginal efficiencies and not through a market 'tâtonnement'.

His last point – though somewhat beyond the bounds of the discussion – was that the rate proposed by Ramsey seems to be the only possibly relevant one for determining the consumption flows of real resources by the community.

ANGELO MARCELLO CARDANI:[2] In his 1977 Presidential Address to the American Economic Association Professor Klein pointed out the increasing need for economic theorists and model builders to devote more attention to the 'Supply side'.[3]

This subject has to be discussed at both normative and positive levels, and two distinct questions arise for Professor Kahn.

On the positive level, Professor Klein's suggestion is to add to the theoretical framework a detailed analysis of the supply structure. The rationale behind it is to explain industrial prices as a result of costs, and therefore in terms of inputs and outputs of the industrial sectors: from this follows a need for a more detailed description of inter-industry flows.

This line of argument seems to be logical and straightforward; it surely stems from the observed increase in the rigidities spreading around into economic systems. The first point is whether this

---

1. A conclusion more easily reached within a real terms analysis à la Fisher.

2. Research Fellow in the Department of Economics, Università Commerciale Luigi Bocconi, Milano.

3. LAWRENCE R. KLEIN, 'The Supply Side', *American Economic Review*, March 1978, pp. 1-7.

line of thought can be considered consistent with Keynes' analysis of supply.

On the normative level, on the other hand, the implications of stressing the supply side are also relevant. They include the results of the difficulties which demand management policies encounter in a world of inflation and unemployment, but, far more relevant, a new strategic evaluation of economic policy.

Demand management policy encounters increasing problems in fighting on a continuously increasing number of fronts: social dynamics augment the number of vested interests of social groups, and therefore the number of targets of the Tinbergen rule increases. On the other hand, the tools of demand management policy are impeded by the institutional forms in which the rigidities that are spreading around the system tend to crystallise.

If these problems exist at the normative level, it seems natural to look for other routes, without abandoning, as far as possible, the traditional ways. It seems much more difficult at the normative level to reconcile Keynesian orthodoxy with a policy based on supply. The first point of disagreement should be the time span: supply policy is necessarily long term. The second point stems directly from this: supply policy implies supply management, and therefore, to a greater or lesser extent, planning.

PIERCARLO GRANDI[1] said that he was very interested in the debate over Keynes and the neo-Keynesians and that, apart from the continuing work of clarifying and going beyond Keynes' work at Cambridge, he had been most impressed by Professor Leijonhufvud's thesis. Would Lord Kahn agree with his claim that most comparisons of the ideas of Keynes with those of subsequent students are nonsensical because the definitions of entities are different and the structures of the models are incompatible?

His second question arises from a study of systems science, as a result of which he had come to feel that structural aspects of economic theories are often considered with less than the necessary attention. One of the rare instances of such attention is Joan Robinson's insistence on the logical incomparability of the states

1. Cybernetic Institute, Università degli Studi, Milano.

229

of an economy before and after a perturbation that causes expectations to change abruptly. Most often discussion centres on detailed issues such as elasticities rather than on differences of approach. Would Lord Kahn agree with the view that, since the structure (or at least behaviour functions) of the economy changes in a dozen years at most, the style of the approach to economics may be more important than a given model?

The third issue is the growing attention among economists to disequilibrium analysis and the ensuing concepts of cost and limitedness of information, irreversibility of decisions, and irreducibility of aggregates to their parts. Does Lord Kahn think, as many contend, that such concepts are at least implicit in Cambridge economics, for example, regarding expectations, choice of techniques, money?

The fourth point concerns monetarism. As it becomes more fashionable, bringing with it some brands of neo-classical economics, many economists preach that government should reduce the scope of its intervention in the economy because it makes so many mistakes that it does more harm than good. Some suggest that this is due to the undue attention of so-called Keynesians to fine tuning and exceedingly short-term policies. What is Lord Kahn's opinion on the past performance of so-called Keynesian economic policy? How was it that Keynes' stress on the long-term interest rate and on the fact that most capital lasts a very long time almost disappeared in short-term policies?

Due to confusion and despair many governments are turning to 'black magic' monetarist economics. Many economists seem to have been attracted by these fashionable positions and Keynesian economics seems to be confined to a few institutions and is in many cases diluted with various neo-classical ideas. Does Lord Kahn think that there are still some economists or schools of thought that are still faithful to the true spirit of Keynes and Cambridge economics and will continue this valuable approach?

ORLANDO D'ALAURO[1] raised two questions. The first concerns some aspects of Keynes' thinking on the subject of interest.

---

1. Professor of Economic and Financial Policy, Università degli Studi, Genova.

Keynes was not, of course, in favour of monetary saving, a point that is not at issue on this occasion. A few years ago when at a meeting in Genoa Professor D'Alauro had the pleasure of welcoming Lord Kahn as lecturer for the Associazione Culturale Italiana, he noted Kahn's scepticism on this point. Moreover, in a recent debate with Eltis he gave one to understand that he was not entirely in agreement with Keynes. However, in the course of the Lectures the relations that are or may as a rule be involved between a variation in money stock and interest rates are not made altogether clear. The question is this: in periods of continuous monetary expansion and of high inflation does Lord Kahn really think that monetary interest rates may not rise? And does he not think that in periods of inflation a policy of negative 'real' interest rates may discourage saving and hence the psychological stimuli to investment? A recent investigation by the Union de Banques Suisses shows that in many countries, notably in Italy and Great Britain, in the past few years normal 'real' interest rates have been negative (in the 2 to 8 per cent range). Does Lord Kahn think that this may have contributed to the difficulty of implementing a counter-inflationary policy?

Professor D'Alauro's second question concerns Lord Kahn's opinion on the fact that Keynes substantially confined his theoretical approach to a closed market. This limitation, as Kahn himself has mentioned, cannot be justified when one considers that the level of interest rates influences – and often more than is believed – the psychological movements of capital (private or public) between the various countries. But the point that simply cannot be ignored is that if countries accept Keynes' recommendations in open market conditions, a policy of full employment is hardly feasible, indeed is highly unlikely. As recent events show, the countries that suffer from inflationary pressures are burdened by recurrent upsets in their balances of trade and of payments, the corrections of which involve more or less large pockets of unemployment. When it comes to the point, perhaps Sauvy has got it right when in his stimulating book *L'économie du diable: chômage et inflation*[1] he argues that the adoption

1. ALFRED SAUVY, *L'Économie du diable, Chômage et inflation*. Paris: Calmann-Lévy, 1976.

of a Keynesian approach may be termed diabolical in that the waste of resources it involves leads both to inflation and unemployment. And the existence of more or less open markets makes this diabolical conclusion inevitable. Perhaps it is time to admit frankly that full-employment policies of the kind Keynes had in mind are incompatible with an open market system. This applies particularly to countries like Italy and Britain, which can go in for autarky – or some measure of autarky – only by serious cuts in normal living conditions and growth rates. Does Professor Kahn think this view exaggerated or that it has a serious basis?

COMMENTS BY RICHARD KAHN

The Discussion is extremely interesting. Of course, it was a discussion of the Lectures which I delivered in June 1978. In replying, I refer to passages in this book – a completely rewritten version of the Lectures. I should explain that the text of the Discussion was not available to me when, in June 1979, I submitted the text of the book.

In accordance with the wishes of the Trustees of the Raffaele Mattioli Foundation, I concentrate on replying to those contributions to the Discussion concerned with the history of economic thought.

Of course, I begin with Professor GIACOMO BECATTINI, who is the leading scholar on the subject of Marshall and his contemporaries. I have learnt much from his books, as well as from his contribution to the Discussion.

I comment with diffidence. Of great interest is the light thrown by Giacomo Becattini on the influence on young Marshall of Ferdinand Lassalle. He quoted from a book on *Foreign Trade*, written in the years 1875-77, of which only four chapters were privately printed, the rest being discarded.[1]

I mention in Section 2 of the First Lecture the little book by Alfred and Mary Marshall (1879).[2] Particularly attributable to Lassalle's influence is the passage

if all trades which made goods for direct consumption agreed to work on and buy each other's goods as in ordinary times, they

1. The passage quoted does not appear in MARSHALL'S *Pure Theory of Foreign Trade* (printed for private circulation, 1879; reprinted by the London School of Economics, Scarce Tracts in Economic and Political Science, No. 1. London: 1930); nor in any of the passages in MARSHALL'S *Principles of Economics* and *Money, Credit and Commerce*, referred to by Pigou, in *Memorials of Alfred Marshall*. London: Macmillan, 1925, p. 24 ff.

MARSHALL'S unpublished book on *Foreign Trade* is reproduced in JOHN K. WHITAKER, *The Early Economic Writings of Alfred Marshall, 1867-1890*, vol. II. London: Royal Economic Society, 1975, pp. 3-181. The passage quoted by Professor Becattini appears on p. 38.

2. ALFRED MARSHALL and MARY PALEY MARSHALL, *The Economics of Industry*. London: Macmillan, First Edition 1879; Second Edition 1884. See pp. 11-14 above. Italian Edition by GIACOMO BECATTINI, *Economia della produzione*. Milano: ISEDI, Istituto Editoriale Internazionale, 1975. More recently Giacomo Becattini has made a further important contribution in the form of *Alfred Marshall. Antologia di scritti economici*. Bologna: Il Mulino, 1981.

would supply one another with the means of earning a moderate rate of profits and of wages . . . Confidence by growing would cause itself to grow.[1]

Lassalle's own proposal was a bolder one. The young Marshalls referred to it as 'the most plausible of all the plans that have been suggested by Socialists for [. . .] "the abolition of commercial risk." They propose that in times of depression Government should step forward and, by guaranteeing each separate industry against risk, cause all industries to work, and therefore to earn and therefore to buy each other's products.'[2]

They proceeded to condemn the proposal:

But they have not yet shown how Government should tell whether a man's distress was really due to causes beyond his own control, nor how its guarantee could be worked without hindering that freedom on which energy and the progress of invention depends.[3]

Marshall's comment, in his unpublished work, follows the passage quoted by Giacomo Becattini:

Lassalle has not thoroughly treated any of the difficulties which beset his system and many of them he has wholly ignored. He has compelled attention to a flaw in that organisation of labour which is brought about by the free play of the interests of individual producers under the sway of untrammelled competition.

Lassalle has compelled attention to the fact that the individual interest of each may not prompt him to continue his work alone at a time at which the continued work of all together would conduce to the collective interest of all. He has not indeed fairly grappled with the task of proving that the net result of the governmental interference which he proposes would be a benefit.[4]

While I am strongly impressed by the tenor of Giacomo Becattini's learned comments, I am unable to accept his suggestion that in Marshall's mind 'the cumulative mechanisms of depression and recovery [. . .] indicate a certain degree of adher-

1. ALFRED MARSHALL and MARY PALEY MARSHALL, *The Economic of Industry*, p. 155.
2. *Ibid.*, p. 155 footnote.
3. *Ibid.*
4. JOHN K. WHITAKER, *The Early Economic Writings of Alfred Marshall, 1867-1890*, vol. II, p. 38.

ence to Lassalle's diagnosis of the anarchy in the capitalistic market'. Giacomo Becattini himself qualified his suggestion by saying that Marshall maintained that 'the deep causes of dis-equilibria [. . .] [are] never unavoidable, never incurable'.

In the fifth (1907) and subsequent editions of his *Principles*, Marshall inserted as an addition to Section 10 of the final chapter XIII of Book VI a considerable part of the early book (1879) written jointly with Mary. It includes the passage:

> The chief cause of the evil [. . .] [of a set-back in trade] could be removed almost in an instant if confidence could return, touch all industries with her magic wand, and make them continue their production and their demand for the wares of others.[1]

Where I reluctantly part company with Giacomo Becattini is over his suggestion that 'there is so little difference between Keynes' and Marshall's basic diagnosis of the nature and functioning of the market'. Giacomo Becattini explained the difference in the long passage of his speech which follows his crucial question why did Marshall 'having identified the po-tential for destabilisation hidden in normal market functioning [. . .] stop at a Platonic reference to the "confidence trick"?' He pointed out that Marshall's dislike for 'counter-cyclical interven-tion [. . .] can be explained by his personal view of the world', of which he then presented a vivid picture. In support of his diagnosis, I refer to the passages in Marshall's *Money, Credit and Commerce* which I quote in Section 2 of my First Lecture. I add one more:

> Those causes of discontinuity which lie within our scope, and are remediable, are chiefly connected in some way or other with the want of knowledge; [. . .][2]
> The sagacity and public spirit of the leading minds both among employers and employed are increasing fast.[3]

Giacomo Becattini asked us 'how far Keynes was tormented by the problem of moulding human nature'. In the course of

---

1. ALFRED MARSHALL, *Principles of Economics*, Ninth (Variorum) Edition, vol. I, p. 711, as explained by the editor, CLAUDE GUILLEBAUD, vol. II, p. 714.
2. ALFRED MARSHALL, *Money, Credit and Commerce*, p. 260.
3. *Ibid.*, p. 262.

The End of Laissez-Faire,[1] Keynes described a quotation from Marshall as 'a fine picture of the great captain of industry [. . .], who serves us in serving himself, just as any other artist does. Yet this one, in his turn, is becoming a tarnished idol. We grow more doubtful whether it is he who will lead us into paradise by the hand.'[2]

Towards the end of his pamphlet Keynes referred to

a latent reaction, somewhat widespread, against basing society to the extent that we do upon fostering, encouraging, and protecting the money-motives of individuals. A preference for arranging our affairs in such a way as to appeal to the money-motive as little as possible, rather than as much as possible, need not be entirely *a priori*, but may be based on the comparison of experiences [. . .]
For my part I think that capitalism, wisely managed, can probably be made more efficient for attaining economic ends than any alternative system yet in sight, but that in itself it is in many ways extremely objectionable. Our problem is to work out a social organisation which shall be as efficient as possible without offending our notions of a satisfactory way of life.[3]

In 'Economic Possibilities for our Grandchildren',[4] Keynes looking a hundred years ahead wrote that 'the *economic problem* may be solved'. (He was unjustifiably optimistic as to the shortness of this period, even though he assumed 'no important wars and no important increase in population'.) 'This means that the economic problem is not – if we look into the future – *the permanent problem of the human race.*'[5]

I see us free, therefore, to return to some of the most sure and certain principles of religion and traditional virtue – that [. . .] the love of money is detestable [. . .] We shall once more value ends above means and prefer the good to the useful. We shall honour those who can teach us how to pluck the hour and the day virtuously and well, the delight-

1. JOHN MAYNARD KEYNES, *The End of Laissez-Faire*, originally published in 1926; KEYNES, vol. IX, pp. 272-94.
2. *Ibid.*, p. 287.
3. *Ibid.*, pp. 293-4.
4. JOHN MAYNARD KEYNES, 'Economic Possibilities for our Grandchildren', originally published in *Nation and Athenaeum*, 11 and 18 October 1930; KEYNES, vol. IX, pp. 321-32.
5. *Ibid.*, p. 326.

ful people who are capable of taking direct enjoyment in things, the lilies of the field who toil not, neither do they spin.[1]

Dr FABIO RANCHETTI reminded us of the importance attached by Keynes to the 'variety of life' as 'the most powerful instrument to better the future'. He was quoting from Keynes in his *General Theory* as an advocate of the capitalist system, which he believed that the adoption of his ideas could save from collapse. Here Keynes was thinking contemporaneously.

In the two passages which I have just quoted Keynes was thinking ahead to the time when it would be possible – indeed desirable – to dispense with capitalism as a means of promoting material welfare and adopt a more satisfactory way of life. Fabio Ranchetti aptly reminded us of another passage, written in the same vein, in Keynes' Preface to *Essays in Persuasion*.

Professor FRANCO BRUNI, learned about Knut Wicksell, made an important contribution towards an understanding of his economics. He asked the question: how Keynesian was Wicksell?

Wicksell's *Lectures on Political Economy* must, I think, be ruled out. The first Swedish edition was published in 1901 – Volume 1, *General Theory* – and 1906 – Volume 2, *Money*. The English translation was not published until 1934. It is difficult to trace any influence on Keynes of this later work of Wicksell's, although part of its contents were transmitted through Gustav Cassel's *Theory of Social Economy*, the English translation of which was published in 1923.[2]

My English translation of *Geldzins und Güterpreise* was not published until 1936, and I had no acquaintance with the book until I embarked on the translation. Apart from any help that Keynes may have derived from Cassel's book, he had to rely on his own knowledge of German, of which he wrote: 'in German I can only clearly understand what I know already: — so that *new* ideas are apt to be veiled from me by the difficulties of language.'[3]

Having worked out his own theory, Keynes discovered that in

---

1. *Ibid.*, pp. 330-1.
2. See KEYNES, vol. v, p. 167.
3. *Ibid.*, p. 178, note 2.

one respect he had been anticipated – to the extent of thirty-two years – by Wicksell, so that he wrote:

At any rate, whether or not I have exaggerated the depth to which Wicksell's thought penetrated, he was the first writer to make it clear that the influence of the rate of interest on the price level operates by its effect on the rate of investment [. . .] [and so on the] demand for actual goods [. . .] it is this increased actual demand which sends up prices.[1]

Another contribution in the field of the history of economic thought was made by Professor LUIGI PASINETTI. While he appears to question my rejection in Section 5 of Lecture VI of a tribute paid to me by Schumpeter, he does little more than point to my leading role in the Cambridge 'Circus' of late 1930 and early 1931. From then until the completion of the *General Theory* in 1936 the process of consultation continued – with Joan and Austin Robinson and myself of the members of the Circus, and with those other economists correspondence with whom occupies considerable parts of Volumes XIII, XIV and XXIX of the Royal Economic Society edition of Keynes' *Collected Writings*. Why does Luigi Pasinetti regard it as extraordinary that Keynes preferred not to work in a vacuum?

On Luigi Pasinetti's account of Keynes as a thinker and writer, I have two comments. It was one of Keynes' great virtues that he was ready to change his mind – either because the situation, actual and prospective, had changed or because he realised that he had been wrong on a logical process of thought. Another great virtue was his readiness to discuss with the young – as well as the not so young – and the pleasure which such discussions gave him. These two virtues contributed enormously to his success. His astonishing creative powers were enhanced by these virtues. I draw attention to my concluding sentence of Lecture V.

If in one of my spoken Lectures I said that it was only after 1928 that Keynes became a serious economist I made a slip. I refer to the first paragraph of Lecture VI. 1925 was the crucial year – the year in which he began to live with Lydia as husband and wife.

1. KEYNES, vol. V, pp. 177-8.

Before I comment on other aspects of the Discussion, I can conveniently make a number of general observations.

Firstly, I cannot refrain from expressing surprise that no reference was made to the overwhelming importance of risk and uncertainty in the actual world. It dominated the thinking of Keynes, the author of *A Treatise on Probability*.[1] The assumption of confident expectations deprives much of contemporary so-called *neo-Keynesian* economics of the right to be described as *Keynesian*. I need only draw attention to the passages from Keynes' reply to Viner's review of the *General Theory* which I quote in Section 7 of Lecture v.

The reason why Keynes' treatment of the *Inducement to Invest* is difficult to follow – and open to improvement – is because he – unlike most economists – was dealing with an uncertain future. I refer to the eloquent quotations from Keynes' Chapter 12 quoted in Section 9 of Lecture v.

I do not in this book deal with wage-inflation – which has become the overwhelmingly serious economic problem of recent years. My reason for this omission is that I am confining myself to the development of monetary thought only up to the publication of the *General Theory*, in 1936.

Keynes did in fact in his *General Theory* set out the theoretical basis for the anti-inflationary policy advocated by the post-Keynesian school. In Section 4 of my fifth Lecture I emphasise the fundamental role in the *General Theory* of the money-wage in determining all prices, incomes – indeed, the money-values of everything.

Hence the post-Keynesian anti-inflationary policy is to deal with the causal root of the trouble – to attack directly the machinery of wage-bargaining. The monetarist alternative is to rely on deep recession, associated with massive unemployment and low profits and heavy losses, to weaken the bargaining power of the trade-unions and to strengthen the resistance of employers. There is little doubt which alternative is preferred by wise trade-union leaders co-operating with wise employers under the in-

1. KEYNES, vol. VIII (originally published 1921).

fluence of Ministers who combine sound (by which, of course, I mean Keynesian) thinking on economic policy with a friendly – as opposed to aggressive – attitude towards labour.

In an article published in 1978 I devoted more attention to early indications of Keynes' awareness of the problem of wage-inflation.[1] In the *General Theory* Keynes wrote that 'the struggle for money-wages is [...] essentially a struggle to maintain a high *relative* wage'[2] – the basis of the emphasis of many post-Keynesians on the 'wage-wage spiral' or 'the leap-frogging effect' – as opposed to the 'wage-price spiral' – as the main cause of rapidly rising wages.

In 1943 and 1944 Keynes corresponded on the subject both with Frank Graham (Professor at Princeton) and with Benjamin Graham (the famous advocate of an international buffer stock).[3] In the course of a letter to the former, Keynes wrote:

How much otherwise avoidable unemployment do you propose to bring about in order to keep the Trade Unions in order? [...]
My own preliminary view is that other, more reasonable, less punitive means must be found.[4]

In the course of a letter to the latter he wrote:

the more aware we were of this risk, the more likely we should be to find a way round other than totalitarianism. But I recognised the reality of the risk [...]
The task of keeping efficiency wages reasonably stable [...] is a *political* rather than an economic problem.[5]

This suggestion that the problem is political points to Government influence on the wage-bargaining process. As Professor PAOLO SAVONA said: 'One may well be wrong in looking for a solution to the crisis in the context of economics. The crisis goes far beyond the calculations of economists.'

1. RICHARD KAHN, 'Some Aspects of the Development of Keynes's Thought', *Journal of Economic Literature*, June 1978, pp. 544-59.

2. KEYNES, vol. VII, p. 252.

3. Quoted by DONALD MOGGRIDGE and SUSAN HOWSON, 'Keynes on Monetary Policy, 1910-1946', *Oxford Economic Papers*, July 1974, p. 244, note 1.

4. *Letter* to Frank D. Graham, *31 December 1943*; published in KEYNES, vol. XXVI, pp. 34-6.

5. *Letter* to Benjamin Graham, *31 December 1943*; published *ibid.*, pp. 36-8.

In two articles, both approved by Keynes in draft, Joan Robinson foresaw the danger.[1] But Keynes had absolutely no idea of the terrifying orders of magnitude of the rates of wage-inflation which in recent years have induced Governments and monetary authorities to pursue crippling policies.

I am not attempting any adequate discussion of *monetarism*, widespread belief in which in recent years is responsible for worldwide economic recession. I agree with Paolo Savona that blame has to be attached to the failure of Keynesians effectively to propagate the policy which wage-inflation calls for. I mean of course Government influence on the processes of wage-bargaining.

Literal belief in monetarism – derived from the Quantity Theory of Money – is a form of *mystique*: what PIERCARLO GRANDI described as 'black magic' economics. By now, however, most monetarists have been forced by experience to abandon the idea of an automatic influence on the behaviour of the price-level of changes in the quantity of money. They have been driven – subconsciously if not consciously – to accept the Keynesian belief in the dependence of the price-level on the behaviour of money-wages. Indeed, in the Public Sector in many countries Governments curb wage-increases by direct invervention.

Monetarism has become a belief that, apart from such direct intervention by Governments in the Public Sector, the only acceptable instrument for curbing the rate of wage-inflation is heavy unemployment.

The level of demand – already directly depressed by the dramatic rise in the price of oil and indirectly as a result of loss of confidence on the part of industrialists – has been further depressed by the reductions in real terms of State expenditure, or at least in its rate of growth, and by increases in taxation.

Fundamentalist monetarists regard a reduction in the Public

---

1. JOAN ROBINSON, 'Full Employment', in *Essays in the Theory of Employment*. London: Macmillan, 1937, reprinted in *Collected Economic Papers*. Oxford: Basil Blackwell, 1973, vol. IV, pp. 176-98; and 'Planning Full Employment', *The Times*, 22 and 23 January 1943, reprinted in *Collected Economic Papers*, vol. I, 1951, pp. 81-8.

Sector Financial Deficit as a means of curbing the rate of increase of the quantity of money. But in many so-called monetarist quarters *mystique* is beginning to give way to commonsense. It is becoming widely recognised that it is the level of unemployment which is the causative influence rather than the behaviour of the quantity of money. Associated with a high level of unemployment is low profitability and the loss of confidence of industrialists, which, through their adverse influence on the rate of industrial investment, deepen the recession, and so raise still further the level of unemployment.

The crucial question which worries everybody – both monetarists and Keynesians – is that insofar as heavy unemployment and low profitability are associated with a fall in the rate of inflation, what is to prevent the rate of inflation from again rising with a recovery in the level of demand? Or does monetarist belief condemn us to a permanent state of stagnation and unemployment? As PAOLO SAVONA put it, 'the outcome of monetarist therapy, if such it can be called [. . .] is leading the western world to a freeze in economic and employment growth'.

Professor ANGELO CARDANI introduced the important topic of the 'supply side', of which much is heard at the present time. Several aspects of the 'supply side' need to be distinguished.

First, there is the restraint on higher levels of output imposed by limited supplies of labour and of plant and equipment. Keynes fully recognised this restraint.

Secondly, Angelo Cardani referred to Professor Klein's suggestion that price formation of industrial products be explained as resulting from costs. So far from this line of thought being inconsistent with Keynes' analysis in the *General Theory*, it is one of the pillars on which his system rests (see Section 4 of Lecture v).

But Angelo Cardani is rightly concerned with present-day emphasis on the 'supply-side'. There is a widespread desire – pathological in character – to attribute the heavy unemployment of today not to failure on the part of the authorities to secure a rise in demand but to constraints which prevent output from responding to a rise in demand. This view is widely held by monetarists, but also by others to whom the word 'Keynesian' is a term of abuse.

It is a tragically paradoxical situation. The authorities, by imposing restraint on demand, have been successful in securing surplus labour and physical capacity on a massive scale. But it is maintained that any reversal of policy on the demand side would be frustrated by scarcity of labour and of physical capacity.

Put in such bald terms, the idea is, of course, ridiculous. Unfortunately there is a small element of validity in the idea, especially when, as at the present time – in many countries – hopes of rapid recovery are low. The object of policy is to curb the rate of inflation. In all advanced industrial countries it has been curbed, but in most of them it remains unduly high.

The result is that incentives to train skilled labour are weak – both to employers and to workers. Advantage is taken of Government schemes to a disappointing extent. This is especially true of Britain, where the outlook is so black. As skilled workers reach the retiring age or become redundant at an earlier age, they are replaced by young trained workers, to an extent little more than is required to meet the existing low demand.

A recovery of demand will be met by shortages of skilled labour. It takes time for the shortages to be remedied by training; and they will be remedied only to the extent that confidence is built up in the recovery being sustained.

To take a less pessimistic view, when demand does begin to expand – in the first place by increasing public expenditure and reducing taxation – so that, subject to a time-lag, the demand for labour also expands, it will be necessary to curb the rate of recovery. As optimism about the future replaces pessimism, unskilled workers will be anxious to acquire skills, employers will be anxious to help them, and the Government's attitude on support of training schemes will be reversed. With the passage of time, the rate at which it will be safe to expand demand will gradually increase.

Supply constraints are also imposed by shortages of certain kinds of plant and equipment at a time of deep depression. Again it seems paradoxical. Once a plant has been closed down, it is in many industries expensive to keep it in mothballs in a state in which its use can easily be resumed, and much of it is scrapped. So long as deep pessimism rules about the future, there is no incentive to invest gross much more than is required for replacement of that plant and equipment which is actually being operated. Technical progress usually needs new plant in which to be embodied.

With recovery many industrialists will prefer to keep pace with the completion of new, more efficient plant, and only to a limited extent reopen plants which have become obsolete with the passage of time. So for this reason too, the rate of recovery should be curbed. As confidence revives, and the rate of investment in new plant and equipment grows, the rate of recovery of demand can be allowed gradually to rise.

Of course, I entirely agree with Angelo Cardani that the difficulties presented in a depression by constraints on the supply side should be largely avoided in a well-planned economy.

I return to contributions to the Discussion on aspects of the history of economic thought.

Professor FERDINANDO TARGETTI suggested that Sraffa's analysis in his *Production of Commodities by Means of Commodities* is similar to Keynesian analysis – Sraffa's analysis being concerned with the relation between the distribution of income and relative prices and Keynes' with the determination of output – although Keynes and Sraffa were concerned with different problems. But so far from there being any similarity of method, Sraffa admits – indeed insists – in his book that his system is underdetermined. 'the number of [variables] [...] exceeds the number of equations by one and the system can move with one degree of freedom.'[1] Given the technical conditions, Sraffa discusses the relationship between the distribution of income, the real wage, the rate of profit, the value of capital and relative prices. 'if one of the variables is fixed the others will be fixed too.'[2] But within wide limits, there is an infinite range of these relationships.

What is missing from the Sraffa system is the Keynesian pro-

1. PIERO SRAFFA, *Production of Commodities by Means of Commodities*. Cambridge: Cambridge University Press, 1960, p. 11.
2. *Ibid.*

cess of causation, which is causation not only of output but, for any given output (such as the maximum output of which productive resources in the short period – equipment and the labour force – are capable), of the distribution of income. The introduction of Keynesian causation closes Sraffa's system. The position is determined, given the technical conditions, by the thriftiness conditions and the rate of growth. In a stationary state the rate of growth is zero and *aggregate* net saving is zero. Given thriftiness conditions determine the one unique distribution of income, the real wage, rate of profit, value of capital and relative prices which result in zero aggregate net saving.

This is quite a different process of thought from Sraffa's tacit assumption that capitalists spend the whole of their profits. Sraffa provides no kind of an explanation why capitalists do not save. That in a stationary state aggregate net saving must be zero is not an explanation – it involves a circular argument.

Dr ALBERTO DI PIERRO introduced into the discussion Frank Ramsey's masterly article on 'A Mathematical Theory of Saving'.[1]

It is based on special assumptions – distributional considerations are ignored and the goal of saving is a state of Bliss – in which the rate of enjoyment is the maximum conceivable. Those families which discount the future at a rate less than the rate of interest end up in this state of Bliss. Those which discount the future at a rate higher than the rate of interest remain at the subsistence level.

Although Ramsey, a brilliant young mathematician, acknowledged help from Keynes, Keynes does not mention the article in the *General Theory*.[2]

Keynes was concerned with the propensity to save of the actual economy in which people are not conscious of the rate at which they discount the future and in which the simplifying assumptions made by Frank Ramsey lack justification.

Alberto Di Pierro's last two questions apply to a socialist

1. FRANK P. RAMSEY, 'A Mathematical Theory of Saving', *Economic Journal*, December 1928, pp. 543-59.

2. But he praised it in his Obituary of 'F. P. Ramsey', *Economic Journal*, March 1930, pp. 153-4; reprinted in KEYNES, vol. x, pp. 335-6.

economy in which investment is determined by the managements of state enterprises. Here Frank Ramsey's concepts are useful as a starting point; but again the problems facing those who have to make the decisions involve great complications.

The IS–LM diagram devised by Professor John Hicks as a simple expository device for presenting the determination of the rate of interest in the *General Theory* was discussed by Professors GIANGIACOMO NARDOZZI and FERDINANDO TARGETTI.

I refer to IS–LM in Section 10 of Lecture v. My reference is brief but highly critical. I blame Keynes for having been too mild with John Hicks. I quote a passage from Joan Robinson in which she mentioned repentance by John Hicks. She was referring to an article published in February 1973, and in particular to the passage from it which I quote at the conclusion of my passage about IS–LM. But four years later John Hicks had relapsed, as indicated in my preceding quotation in Section 10 of Lecture v.

Since then John Hicks has published a far more critical assessment of the usefulness of the IS–LM apparatus:

I accordingly conclude that the only way in which IS–LM analysis usefully survives – as anything more than a classroom gadget, to be superseded, later on, by something better – is in application to a particular kind of causal analysis, where the use of equilibrium methods, even a drastic use of equilibrium methods, is not inappropriate. I have deliberately interpreted the equilibrium concept, to be used in such analysis, in a very stringent manner (some would say a pedantic manner) not because I want to tell the applied economist, who uses such methods, that he is in fact committing himself to anything which must appear to him to be so ridiculous, but because I want to ask him to try to assure himself that the divergences between reality and the theoretical model, which he is using to explain it, are no more than divergences which he is entitled to overlook. I am quite prepared to believe that there are cases where he is entitled to overlook them. But the issue is one which needs to be faced in each case. When one turns to questions of policy, looking toward the future instead of the past, the use of equilibrium methods is still more suspect.[1]

1. JOHN R. HICKS, 'IS–LM; an explanation', *Journal of Post Keynesian Economics*, Winter 1980-1981, pp. 152-3.

Both Luigi Pasinetti and Giangiacomo Nardozzi referred to statements made by Professor Modigliani in the course of the first Raffaele Mattioli Lectures. 'There is fundamentally no difference between "Keynesianism" and "monetarism"' – is the quotation given by Pasinetti – and 'we are all monetarists now' – is the quotation given by Nardozzi, who also said that 'this conciliatory position may be seen as the end-result of the IS–LM scheme'. I await with keen anticipation the text of Professor Modigliani's Lectures, especially keen in view of these quotations, which to me appear complete nonsense. The last one strengthens my belief that the IS–LM scheme has very seriously confused the development of economic thought.

This belief is reinforced by Ferdinando Targetti's reference to the 'neo-classical analysis of IS–LM' as an aggregate version of 'a theory of general equilibrium of prices and quantities'. I emphatically agree with him that with such a theory 'one cannot have either a theory of prices and distribution or a theory of output and employment'.

I turn now to the topic of the rate of interest. Ferdinando Targetti is not satisfied with Keynes' monetary theory of the rate of interest. As presented in the *General Theory*, it is open to criticism on a number of scores. This does not detract from the claim that Keynes' great contribution was to identify the process of causation. As a matter of proximate causation, the rate of interest is not *determined* by the interaction of the forces of productivity of capital and of thrift. These real forces, given time, can, however, exercise an indirect influence on the rate of interest, by gradually influencing the position of the liquidity preference schedule. In Section 6 of Lecture v I quoted Keynes' statement in the *General Theory* that

the rate of interest is a highly conventional, rather than a highly psychological phenomenon. For its actual value is largely governed by the prevailing view as to what its value is expected to be.[1]

If the public are confident that the monetary authority intend – by expanding the quantity of money – to bring rates of

---

1. KEYNES, vol. VII, p. 203.

interest down sufficiently to secure full employment, the liquidity preference schedule will shift so as to bring current rates down to that level even without an expansion of the quantity of money. This level of rates of interest Keynes suggested might be called the 'neutral' or 'optimum' rate.

Keynes supplied the answer to the question as to what

tacit assumption is required to make sense of the classical theory of the rate of interest. This theory assumes either that the actual rate of interest is always equal to the neutral rate [. . .] or alternatively that the actual rate of interest is always equal to the rate of interest which will maintain employment at some specified constant level. If the traditional theory is thus interpreted, there is little or nothing in its practical conclusions to which we need take exception. The classical theory assumes that the banking authority or natural forces cause the market-rate of interest to satisfy one or other of the above conditions [. . .] we are safely ensconced in a Ricardian world.[1]

As PAOLO SAVONA suggested, 'it cannot be argued that the neo-classical model is *always* wrong and that the market *never* works'. But I am unable to agree with him that 'the same goes for monetarism or rather its policy in the oil crisis'.

Keynes was not abandoning his Liquidity Theory as a statement of causation. But given tranquil conditions and a rationally conducted monetary authority (*not afraid of increasing the quantity of money*), the state of expectations about the future of rates of interest (the liquidity preference schedule) will shift until actual rates are close to 'optimum' rates.

This day-dream is based on the assumptions of conditions of tranquillity.

Keynes had little confidence that

the influence of banking policy on the rate of interest will be sufficient by itself to determine an optimum rate of investment. I conceive, therefore, that a somewhat comprehensive socialisation of investment will prove the only means of securing an approximation to full employment [. . .] It is not the ownership of the instruments of production which it is important for the State to assume. If the State is able to determine the aggregate amount of resources devoted to augmenting

1. KEYNES, vol. VII, pp. 243-4.

the instruments and the basic rate of reward to those who own them, it will have accomplished all that is necessary.[1]

FRANCO BRUNI attributes Keynesian unemployment to stickiness of prices and wages – a widely held view. Keynes was not, however, prepared to rely for the necessary expansion of the quantity of money measured in real terms on a fall in money-wages, as opposed to an expansion of the quantity of money in nominal terms. I refer in Section 4 of Lecture v to the extreme difficulties envisaged by Keynes in practice of securing a large fall in money-wages – and the hardship imposed on those groups of workers least able to resist the pressure imposed by heavy unemployment in their own sectors. Above all, he emphasised the adverse effect on the rate of investment of a wage-reduction which leads 'to the expectation, or even the serious possibility, of a further wage-reduction in prospect'. With falling wages go falling prices and falling profits in terms of money. The expectation of falling profits exercises an adverse influence on the rate of investment, and so on levels of output and employment.

In a world, like the real world, in which great uncertainty prevails – and in a world, like the real world, in which monetary authorities are irrationally terrified of increasing the quantity of money as a means of bringing down rates of interest – the application of the Keynesian theory of the rate of interest is difficult. But my answer to Ferdinando Targetti is that this does not mean that the theory is invalid.

Keynes' emphasis in the *General Theory* on money-rates of interest as determining investment is open to criticism as being far too narrow. As I indicate already in Section 2 of Lecture II, there is a range of close substitutes to money – including equities, prices of which, in relation to expected earnings, play a much more important part than money-rates of interest in the determination of rates of industrial investment. In his post-*General Theory* contributions on the subject of *Finance*, Keynes indicated the lines on which his Theory could fruitfully be broadened (see Section 11 of Chapter v).

Franco Bruni, in addition to stickiness of prices and wages,

1. *Ibid.*, p. 378.

251

mentioned stickiness of the rate of interest. Although his phrase *liquidity trap* was devised by Dennis Robertson, and not Keynes, Keynes does refer to the possibility that 'after the rate of interest has fallen to a certain level [a long-term rate of about 2 per cent per annum] 'liquidity-preference may become virtually absolute'[1] because it 'leaves more to fear than to hope, and offers, at the same time, a running yield which is only sufficient to offset a very small measure of fear'.[2] This idea of a 'psychological minimum' Keynes qualified by the suggestion that 'Public opinion can be fairly rapidly accustomed to a modest fall in the rate of interest and the conventional expectation of the future may be modified accordingly'.[3]

Keynes added that 'if such a situation were to arise, it would mean that the public authority itself could borrow through the banking system on an unlimited scale at a nominal rate of interest'.[4] This supports Franco Bruni's suggestion, in contrasting Keynes with Wicksell, that while Keynes 'certainly did not reject monetary policy' he 'thought it possible to stabilize (mainly by fiscal policy) the real side of the economy'.

Professor ORLANDO D'ALAURO asked about money-rates of interest at times of rapid inflation. Of course, money-rates adjust to the rate of inflation. The operative rate is the real rate – the expected money-rate *minus* the expected rate of increase of prices. Money-rates are especially high in those countries in which, and at those times when, the rate of inflation is especially high.

The following table was drawn up in November 1981:

	Yield on 10 year Government Bonds	Rate of increase of prices	Real rate of interest
	(Annual percentage rate)		
France	16.3	14.1	1.9
United Kingdom	15.6	11.7	3.5
United States	13.1	10.2	2.6

1. KEYNES, vol. VII, p. 207.
2. *Ibid.*, p. 202.
3. *Ibid.*, p. 204.
4. *Ibid.*, p. 207.

| Germany | 9.4 | 7.0 | 2.2 |
| Japan | 8.0 | 3.9 | 3.9 |

For those five countries in November 1981 real rates of interest were all positive – varying between 1.9 per cent (France) and 3.9 per cent (Japan): a surprisingly narrow range.

I agree that a negative real rate of interest – as has often ruled, though usually small – is, taken by itself, a stimulating factor, which, however, it is difficult or impossible to identify because it is associated with deep depression of the economy and so of entrepreneurs' spirits.

The table indicates that international mobility of funds results in a tendency towards equalisation of real rates of interest rather than money-rates. In a rough and ready sense, the reason is clear. Arbitrage does not result in equality of spot money-rates but in equality of spot money-rates *plus* or *minus* discounts or premiums on forward markets. These discounts and premiums are partly dependent on expectations of changes in spot rates. These expectations largely depend on differential rates of inflation.

Orlando D'Alauro asked me why Keynes' *General Theory* deals almost exclusively with a closed economy. This differentiates the *General Theory* from almost all other writings of Keynes. I explain near the opening of Section 10 of Chapter v that the reason is that the book's 'main purpose is to deal with difficult questions of theory, and only in the second place with the application of this theory to practice'. I point to certain passages which deal with some of the problems of an open economy.

On the rate of interest Keynes wrote:

in a country linked to an international gold-standard, a rate of interest lower than prevails elsewhere will be viewed with a justifiable lack of confidence; yet a domestic rate of interest dragged up to a parity with the *highest* rate [. . .] prevailing in any country [. . .] may be much higher than is consistent with domestic full employment.[1]

In answer to Orlando D'Alauro's final question of the compatibility of Keynesian full employment policies with an open market

1. *Ibid.*, p. 203.

system, of course I am, like most economists, fully aware of the extremely serious problem. Resort to autarky I regard as a policy of despair, and I should be in favour of it only if international economic co-operation between the authorities of the leading industrial countries completely broke down. I am somewhat hopeful of a gradual expansive movement occurring – perhaps under the auspices of the OECD – as a result of the frustrating experience of recent years of monetarism and, its consequence, deep economic recession. I appreciate the enormous difficulties involved; but I have not yet entirely despaired of an internationally co-ordinated progressive movement.

It would be tragic if Italy and Britain were driven to autarky. I need not spell out what it would mean in terms of human misery.

GIANGIACOMO NARDOZZI and FERDINANDO TARGETTI discussed the determination in the *General Theory* of the rate of investment.

Keynes' idea of 'animal spirits' as entering into the determination of the rate of investment has, it seems to me, led to misunderstanding. Giangiacomo Nardozzi seems to think that the use of this phrase means that it is impossible to evolve a theory of the rate of investment, so that the rate of investment is exogenous. 'Why should a theory [the Cambridge approach] that fails to account for ... investment ... be thought better than a theory that accounts for and considers these aspects?' I take it that the alternative, and superior, theory is monetarism. This attitude I find most surprising.

Ferdinando Targetti made the same criticism. 'Investment theory is back to square one with a non-explanation of the "animal spirits" variety.'

The term 'animal spirits' appears in the *General Theory* – not in the fundamental Chapter 11 but near the end of the more light-hearted, though most important, Chapter 12. (The term is not mentioned in the Index.) In the course of a passage which I quote at length in Section 9 of Lecture v Keynes wrote:

a large proportion of our positive activities depend on spontaneous optimism rather than on a mathematical expectation [. . .] Most, probably, of our decisions to do something positive, the full consequences of which will be drawn out over many days to come, can only be taken as a result of animal spirits – of a spontaneous urge to action rather than inaction, and not as the outcome of a weighted average of quantitative benefits multiplied by quantitative probabilities [. . .] Only a little more than an expedition to the South Pole, is [enterprise] based on an exact calculation of benefits to come.[1]

I emphasise the word 'exact'. Keynes – in a passage in which he gave full rein to his rhetoric – was not meaning to repudiate his prosaic but fundamental preceding chapter. The passage illustrates the domination over Keynes' thinking of the high degree of uncertainty in the real world. But his use of the term 'animal spirits' cannot be held to mean that the state of expectations which, in a given situation, determines the rate of investment, does not fluctuate, with consequent fluctuations in the rate of investment. What Keynes had in mind was the impossibility of expressing the state of expectations in actuarial form. To speak as though the height of animal spirits is constant – so that the rate of investment is exogenously determined – is to ignore a large part of the *General Theory*.

Immediately following the passage which I have quoted, Keynes referred to 'animal spirits' being 'dimmed'. The height of animal spirits varies with the degree of optimism about the future, and the degree of confidence, and so consequently does the rate of investment.

But I agree with Ferdinando Targetti that Keynes' use of the term 'animal spirits' indicates awareness – probably unconscious – of the Marxian imperative: 'Accumulate! That is Moses and the Prophets.' Dennis Robertson concluded his *A Study of Industrial Fluctuation* with a quotation from Whitman:

> Urge and urge and urge
> Always the procreant urge of the world?[2]

To quote Keynes:

if the animal spirits are dimmed and the spontaneous optimism falters, leaving us to depend on nothing but a mathematical expectation,

1. KEYNES, vol. VII, pp. 161-2.
2. DENNIS H. ROBERTSON, *A Study of Industrial Fluctuation*. London: P. S. King & Son, 1915, p. 254.

enterprise will fade and die; – though fears of loss may have a basis no more reasonable than hopes of profit had before.

[. . .] it is our innate urge to activity which makes the wheels go round, our rational selves choosing between the alternatives as best we are able, calculating where we can, but often falling back for our motive on whim or sentiment or chance.[1]

The fruitful use made by Joan Robinson of the concept of animal spirits is indicated in the Index to her five volumes of *Collected Economic Papers*. For example, 'investment is determined, in one sense, by profit expectations, the "animal spirits", of entrepreneurs which incline them to take the risks of investment, and the state of supply of finance';[2] and in another passage she refers to 'the urge to accumulate ("animal spirits")'.[3]

The concept plays an important part in modern theories of the determination of the rate of growth of joint-stock-companies. The Directors and higher Management of most large companies own a small stake in the equity. Decisions as to the rate of growth often invoke a conflict between the sense of loyalty to the shareholders and the desire to keep them contented, and the Napoleonic urge to grow – 'animal spirits'.

Ferdinando Targetti quoted Joan Robinson as 'having several times correctly pointed out that Chapter 11 of the *General Theory* must be discarded as one of the weakest in the masterpiece'. He inferred that 'investment theory is back to square one with a non-explanation of the "animal spirits" variety'. Joan Robinson informs me that if she did use the word 'discard', what she meant was that Chapter 11 needs to be completely rewritten. This I certainly cannot claim to have done in Sections 7 to 11 of Lecture v. I state that 'the subject of Chapter 11 is the most important one in the *General Theory*. But this Chapter is one of

1. KEYNES, vol. VII, pp. 162-3.

2. JOAN ROBINSON, 'La Théorie de la Répartition', originally published in *Economie Appliquée*, October-December 1957, pp. 523-38; reprinted as 'The Theory of Distribution', in *Collected Economic Papers*, vol. II, pp. 145-58 (the quotation on p. 146).

3. JOAN ROBINSON, 'Findlay's Robinsonian Model of Accumulation: A Comment', *Economica*, November 1963, pp. 408-11; reprinted as 'Robinson on Findlay on Robinson', in *Collected Economic Papers*, vol. III, pp. 48-51 (the quotation on p. 50).

the most confused.' I cannot claim more than to have indicated the lines on which the theory of the inducement to invest needs to be rewritten. I draw special attention to Keynes' reply to Viner's review of the *General Theory*, in the course of which he admitted that 'his theory requires considerable amendment'. Finally, I elaborate on his important contributions on the subject of Finance (made in 1937 and 1938).

I emphatically agree with PIERCARLO GRANDI that 'the approach to an analysis of the economy may be more important than a given model'. His suggestion that 'behaviour functions change every dozen years at most' is an under-statement – they change far more rapidly.

I agree also about the concepts which he attributes to Cambridge economics, partly implicit, but often explicit.

I do not attribute the attraction of monetarism to 'undue attention of so-called Keynesians to fine tuning', but I do not deny the charge. I have already discussed briefly the reasons for the vogue of monetarism.

In answer to Piercarlo Grandi's final question, there are distinct signs of a revival of Keynesian thought, the result partly of disgust over the failure of monetarist policy.

The contribution to the discussion by Dr PIETRO MANES provided an eloquent confirmation of my attitude. How true it is – and how tragic – that 'a large part of what is said and written today in economics is nonsense'. With the diagnosis suggested by Pietro Manes I am entirely in agreement.

By concluding on an optimistic note – though somewhat subdued – I indicate my present state of mind.

My Comments on the illuminating Discussion have been lengthy. The reason is the wide range covered by the contributors. At the same time I am conscious that I have seriously failed to deal with every point raised and every question asked. For this I apologise.

RICHARD KAHN

BIOGRAPHY OF RICHARD KAHN

This Biography is by no means a complete Biography. Many parts of this Book cover those sections of Kahn's intellectual life which involved association with Keynes. Lecture VI deals with personal aspects of Keynes' relationship with a number of economists including Kahn.

This Biography is designed to indicate how extensive have been Kahn's activities and that his reputation is by no means exclusively based on his co-operation with Keynes.

RICHARD KAHN was born on 10 August 1905 in London, son of a Government Inspector of Schools. From 1918 to 1924 he was educated at St Paul's School, London; from October 1924 at King's College, Cambridge. From 1924 to 1927 he studied mathematics and physics, obtaining a second-class degree in physics in June 1927. Then encouraged by his father and by Gerald Shove, in charge at the College of the teaching of economics, he began to study economics, starting with Marshall's *Principles*. In the academic year 1927-1928 he was taught by Keynes as well as by Shove – much encouraged by both. He attended University lectures delivered, among others, by Pigou, Keynes, Shove and Dennis Robertson (Piero Sraffa's lectures in the subsequent academic year). In June 1928 he sat for the degree examination in economics (Part II of the Economics Tripos) and was placed in the First Class.

In September 1928 he began working on the Economics of the Short Period, the subject of one of the most successful sections of Marshall's *Principles*, owing much to the personal influence of Sraffa and of Shove, and encouraged by Keynes. At the beginning of December 1929 he submitted his Dissertation on *The Economics of the Short Period* to the Fellowship Electors of King's College and was elected to a Fellowship in March 1930.[1]

Kahn was appointed a University Lecturer in 1933, a Professor of Economics in 1951, reaching the retiring age in 1972. He was

---

1. An Italian edition (*L'economia del breve periodo*: translation by Pier Luigi Cecioni) by Professor Marco Dardi of the Florence University, has been published by Boringhieri Editore, Torino, 1983. Included are introductions both by the editor and by the author.

a member of the College economics teaching staff from 1936 until becoming Professor.

During most of his working life Kahn was heavily involved in the financial administration of the College. In 1935 he was appointed Second Bursar, working closely with Keynes, who, as First Bursar since the early nineteen-twenties, with his remarkable success in building up the finances of the College, exerted a fruitful influence generally on College policy.

On Keynes' death in April 1946 Kahn succeeded him as First Bursar. On becoming Professor in October 1951 he had, under University regulations, to give up the Bursarship, though continuing for a time to be involved in College finance. As a Trustee of Keynes, in co-operation with his co-Trustee – the late Geoffrey Keynes and more recently Geoffrey's son, Richard – he was responsible for the stock-exchange portfolio of the Keynes Trust until, on the death of Lady Keynes in June 1981, it reverted to the College. In a more informal capacity he undertook responsibility for Lady Keynes' portfolio and supervised the management of her 700 acre farm at Tilton (the Keynes' country home at the northern foot of the South Downs, in the Bloomsbury area) on which Keynes had embarked in 1937.

Kahn's close association with Keynes – which lay in the realm of thought, rather than administration – had already begun after submission of his Fellowship Dissertation in December 1930. It is described in the course of Lecture VI.

From December 1939 until September 1946 Kahn served as a temporary Civil Servant concerned largely with helping to ensure that the supply of goods to civilians was restricted to an essential level, so as to the maximum possible extent to encourage the diversion of labour, raw materials, equipment, buildings and shipping space to the production of munitions and the building up of the Armed Forces; and at the same time to help to ensure efficiency in the limited production of civilian goods, and equity in their distribution (culminating in clothes rationing).

His work as a civil servant lay in different fields from that of Keynes. Indeed when he entered the Civil Service in December 1939 Keynes was still regarded with suspicion in the Treasury (his work there did not start until June 1940), with the result, because of his close association with Keynes, that the Board of Trade obtained Treasury consent to his recruitment only on condition that he would not be concerned with issues of overseas finance (a condition inconsistent with his contribution to the reduction of demands for imports by civilian consumption).

From October 1941 until January 1943 Kahn served, still a Civil Servant, in the Middle East – as Economic Adviser to the Minister of State and a member of the staff of the Middle East Supply Centre. The main objective was to restrict the use of ocean shipping space for non-military purposes to the maximum extent consistent with the avoidance of famine and serious unrest.

Considerable help towards the achievement of this objective was provided by the encouragement of local production of wheat and other cereals, partly by influencing the cropping programme, partly by insisting on high milling extraction rates and the inclusion of flour made from locally produced cereals – rice, barley and millet; and partly by curbing absorption by the black market.

In January 1943 Kahn returned to London. Until mid-1944 he worked in the Raw Materials Department of the Ministry of Supply on the post-War problems of supply, including domestic production, of raw materials.

(Here he developed an interest in Keynes' proposed international buffer stocks. This developed in subsequent years into one of his numerous – as yet – unpublished papers. Apart from a general paper, he wrote papers on buffer stocks for tin and sugar – on tin carried out for the Food and Agriculture Organisation of the United Nations and on sugar for the International Sugar Council.)

About the middle of 1944 Kahn was transfered to the Ministry of Production as Head of their General Division. One of his functions was to co-operate in the planning of supplies for liberated and conquered territories.

After the end of the War the Ministry of Production and the Board of Trade were merged and Kahn became Head of the General Division of the Board of Trade. In this capacity he supervised the setting up and the operation of the Tripartite Industrial Working Parties, to the Reports of which Stafford

Cripps, the President of the Board of Trade, pinned hopes which were in the outcome only partly justified. (The Working Parties consisted of four representatives of the employers and four of the trade-unions – largely conservative and backward looking in their outlook: four independent members provided the progressive element.)

Kahn returned to Cambridge in September 1946. He had lost contact over seven years with developments in economic theory. For some time he was heavily preoccupied as First Bursar with getting the administration of the College back on to a peacetime footing, with liquidating Keynes' estate and setting up the Keynes Trust and, until he was joined in 1949 by Nicholas Kaldor, in conducting single-handed the economics teaching of the College (Shove having died after a protracted illness). Kahn, having for so long lost contact with the development of economic thought, chose for his University lectures the early Fabians. His experience in the Board of Trade in the first post-War year had led him to take a historical interest into the reasons for, and objectives of, the policy of nationalising certain industries, the methods of expropriation, and the proposed methods of administration.

In the course of the years which followed Kahn's publications were ephemeral in character – concerned with Government economic policy and published mainly in the Reviews of the Joint Stock Books and in the *Listener*. A plan for publishing a selection has not – at any rate as yet – been executed, apart from those published in *Selected Essays on Employment and Growth*,[1] which include Kahn's written evidence to the Radcliffe Committee on the Working of the Monetary System (May 1958)[2] and an article on 'The Pace of Development', based on a lecture delivered at the Hebrew University of Jerusalem.[3]

1. Cambridge University Press, 1972. Italian translation by Gabriele Pastrello, published by Giulio Einaudi, Torino, 1976.

2. RADCLIFFE COMMITTEE ON THE WORKING OF THE MONETARY SYSTEM, *Principal Memoranda of Evidence*, Memorandum of Evidence submitted by RICHARD KAHN, 27 May 1958, London: His Majesty's Stationery Office, 1959; reprinted in *Selected Essays on Employment and Growth*. Cambridge: Cambridge University Press, 1972, pp. 124-52.

3. Published in *The Challenge of Development*. Jerusalem: Hebrew University, 1958, pp. 163-98; reprinted in *Selected Essays on Employment and Growth*, pp. 153-91.

Of the post-War theoretical articles published in this volume, the more important are 'Some Notes on Liquidity Preference',[1] 'Exercises in the Analysis of Growth',[2] and 'Notes on the Rate of Interest and the Growth of Firms' (1971) (not previously published),[3] in which the relation between a firms's valuation ratio (the ratio of the market price of its shares to the value of its assets, as assessed by the management), and its rate of growth is expressed in terms of a simple formula and then the implications are examined. Kahn's analysis was inspired by a book by Robin Marris.[4] It was drafted with the help of Joan Robinson. In the book is reprinted Kahn's 'multiplier' article on 'The Relation of Home Investment to Unemployment' (*Economic Journal*, June 1931).[5]

In a contribution to a Conference on Involuntary Unemployment, Kahn discussed the difficulties of definition in Chapter 2 of Keynes' *General Theory*, indicated the origin in the *General Theory* of wage inflation as the cause of cost inflation, and reproduced the estimates made by Keynes during the War of the extent to which after the War it would be safe to carry full employment without risking inflation (involving 5 per cent unemployment), in the absence of Government measures, including regional control of location of industry.[6]

Kahn spent the year 1955 at Geneva as a member of the Research Division of the Economic Commission for Europe (of the United Nations) and co-operated in preparing their *Economic*

1. RICHARD KAHN, 'Some Notes on Liquidity Preference', *Manchester School of Economic and Social Studies*, September 1954, pp. 229-57; reprinted in *Selected Essays on Employment and Growth*, pp. 72-96.

2. RICHARD KAHN, 'Excercises in the Analysis of Growth', *Oxford Economic Papers*, June 1959, pp. 146-63; reprinted in *Selected Essays on Employment and Growth*, pp. 192-207.

3. RICHARD KAHN, 'Notes on the Rate of Interest and the Growth of Firms'; published in *Selected Essays on Employment and Growth*, pp. 208-32.

4. ROBIN MARRIS, *The Economic Theory of 'Managerial' Capitalism*. London: Macmillan, 1964.

5. RICHARD KAHN, 'The Relation of Home Investment to Unemployment', *Economic Journal*, 1931, pp. 173-98; reprinted in *Selected Essays on Employment and Growth*, pp. 1-27.

6. RICHARD KAHN, 'Unemployment as seen by the Keynesians' in GEORGE DAVID N. WORSWICK, *The Concept and Measurement of Involuntary Unemployment*. London: George Allen and Unwin; Boulder, Colorado: Westview Press, 1976, pp. 19-25.

Survey of Europe in 1955.[1] His particular concern was with obstacles to industrial investment in Western Europe. He published an article on 'Short-Term Business Indicators in Western Europe' in the ECE *Economic Bulletin for Europe.*[2]

In June 1959 Kahn was appointed a member of a Group of Experts (of which he was informal Chairman) of the OEEC (the predecessor of the OECD) – to study the problem of rising prices.[3] In the Chapter on 'The Role of Wages'[4] the Group, referring to the 'pressure of wage increases resulting from wage negotiations',[5] stated that:

The importance of this factor has differed greatly among the countries [. . .] it is possible to state broadly that negotiated wage increases have played a large part in some countries and that, apart from the cases of extreme excess demand, this factor is decisive in explaining why some countries have failed to a far greater extent than others to achieve price stability.[6]

The Group introduced the concept of the Wage-Wage Spiral – 'leap-frogging'.[7] 'We believe that the "wage-wage spiral" has been one of the main causes of excessive wage increases.'[8] That was in 1961 – when the state of thought about inflation was still primitive.

In the course of the sixties Kahn devoted considerable effort to work for the Government. Later he served for three years as a part-time member of the National Coal Board.

In the course of the years 1965 to 1969 Kahn served as a

1. UNITED NATIONS, Economic Commission for Europe, *Economic Survey of Europe in 1955.* Including Studies of Investment Problems and Policies of European Countries and Labour Market Problems in Western Europe, Geneva: UN, Department of Economic and Social Affairs, Research Planning Division, 1956.

2. [RICHARD KAHN], 'Short-Term Business Indicators in Western Europe', in UNITED NATIONS, Economic Commission for Europe, *Economic Bulletin for Europe*, November 1955, pp. 34-78.

3. ORGANISATION FOR ECONOMIC COOPERATION AND DEVELOPMENT, *The Problem of Rising Prices.* Document by William Fellner, Milton Gilbert, Bent Hansen, Richard Kahn, Friedrich Lutz, Pieter de Wolff. Paris: OECC, 1961.

4. *Ibid.*, Chapter v, pp. 45-68.

5. *Ibid.*, p. 45.

6. *Ibid.*

7. *Ibid.*, pp. 53-5.

8. *Ibid.*, p. 54.

member of four Groups of Experts of the United Nations Conference on Trade and Development (UNCTAD). The authors of the Report on *International Monetary Issues and the Developing Countries*[1] considered the need for a reform of the international monetary system which would make it more responsive to the needs for economic growth of both developed and developing countries. They advocated that part of the additional international liquidity created by the International Monetary Fund should be placed at the disposal of the International Bank – the famous 'Link'.[2]

The authors of the Report on *Trade Expansion and Economic Co-operation among Developing Countries*[3] dealt with the possibilities of expansion of trade among developing countries by commercial policy measures, the co-ordination on investment and production programmes, and the regional integration of national markets. The authors of the Report on *Payments Arrangements among the Developing Countries for Trade Expansion*[4] considered the contributions which could be made towards the expansion of trade among developing countries by payments arrangements (clearing arrangements, credit arrangements and monetary unions). The authors of the Report on *International Monetary Reform and Co-operation for Development*[5] were in a position to formulate more concrete proposals for a 'Link' on the basis of the newly accepted Special Drawing Rights to be issued by the International Monetary Fund. They also made proposals about the share of developing countries in increases in IMF quotas.

In June 1974 Kahn read a paper on 'Historical Origins of the International Monetary Fund' to the Second Keynes Seminar held at the University of Kent.[6] He described the development

1. UNITED NATIONS CONFERENCE ON TRADE AND DEVELOPMENT, *International Monetary Issues and The Developing Countries*. New York: UN, 1965.

2. See Chapter IV, 'The Possibility of "a Link"', *ibid.*, pp. 26-31.

3. UNITED NATIONS CONFERENCE ON TRADE AND DEVELOPMENT, *Trade Expansion and Economic Co-operation among Developing Countries*. Geneva: UN, 1966,

4. UNITED NATIONS CONFERENCE ON TRADE AND DEVELOPMENT, *Payments Arrangements among the Developing Countries for Trade Expansion*. Geneva: UN, 1966.

5. UNITED NATIONS CONFERENCE ON TRADE AND DEVELOPMENT, *International Monetary Reform and Co-operation for Development*. New York: UN, 1969.

6. RICHARD KAHN, 'Historical Origins of the International Monetary Fund', in ANTHONY P. THIRLWALL (ed.), *Keynes and International Monetary Relations*, pp. 3-35.

of Keynes' thought on the subject of an international monetary institution, and the discussions with the Americans, culminating in the Bretton Woods Conference of July 1944. This was followed by the Savannah Conference of March 1946 – the first meetings of the Governors of the Fund and of the Bank – a grievous disappointment to Keynes. At the age of 62 he died four weeks after his departure from Savannah.

Kahn's interest in the development of Keynes' basic thinking was not renewed until 1974. On 6 November 1974 he delivered to the British Academy the Fourth Keynes Lecture 'On Re-Reading Keynes'.[1] In June 1978 he published an article on 'Some Aspects of the Development of Keynes' Thought'.[2]

In 1964 a life Peerage was conferred on Kahn.

1. RICHARD KAHN, 'On Re-Reading Keynes', *Proceedings of the British Academy*, vol. LX, 1974, pp. 361-92.
2. RICHARD KAHN,' Some Aspects of the Development of Keynes's Thought', *Journal of Economic Literature*, June 1978, pp. 544-59.

THE COLLECTED WRITINGS OF
JOHN MAYNARD KEYNES

THE COLLECTED WRITINGS OF
JOHN MAYNARD KEYNES[1]

Published by the Royal Economic Society, Cambridge.

Managing Editors of the Series: Sir Austin Robinson, Donald Moggridge

Editors of the Individual Volumes: Elizabeth Johnson, Donald Moggridge

I. *Indian Currency and Finance* (1971)[2]

Keynes' first book, published in 1913, contains his earliest theoretical thinking on a gold exchange standard and a managed paper currency.

II. *The Economic Consequences of the Peace* (1971)

The book which first made Keynes famous when published in 1919. This edition includes the special prefaces written for the French and Roumanian translations.

III. *A Revision of the Treaty* (1971)

A sequel to *The Economic Consequences of the Peace* made necessary by the subsequent flow of events, first published in 1922.

IV. *A Tract on Monetary Reform* (1971)

This book published in 1923 was chiefly composed of abbreviated versions of articles that Keynes had contributed to the Reconstruction Supplements of the Manchester Guardian Commercial that he had edited. It is important as showing Keynes' theoretical thinking about money at that date.

V. *A Treatise on Money: The Pure Theory of Money* (1971)

VI. *A Treatise on Money: The Applied Theory of Money* (1971)

Volumes V and VI represented when published in 1930 six years of intensive work and argument with Robertson and others. This new edition includes the very important special prefaces that he wrote for the German and Japanese translations, when he himself was well on the way to *The General Theory*.

---

1. References to *The Collected Writings of John Maynard Keynes* are given in the form: KEYNES, vol. 1 (etc.).

2. Date of publication in this edition given in brackets.

VII. *The General Theory of Employment, Interest and Money* (1973)
This new edition includes the extremely important special prefaces written for the German, Japanese and French translations. These, and particularly that of the French edition, set out more clearly his reasons for adopting the controversial note that had distressed some of his friends.

VIII. *A Treatise on Probability* (1973)
This book grew out of Keynes' earliest interests as a mathematician in the theory of probability and out of the dissertation at King's College, Cambridge, which secured his election to a Fellowship in 1909. He revised it after his return to academic life in 1919 and published it in 1921. A valuable editorial foreword by Professor Richard B. Braithwaite relates Keynes' work to the subsequent development of this subject.

IX. *Essays in Persuasion* (1972)

X. *Essays in Biography* (1972)
Volumes IX and X, first published in 1931 and 1933, have been enlarged to include later writings of a similar character. The first includes his later 'Means to Prosperity' and 'How to Pay for the War'. The second includes his later essays on Malthus, Jevons and Newton as well as his 'Two Memoirs' posthumously published in 1949.

XI. *Economic Articles and Correspondence: Academic* (1983)

XII. *Economic Articles and Correspondence: Investment and Editorial* (1983)
Volumes XI and XII collect all these economic articles, published in various journals, which are not reprinted in other volumes in the series and certain unpublished writings.

XIII. *The General Theory and After: Preparation* (1973)

XIV. *The General Theory and After: Defence and Development* (1973)
Volumes XIII and XIV provide all the material relevant to an appraisal of the development of Keynes' thinking in the monetary field from the time of the *Tract* in 1923 to the *Treatise* in 1930, onward to *The General Theory* in 1936, and after its publication. They contain not only the various drafts of the book but also the complete and

fascinating correspondence and arguments with Dennis H. Robertson, Ralph G. Hawtrey, Arthur C. Pigou, Roy F. Harrod, Richard Kahn, Joan Robinson and others. They are indispensable to any serious discussion of modern economic theory.

xv. *Activities 1906-1914: India and Cambridge* (1971)

xvi. *Activities 1914-1919: The Treasury and Versailles* (1971)
Volumes xv and xvi represent the first two in a series that makes available Keynes' correspondence, memoranda, letters to the newspapers, shorter articles and other hitherto unpublished writings. The first covers his period in the India Office and his membership of the Royal Commission on Indian Finance and Currency. The second covers all his work in the Treasury 1914-1919, ending in his resignation in despair over the Treaty of Versailles.

xvii. *Activities 1920-1922: Treaty Revision and Reconstruction* (1977)

xviii. *Activities 1922-1932: The End of Reparations* (1978)
Volumes xvii and xviii cover the attempts during 1920-1932 at international financial reconstruction and end the story of post-1918 reparations.

xix. *Activities 1922-1929: The Return to Gold and Industrial Policy* (1981)

xx. *Activities 1929-1931: Rethinking Employment and Unemployment Policies* (1981)

xxi. *Activities 1931-1939: World Crisis and Policies in Britain and America* (1982)
Volumes xix, xx and xxi are concerned with Keynes' activities between 1922 and 1939.

xxii. *Activities 1939-1945: Internal War Finance* (1978)
This volume deals with Keynes' contributions to the internal financing of the second War.

xxiii. *Activities 1940-1943: External War Finance* (1979)
This volume records Keynes' involvement in Stage ii negotiations and the post-War American loan.

XXIV. *Activities 1944-1946: The Transition to Peace* (1979)
This volume focuses on discussions concerning the Lend Lease Agreement.

XXV. *Activities 1940-1944: Shaping the Post-War World: the Clearing Union* (1980)

XXVI. *Activities 1941-1946: Shaping the Post-War World: Bretton Woods and Reparations* (1980)

XXVII. *Activities 1940-1946: Shaping the Post-War World: Employment and Commodities* (1980)
Volumes XXV, XXVI and XXVII are concerned with Keynes' efforts to shape the post-War world. The first has as its focus the origins of the Clearing Union and the progress of subsequent discussions in both London and Washington up to April 1944. Two further ones are concerned with the negotiations surrounding the founding of the International Monetary Fund and World Bank after that date and with Keynes' activities in such areas as employment policy, commodity policy, relief and reparations.

XXVIII. *Social, Political and Literary Writings* (1982)
This volume includes Keynes' very interesting correspondence as chairman of the *New Statesman* with Kingsley Martin, its editor; his writings on the arts; a previously unpublished study of ancient currencies; and his preface with Piero Sraffa to the Abstract of Hume's *Treatise of Human Nature*.

XXIX. *The General Theory and After: A Supplement* (1979)
This volume supplements volumes XIII and XIV and in it are collected together papers relating to the composition and defence of *The General Theory* discovered at Tilton in 1976.

XXX. *Bibliography and Index* (not yet published)
This volume will provide a general index to the whole edition.

ROYAL ECONOMIC SOCIETY

In 1984 the annual subscription is £ 21.00, and payable also in US $ 48. Members receive four numbers a year of the *Economic Journal* and can buy all published volumes in the Keynes' series for personal use at the reduced price (£ 18.00 per volume). Applications for membership should be made to The Membership Secretary, Royal Economic Society, PO Box 86, CAMBRIDGE, CB4 3EY, England.

Available from booksellers, all published volumes £ 24.00, Paperback of *The General Theory* £ 6.95

Macmillan (World-wide, except the U.S.A. and Canada)
Cambridge University Press (U.S.A. & Canada only)

BIBLIOGRAPHY

BECATTINI Giacomo, *Alfred Marshall. Antologia di scritti economici.* Bologna: Il Mulino, 1981.

BRESCIANI-TURRONI Costantino, *Le vicende del marco tedesco.* Milano: Università Bocconi Editrice, 1931. English Edition substantially revised by the author, with a Foreword by Lionel Robbins: *The Economics of Inflation. A Study of Currency Depreciation in Post-War Germany.* London: George Allen and Unwin, 1937.

Britain's Industrial Future. Report of the Liberal Industrial Inquiry, 1928 (the 'Yellow Book'). London: Ernest Benn, 1928; see also KEYNES, vol. XIX, Part II, pp. 731-8.

Challenge of Development, The. Symposium held on 26, 27 June 1957 at the Eliezer Kaplan School of Economics and Social Sciences. Jerusalem: The Hebrew University, 1958.

COUTTS Kenneth, GODLEY Wynne and NORDHAUS William, *Industrial Pricing in the United Kingdom.* Cambridge: Cambridge University Press, 1978.

CRABTREE Derek and THIRLWALL Anthony P. (eds.), *Keynes and the Bloomsbury Group.* Proceedings of the Fourth Keynes Seminar held at the University of Kent at Canterbury, 1978. London: Macmillan, 1980.

DAVIS Ronnie J. and CASEY Francis J., Jr, 'Keynes's Misquotation of Mill', *Economic Journal,* June 1977, pp. 329-30.

DUESENBERRY James S., *Income, Saving and the Theory of Consumer Behavior.* First published as Harvard Economic Study, Number 87, Cambridge, Mass.: Harvard University Press, 1949; reprinted as a Galaxy Book, New York: Oxford University Press, 1967.

DURNFORD Hugh G., 'The Bursar', in *John Maynard Keynes, 1883-1946. Fellow and Bursar. A Memoir,* pp. 15-20.

ESHAG Éprime (ed.), 'Michal Kalecki Memorial Lectures', *Oxford Bulletin of Economics and Statistics,* Special Issue, February 1977.

FETTER Frank Whitson, 'Lenin, Keynes and Inflation', *Economica,* February 1977, pp. 77-80.

FISHER Irving, *The Rate of Interest, its Nature, Determination and Relation to Economic Phenomena.* New York: Macmillan, 1907.

FISHER Irving, *The Purchasing Power of Money. Its Determination and Relation to Credit Interest and Crises.* New York: Macmillan, 1911.

FISHER Irving, *The Theory of Interest. As Determined by Impatience to Spend Income and Opportunity to Invest It.* New York: Macmillan, 1930.

GAYER Arthur D. (ed.), *The Lessons of Monetary Experience. Essays in Honor of Irving Fisher*. Presented to him on the occasion of his Seventieth Birthday. New York and London: George Allen and Unwin, 1937.

HANSEN Alvin H., 'A Fundamental Error in Keynes's "Treatise on Money"', *American Economic Review*, September 1932, p. 462; reprinted in KEYNES, vol. V, pp. 329-30.

HARROD Roy F., 'Mr. Keynes and Traditional Theory', *Econometrica*, January 1937, pp. 74-86.

HARROD Roy F., *Towards a Dynamic Economics*. London: Macmillan, 1948.

HARROD Roy F., *The Life of John Maynard Keynes*. London: Macmillan, 1951.

HAYEK Friedrich A., *Prices and Production*. London: George Routledge & Sons, First Edition with a Foreword by Lionel Robbins, 1931: Second, revised and enlarged Edition, 1935.

HAYEK Friedrich A., 'Reflections on the Pure Theory of Money of Mr. J. M. Keynes', *Economica*, August 1931, pp. 270-95.

HICKS John R., 'Mr. Keynes and the "Classics"; A Suggested Interpretation', *Econometrica*, April 1937, pp. 147-59; reproduced in *Critical Essays in Monetary Theory*, pp. 126-42.

HICKS John R., Obituary of 'Dennis Holmes Robertson, 1890-1963', *Proceedings of the British Academy*, vol. L, 1964, pp. 305-16.

HICKS John R., *Capital and Growth*. Oxford: Clarendon Press, 1965.

HICKS John R., *Critical Essays in Monetary Theory*. Oxford: Clarendon Press, 1967.

HICKS John R., 'Recollections and Documents', *Economica*, February 1973, pp. 2-11.

HICKS John R., *The Crisis in Keynesian Economics*, Yrjö Jahnsson Lectures organized by the Yrjö Jahnsson Foundation, Helsinki. Oxford: Basil Blackwell, 1974.

HICKS John R., *Economic Perspectives. Further Essays on Money and Growth*. Oxford: Clarendon Press, 1977.

HICKS John R., 'IS–LM; an Explanation', *Journal of Post Keynesian Economics*, Winter 1980-1981, pp. 139-54.

HOUSE OF LORDS, *Official Report*. 'Speech of Lionel Robbins'. The Parliamentary Debates; Fifth Series – Volume CCLXXVI; First Session of the Forty-Fourth Parliament of the United Kingdom of Great

Britain and Northern Ireland; Third volume of Session 1966-1967 comprising period from Monday, 11 July to Friday, 12 August 1966. London: Her Majesty's Stationery Office, 1966, Session of 28 July 1966, cols. 950-957.

Howson Susan and Winch Donald, *The Economic Advisory Council 1930-1939. A Study in Economic Advice during Depression and Recovery.* Cambridge: Cambridge University Press, 1977.

Hume David, *Political Discourses.* Edinburgh: R. Fleming, 1752.

Johannsen Nicholas A. L. J., *A Neglected Point in Connection with Crises.* New York: The Bankers Publishing Company, 1908.

Kahn Richard, 'The Economics of the Short Period'. Fellowship Dissertation, Cambridge: King's College, December 1929. Italian Edition (*L'economia nel breve periodo*, translation by Pier Luigi Cecioni) by Marco Dardi. Included are introductions both by the editor and by the author. Torino: Editore Boringhieri, 1983.

Kahn Richard, 'The Relation of Home Investment to Unemployment', *Economic Journal*, June 1931, pp. 173-98; reprinted in *Selected Essays on Employment and Growth*, pp. 1-27.

Kahn Richard, 'The Financing of Public Works: A Note', *Economic Journal*, September 1932, pp. 492-5.

Kahn Richard, 'Public Works and Inflation', *Journal of the American Statistical Association*, Supplement, March 1933, pp. 168-73. Papers and Proceedings of the Ninety-fourth Annual Meeting of the American Statistical Association (edited by Frank Alexander Ross), held at Cincinnati, Ohio, 28-31 December 1932; reprinted in *Selected Essays on Employment and Growth*, pp. 28-34.

Kahn Richard, Review of 'Oxford Studies in the Prices Mechanism', *Economic Journal*, March 1952, pp. 119-30.

Kahn Richard, 'Some Notes on Liquidity Preference', *Manchester School of Economic and Social Studies*, September 1954, pp. 229-57; reprinted in *Selected Essays on Employment and Growth*, pp. 72-96.

[Kahn Richard], 'Short-Term Business Indicators in Western Europe', in United Nations, Economic Commission for Europe, *Economic Bulletin for Europe*, November 1955, pp. 34-78.

Kahn Richard, 'Memorandum of Evidence' (1958). Submitted to the Radcliffe Committee, in Radcliffe Committee on the Working of the Monetary System, *Principal Memoranda of Evidence*, pp. 138-46.

Kahn Richard, 'The Pace of Development'. Lecture delivered at the

Eliezer Kaplan School of Economics and Social Sciences, *The Challenge of Development*, pp. 163-98; reprinted in *Selected Essays on Employment and Growth*, pp. 153-91.

KAHN Richard, 'Exercises in the Analysis of Growth', *Oxford Economic Papers*, June 1959, pp. 146-63; reprinted in *Selected Essays on Employment and Growth*, pp. 192-207.

KAHN Richard, 'Notes on the Rate of Interest and the Growth of Firms' (1971), in *Selected Essays on Employment and Growth*, pp. 208-32.

KAHN Richard, *Selected Essays on Employment and Growth*. Cambridge: Cambridge University Press, 1972. Italian translation by Gabriele Pastrello; included are Introduction by Joan Robinson and Preface by the author: KAHN Richard, *L'occupazione e la crescita*, Torino: Giulio Einaudi editore, 1976.

KAHN Richard, 'On Re-Reading Keynes'. Keynes Lecture delivered on 6 November 1974, *Proceedings of the British Academy*, vol. LX, 1974, pp. 361-92.

KAHN Richard, 'Unemployment as seen by the Keynesians', in WORSWICK George David N. (ed.), *The Concept and Measurement of Involuntary Unemployment*, pp. 19-25.

KAHN Richard, 'Some Aspects of the Development of Keynes's Thought', *Journal of Economic Literature*, June 1978, pp. 544-59.

KALDOR Nicholas, 'Prof. Pigou on Money Wages in Relation to Unemployment', *Economic Journal*, December 1937, pp. 745-53.

KEYNES John Maynard, *Indian Currency and Finance*. London: Macmillan, 1913; reprinted in KEYNES, vol. I.

KEYNES John Maynard, *The Economic Consequences of the Peace*. London: Macmillan, 1919 (reprinted 1920, 1924); reprinted in KEYNES, vol. II.

KEYNES John Maynard, *A Treatise on Probability*. London: Macmillan, 1921; reprinted in KEYNES, vol. VIII.

KEYNES John Maynard, *A Revision of the Treaty*. London: Macmillan, 1922; reprinted in Keynes, vol. III.

KEYNES John Maynard, 'The Stabilisation of the European Exchanges: A Plan for Genoa', *Manchester Guardian Commercial* ('Reconstruction in Europe', Supplement Number 1), 20 April 1922; reprinted in KEYNES, vol. XVII, pp. 355-69.

KEYNES John Maynard, *A Tract on Monetary Reform*. London: Macmillan, 1923 (reprinted in 1924, 1929 and 1932); reprinted in KEYNES, vol. IV.

KEYNES John Maynard, 'The Speeches of the Bank Chairmen', *The Nation and Athenaeum*, 23 February 1924; reprinted in KEYNES, vol. IX, pp. 188-92 (see also *Essays in Persuasion* as '1 February 1924', pp. 220-25).

KEYNES John Maynard 'Alfred Marshall, 1842-1924', *Economic Journal*, September 1924, pp. 311-72; reprinted in PIGOU Arthur C., *Memorials of Alfred Marshall*, p. 165; in KEYNES J. M., *Essays in Biography*, pp. 150-266, and in KEYNES, vol. X, pp. 161-231.

KEYNES John Maynard. *Official Papers of Alfred Marshall*. London: Macmillan, 1925.

KEYNES John Maynard, 'The Return Towards Gold', *The Nation and Athenaeum*, 21 February 1925; reprinted in Keynes, vol. IX, pp. 192-200.

KEYNES John Maynard, 'The Committee on the Currency', *Economic Journal*, June 1925, pp. 299-304. Report of the Committee on the Currency and Bank of England Note Issue; reprinted in KEYNES, vol. XIX, Part I, pp. 207-30.

KEYNES John Maynard, 'The Economic Consequences of Mr Churchill', *Evening Standard*, 22, 23 and 24 July 1925. Published as a pamphlet, London: Hogarth Press, 1925; reprinted in KEYNES, vol. IX, pp. 207-30.

KEYNES John Maynard, *The End of Laissez-Faire*. Published as a pamphlet, London: Hogarth Press, 1926; reprinted in KEYNES, vol. IX, pp. 272-94.

KEYNES John Maynard, 'A Cure for Unemployment', *Evening Standard*, 19 April 1929; reprinted in KEYNES, vol. XIX, Part II, pp. 808-12.

KEYNES John Maynard and HENDERSON Hubert H., *Can Lloyd George Do It? An Examination of the Liberal Pledge*. London: The Nation and Athenaeum (12 May) 1929; pamphlet in support of Lloyd George's Pledge in the 1929 General Election to reduce unemployment by a programme of public spending; reprinted in KEYNES, vol. IX. pp. 86-125.

KEYNES John Maynard, *A Treatise on Money*. Vol. I, *The Pure Theory*;

vol. II, *The Applied Theory*. London: Macmillan, 1930; reprinted in
KEYNES, vols. V and VI.

KEYNES John Maynard, Obituary of 'F. P. Ramsey', *Economic Journal*,
March 1930, pp. 153-4; reprinted in KEYNES, vol. X, pp. 335-6.

KEYNES John Maynard, 'Economic Possibilities for our Grandchildren', *The Nation and Athenaeum*, 11 and 18 October 1930; reprinted in Keynes, vol. IX, pp. 321-32.

KEYNES John Maynard, 'Sir Oswald Mosley's Manifesto', London:
The Nation and Athenaeum, (13 December) 1930; reprinted in
KEYNES, vol. XX, pp. 473-6.

KEYNES John Maynard, *Essays in Persuasion*. London: Macmillan,
1931; reissued London: Rupert Hart-Davis, 1951; reprinted with
additions in KEYNES, vol. IX.

KEYNES John Maynard, 'An Economic Analysis of Unemployment',
in WRIGHT Quincy (ed.), *Unemployment as a World Problem*. Chicago,
Illinois: University of Chicago Press, 1931, pp. 3-42; reprinted in
KEYNES, vol. XIII, pp. 343-67.

KEYNES John Maynard, 'Proposals for a Revenue Tariff', *New Statesman and Nation*, 7 March 1931; reprinted in KEYNES, vol. IX,
pp. 231-8.

KEYNES John Maynard, 'A Rejoinder' [to Mr Dennis H. Robertson],
Economic Journal, September 1931, pp. 412-23; see KEYNES, vol. XIII,
p. 219-36.

KEYNES John Maynard, 'We Must Restrict our Imports', *Evening
Standard*, 10 September 1931; reprinted as 'On the Eve of Gold
Suspension'; in KEYNES, vol. IX, pp. 238-42.

KEYNES John Maynard, 'The Future of the World', *Sunday Express*,
27 September 1931; reprinted as 'The End of the Gold Standard'
in KEYNES, vol. IX, pp. 245-9.

KEYNES John Maynard, 'The Pure Theory of Money. A Reply to Dr.
Hayek', *Economica*, November 1931, pp. 387-97; reprinted in
KEYNES, vol. XIII, pp. 243-56.

KEYNES John Maynard, 'Keynes' Fundamental Equations: A Note',
American Economic Review, December 1932, pp. 691-2; reprinted in
KEYNES, vol. V, pp. 330-1.

KEYNES John Maynard, *Essays in Biography*. London: Macmillan, 1933; new edition with additions, London: Rupert Hart-Davis, 1951; reprinted in KEYNES, vol. X.

KEYNES John Maynard, *The Means to Prosperity*. London: Macmillan, 1933 (enlarged version of four articles in *The Times* of 13, 14, 15 and 16 March 1933); reprinted expanded form in KEYNES, vol. IX, pp. 335-66.

KEYNES John Maynard, *The General Theory of Employment, Interest and Money*. London: Macmillan, 1936; reprinted in KEYNES, vol. VII.

KEYNES John Maynard, 'The Theory of the Rate of Interest', in GAYER Arthur D. (ed.), *The Lessons of Monetary Experience. Essays in Honor of Irving Fisher*, pp. 145-52; reprinted in KEYNES, vol. XIV, pp. 101-8.

KEYNES John Maynard, 'The General Theory of Employment' *Quarterly Journal of Economics*, February 1937, pp. 209-23; reprinted in KEYNES, vol. XIV, pp. 109-23.

KEYNES John Maynard, 'Alternative Theories of the Rate of Interest', *Economic Journal*, June 1937, pp. 241-52; reprinted in KEYNES, vol. XIV, pp. 201-15.

KEYNES John Maynard, 'The "Ex-Ante" Theory of the Rate of Interest', *Economic Journal*, December 1937, pp. 663-9; reprinted in KEYNES, vol. XIV, pp. 215-23.

KEYNES John Maynard, 'Prof. Pigou on Money Wages in Relation to Unemployment', *Economic Journal*, December 1937, pp. 743-5; reprinted in KEYNES, vol. XIV, pp. 262-5.

KEYNES John Maynard, *How to Pay for the War. A Radical Plan for the Chancellor of the Exchequer*. London: Macmillan, 1940; reprinted in KEYNES, vol. IX, pp. 367-439. An early version was published in two articles in *The Times*: 'Paying for the War. The control of consumption', 14 November 1939; 'How to pay for the War. Compulsory savings', 15 November 1939. The original articles are reprinted in KEYNES, vol. XXII, pp. 41-51.

John Maynard Keynes, 1883-1946. Fellow and Bursar. A Memoir. Prepared by direction of the Council of King's College. Cambridge: Printed for King's College, 1949.

'Keynes in Italia'. Bibliographic catalogue edited by the University of Florence. *Studi e Informazioni*, Firenze: Banca Toscana, June 1983.

KEYNES Milo (ed.), *Essays on John Maynard Keynes*. Cambridge: Cambridge University Press, 1975.

KLEIN Lawrence R., 'The Supply Side', *American Economic Review*, March 1978, pp. 1-7.

LAIDLER David, 'On Wicksell's Theory of Price Level Dynamics', *Manchester School of Economic and Social Studies*, June 1972, pp. 125-44.

LEIGH Arthur H., 'John Locke and the Quantity Theory of Money', *History of Political Economy*, Summer 1974, pp. 200-19.

LEIJONHUFVUD Axel, *On Keynesian Economics and the Economics of Keynes. A Study in Monetary Theory*. New York and London: Oxford University Press, 1968.

Liberal Party, *We Can Conquer Unemployment. Mr. Lloyd George's Pledge*. London: Cassel, 1929.

LOCKE John, *Some Considerations of the Consequences of the Lowering of Interest and Raising the Value of Money*. London: Printed for Awnsham and John Churchill, 1692.

MACMILLAN COMMITTEE OF FINANCE AND INDUSTRY, *Minutes of Evidence*, vol. II, Oral Evidence. London: His Majesty's Stationery Office, 1931, pp. 78-93.

MACMILLAN COMMITTEE OF FINANCE AND INDUSTRY, *Minutes of Evidence*, vol. II. Oral Evidence of Sir Richard V. N. Hopkins, Controller of the Finance and Supply Services Department, of the H. M. Treasury, 16 and 22 May 1930, London: His Majesty's Stationery Office, 1931, pp. 1-26, question nos. 5310-5710; see also KEYNES, vol. XX, pp. 166-79.

MACMILLAN COMMITTEE ON FINANCE AND INDUSTRY, *Report*. Presented to Parliament by the Financial Secretary to the Treasury by Command of His Majesty, June 1931. Cmd 3897. London: His Majesty's Stationery Office, 1931.

MALTHUS Thomas R., *Principles of Political Economy, Considered with a View to their Practical Application*. London: John Murray, 1820. Second Edition with considerable additions from the author's own manuscript and an original Memoir, London: William Pickering, 1836.

MARRIS Robin, *The Economic Theory of 'Managerial' Capitalism*. London: Macmillan, 1964.

MARSHALL Alfred, *The Pure Theory of Foreign Trade. The Pure Theory of Domestic Values*. Printed for private circulation, 1879. Reprinted by the London School of Economics, Scarce Tracts in Economic and Political Science. No. 1. London, 1930. Also in WHITAKER John K., *The Early Economic Writings of Alfred Marshall, 1867-1870*. vol. 2, pp. 117-66, 186-236.

MARSHALL Alfred and Mary Paley, *The Economics of Industry*. London: Macmillan, First Edition, 1879; Second Edition, 1884.

MARSHALL Alfred, *Principles of Economics*. London: Macmillan, First Edition, 1890; Ninth (Variorum) Edition, two volumes, for The Royal Economic Society, with annotations by Claude W. Guillebaud, 1961.

MARSHALL Alfred, *Industry and Trade*. A study of industrial technique and business organization; and of their influences on the conditions of various classes and nations. London: Macmillan, First Edition, August 1919; Second Edition, December 1919; Third Edition, August 1920; Reprinted 1921.

MARSHALL Alfred, *Money, Credit and Commerce*. London: Macmillan, 1923.

Memoranda on Certain Proposals Relating to Unemployment [Government White Paper]. Presented by the Minister of Labour to Parliament by Command of His Majesty; May 1929. Cmd. 3331. London: His Majesty's Stationery Office, 1929.

MILGATE Murray, 'Keynes on the "Classical" Theory of Interest', *Cambridge Journal of Economics*, March 1977, pp. 307-15.

MILL John Stuart, *Principles of Political Economy, with Some of Their Applications to Social Philosophy*. First Edition in two volumes, London: John W. Parker, 1848. Second Edition in two volumes, 1849. People's Edition, London: Longmans, Green, 1891.

MINSKY Hyman P., *John Maynard Keynes*. London: Macmillan, 1975.

MOGGRIDGE Donald E., *British Monetary Policy. 1924-1931*. The Norman Conquest of $ 4.86. Cambridge: Cambridge University Press, 1972.

MOGGRIDGE Donald E., 'From the *Treatise* to *The General Theory*: An Exercise in Chronology', *History of Political Economy*, Spring 1973, pp. 72-88.

MOGGRIDGE Donald E. (ed.), *Keynes: Aspects of the Man and his Work*. Proceedings of the First Keynes Seminar held at the University of Kent at Canterbury, 1972. London: Macmillan, 1974.

MOGGRIDGE Donald E. and HOWSON Susan, 'Keynes on Monetary Policy, 1910-1946', *Oxford Economic Papers*, July 1974, pp. 226-47.

MOGGRIDGE Donald E., *Keynes*. London: Macmillan, 1976.

MUMMERY Albert F. and HOBSON John A., *The Physiology of Industry*. London: John Murray, 1889.

OHLIN Bertil, 'Some Notes on the Stockholm Theory of Savings and Investment', *Economic Journal*, Part I: March 1937, pp. 53-69; Part II: June 1937, pp. 221-40.

OHLIN Bertil, 'Some Comments on Keynesianism and the Swedish Theory of Expansion Before 1935', in PATINKIN Don and LEITH J. Clark (eds.), *Keynes, Cambridge and 'The General Theory'*. Appendix III, pp. 149-65.

ORGANIZATION FOR EUROPEAN ECONOMIC COOPERATION, *The Problem of Rising Prices*. Document by William Fellner, Milton Gilbert, Bent Hansen, Richard Kahn, Friedrich Lutz, Pieter de Wolff. Paris: OEEC, 1961.

PATINKIN Don, *Money, Interest and Prices*. First Edition, Evanston, Illinois: Row, Peterson, 1956; Second Edition, New York: Harper and Row, 1965.

PATINKIN Don, *Keynes' Monetary Thought. A Study of its Development* Durham, North Carolina: Duke University Press, 1976.

PATINKIN Don and LEITH J. Clark (eds.), *Keynes, Cambridge and 'The General Theory'*. The process of criticism and discussion connected with the development of 'The General Theory'. Proceedings of a conference held at the University of Western Ontario. London: Macmillan, 1977.

PATINKIN Don, 'Keynes's Misquotation of Mill: Comment', *Economic Journal*, June 1978, pp. 341-2.

PATINKIN Don, 'Keynes and the Multiplier', *Manchester School of Economic and Social Studies*, September 1978, pp. 209-23.

PIGOU Arthur C., *Wealth and Welfare*. London: Macmillan, 1912.

PIGOU Arthur C., *Unemployment*. New York: Henry Holt and Co.; London: Williams and Norgate, 1913.

PIGOU Arthur C., 'The Value of Money', *Quarterly Journal of Economics*, November 1917, pp. 38-65.

PIGOU Arthur C., 'The Problem of the Currency', *Contemporary Review*, February 1920, pp. 169-76.

PIGOU Arthur C., *The Economics of Welfare*. London: Macmillan,

First Edition, 1920 (reprinted, 1921; Second Edition, 1924; Third Edition, 1929), Fourth Edition, 1932.

PIGOU Arthur C., 'Unemployment', *Contemporary Review*, July-December 1921, pp. 737-42; revised and reprinted as 'Unemployment and the Great Slump', in *Essays in Applied Economics*, pp. 34-40.

PIGOU Arthur C., *Essays in Applied Economics*. London: P. S. King & Son, 1923.

PIGOU Arthur C. (ed.) *Memorials of Alfred Marshall*. London: Macmillan, 1925.

PIGOU Arthur C., *Industrial Fluctuations*. London: Macmillan, 1927.

PIGOU Arthur C., *The Theory of Unemployment*. London: Macmillan, 1933.

PIGOU Arthur C., 'Mr. J. M. Keynes' General Theory of Employment, Interest and Money', *Economica*, May 1936, pp. 115-32.

PIGOU Arthur C., *Socialism versus Capitalism*. London: Macmillan, 1937.

PIGOU Arthur C., 'Real and Money Wage Rates in Relation to Unemployment', *Economic Journal*, September 1937, pp. 405-22.

PIGOU Arthur C., 'Money Wages in Relation to Unemployment', *Economic Journal*, March 1938, pp. 134-8.

PIGOU Arthur C., *Employment and Equilibrium. A Theoretical Discussion*. London: Macmillan, First Edition 1941; Second revised Edition, 1949.

PIGOU Arthur C., 'John Maynard Keynes, 1883-1946', *Proceedings of the British Academy*, 1946, pp. 395-414.

PIGOU Arthur C., 'The Economist', in *John Maynard Keynes, 1883-1946. Fellow and Bursar. A Memoir*, pp. 21-23.

PIGOU Arthur C., *Keynes's 'General Theory': A Retrospective View*. London: Macmillan, 1950.

RADCLIFFE COMMITTEE ON THE WORKING OF THE MONETARY SYSTEM, *Principal Memoranda of Evidence*, 'Memorandum of Evidence' submitted by Richard Kahn, vol. III, Part XIII, no. 19, pp. 138-46, 27 May 1958. London: His Majesty's Stationery Office, 1960; reprinted in KAHN Richard, *Selected Essays on Employment and Growth*, pp. 124-52.

RAMSEY Frank P., 'A Mathematical Theory of Saving', *Economic Journal*, December 1928, pp. 543-59.

RICARDO David, *Works and Correspondence*. Edited by Piero Sraffa with the collaboration of Maurice H. Dobb. Eleven volumes, Cambridge: Cambridge University Press: I. *On the Principles of Political Economy and Taxation*; II. *Notes on Malthus's Principles of Political Economy*; III. *Pamphlets and Papers, 1809-1811*; IV. *Pamphlets and Papers, 1815-1823*, 1951; V. *Speeches and Evidence*; VI. *Letters 1810-1815*; VII. *Letters 1816-1818*; VIII. *Letters 1819 - June 1821*; IX. *Letters July 1821-1823*, 1952; X. *Biographical Miscellany*, 1955; XI. *General Index*, 1973.

ROBBINS Lionel, *Autobiography of an Economist*. London: Macmillan, 1971.

ROBERTSON Dennis H., *A Study of Industrial Fluctuation*. An enquiry into the character and causes of the so-called cyclical movements of trade. London: P. S. King & Son, 1915. Reprinted by the London School of Economics and Political Science, with a new introduction by the author, and an appendix by M. Labordere 'Autour de la Crise Americaine de 1907 ou Capitaux-reels et Capitaux-apparents'. Series of Reprints of Scarce Works on Political Economy, No. 8. London, 1948.

ROBERTSON Dennis H., *Money*. London: Nisbet & Co., Cambridge: Cambridge University Press, First Edition 1922 (with an introduction by John Maynard Keynes); Second Edition revised and reset, 1928; revised with additional chapters and with an introduction by Claude W. Guillebaud, 1948.

ROBERTSON Dennis H., *Banking Policy and the Price Level. An Essay in the Theory of the Trade Cycle*. London: P. S. King & Son, 1926.

ROBERTSON Dennis H., 'Increasing Returns and the Representative Firm', *Economic Journal*, March 1930, pp. 79-116.

ROBERTSON Dennis H., 'Mr. Keynes' Theory of Money', *Economic Journal*, September 1931, pp. 395-411.

ROBERTSON Dennis H., 'Saving and Hoarding', *Economic Journal*, September 1933, pp. 399-413. Reprinted in *Essays in Monetary Theory*, pp. 65-82.

ROBERTSON Dennis H., *Essays in Monetary Theory*. London: P. S. King & Son, 1940.

ROBINSON Austin, 'John Maynard Keynes, 1883-1946', *Economic Journal*, March 1947, pp. 1-68.

ROBINSON Austin, Obituary of 'Pigou Arthur Cecil, 1877-1959'. *Dic-*

tionary of National Biography, 1951-1960. Oxford: Oxford University Press, 1971, pp. 814-17.

ROBINSON Austin, 'A personal view', in KEYNES Milo (ed.), *Essays on John Maynard Keynes*, pp. 9-23.

ROBINSON Austin, 'Keynes and his Cambridge Colleagues', in PATINKIN Don and LEITH J. Clark (eds.), *Keynes, Cambridge and 'The General Theory'*, pp. 25-38.

ROBINSON Joan, 'A Parable on Savings and Investment', *Economica*, February 1933, pp. 75-84.

ROBINSON Joan, *Essays in the Theory of Employment.* London: Macmillan, 1937 (re-issued Oxford: Basil Blackwell, 1947); reprinted in *Collected Economic Papers*, vol. IV, pp. 174-246.

ROBINSON Joan, Review of 'The Economics of Inflation' by Bresciani-Turroni, *Economic Journal*, September 1938, pp. 507-13. Reprinted as 'The Economics of Hyper-Inflation' in *Collected Economic Papers*, vol. I, pp. 69-77.

ROBINSON Joan, 'Planning Full Employment', *The Times*, 22 and 23 January 1943; reprinted in *Collected Economic Papers*, vol. I, pp. 81-8.

ROBINSON Joan, *Collected Economic Papers.* Oxford: Basil Blackwell, vol I, 1951; vol. II, 1960; vol. III, 1955; vol. IV, 1973; vol. V, 1979; General Index, 1980.

ROBINSON Joan, *The Accumulation of Capital.* London: Macmillan, 1956.

ROBINSON Joan, 'La Théorie de la Répartition', *Economie Appliquée*, October-December 1957, pp. 523-38; reprinted as 'The Theory of Distribution' in *Collected Economic Papers*, vol. II, pp. 145-58.

ROBINSON Joan, 'Findlay's Robinsonian Model of Accumulation: A Comment', *Economica*, November 1963, pp. 408-11; reprinted as 'Robinson on Findlay on Robinson' in *Collected Economic Papers*, vol. III, pp. 48-51.

ROBINSON Joan, 'A Lecture delivered at Oxford by a Cambridge Economist', in *Collected Economic Papers*, vol. IV, pp. 254-63.

ROBINSON Joan, 'Michal Kalecki on the Economics of Capitalism', Contribution in ESHAG Éprime (ed.), 'Michal Kalecki Memorial Lectures', *Oxford Bulletin of Economics and Statistics*, pp. 7-18; reprinted in ROBINSON Joan, *Collected Economic Papers*, vol. V, pp. 184-96.

ROBINSON Joan, *Contributions to Modern Economics*. Oxford: Basil Blackwell, 1978.

RONCAGLIA Alessandro, *Sraffa e la teoria dei prezzi*, Roma-Bari: Gius. Laterza & Figli, First Edition 1975; Second Edition (revised and enlarged), 1981.

SALTMARSH John and WILKINSON Patrick, *Arthur Cecil Pigou, 1877-1959*. Cambridge: King's College, 1960.

SAUVY Alfred, *L'économie du diable: chômage et inflation*. Paris: Calmann-Levy, 1976.

SCHUMPETER Joseph A., *History of Economic Analysis*. Edited from manuscript by Elizabeth Boody Schumpeter. New York: Oxford University Press; London: George Allen and Unwin, 1954.

SHOVE Gerald F., 'Increasing Returns and the Representative Firm', *Economic Journal*, March 1930, pp. 79-116.

SKIDELSKY Robert, *Oswald Mosley*. London: Macmillan, 1975.

SMITH Adam, *An Inquiry into the Nature and Causes of the Wealth of Nations*. Two volumes. London: Printed for W. Strahan and T. Cadell, 1776. The edition quoted in the Lectures is the text edited by Edwin Cannan and published by Methuen & Co. (London: Fourth Edition, 1935).

SRAFFA Piero, 'Italian Banking To-Day', *Manchester Guardian*, Supplement 'Reconstruction in Europe', 7 December 1922, pp. 675-6. Also published in French, Italian, German and Spanish.

SRAFFA Piero, 'Sulle relazioni fra costo e quantità prodotta', *Annali di Economia*, vol. II (1925-1926), Milano: Università Bocconi Editrice, 1926, pp. 277-328; reprinted in *La Rivista Trimestrale*, March 1964, pp. 177-213.

SRAFFA Piero, 'The Laws of Returns under Competitive Conditions', *Economic Journal*, December 1926, pp. 535-50; reprinted in CLEMENCE Richard V. (ed.), *Readings in Economic Analysis*, vol. II, Cambridge, Mass.: Addison-Wesley Press, 1950, pp. 54-69, and in STIGLER George I. and BOULDING Kenneth E. (eds.), *Readings in Price Theory*, London: Allen and Unwin, 1953, pp. 180-97.

SRAFFA Piero, 'Increasing Returns and the Representative Firm', *Economic Journal*, March 1930, pp. 79-116.

SRAFFA Piero, *Production of Commodities by Means of Commodities. Prelude to a Critique of Economic Theory*. Cambridge: Cambridge University Press, 1960. Italian Edition: SRAFFA Piero, *Produzione di merci a mezzo di merci. Premessa a una critica della teoria economica*. Torino: Giulio Einaudi Editore, 1960.

Symposium on 'Increasing Returns and the Representative Firm', *Economic Journal*, March 1930, pp. 79-116; contributions by Dennis H. ROBERTSON, Gerald F. SHOVE and Piero SRAFFA.

TARSHIS, Lorie, 'Keynes as seen by his Students in the 1930s', in PATINKIN Don and LEITH J. Clark (eds.), *Keynes, Cambridge and 'The General Theory'*, pp. 39-63.

THIRLWALL Anthony P. (ed.), *Keynes and International Monetary Relations*. Proceedings of the Second Keynes Seminar held at the University of Kent at Canterbury, 1974. London: Macmillan, 1976.

THIRLWALL Anthony P. (ed.), *Keynes and Laissez-Faire*. Proceedings of the Third Keynes Seminar held at the University of Kent at Canterbury, 1976. London: Macmillan, 1978.

THIRLWALL Anthony P. (ed.), *Keynes as a Policy Adviser*. Proceedings of the Fourth Keynes Seminar held at the University of Kent at Canterbury, 1980. London: Macmillan, 1982.

TRANSVAAL INDIGENCY COMMISSION, *Report. 1906-1908*. Presented to both Houses of Parliament by Command of His Excellency the Governor. Pretoria: Government Printing and Stationery Office, 1908.

UNITED NATIONS, Economic Commission for Europe, *Economic Survey of Europe in 1955*. Including studies of Investment problems and policies of European countries and labour market problems in Western Europe, Geneva: UN, Department of Economic and Social Affairs, Research Planning Division, 1956.

UNITED NATIONS CONFERENCE ON TRADE AND DEVELOPMENT, *International Monetary Issues and The Developing Countries*. Report of the Group of Experts. New York: UN, 1965.

UNITED NATIONS CONFERENCE ON TRADE AND DEVELOPMENT, *Trade Expansion and Economic Co-operation among Developing Countries*. Report of the Group of Experts. Geneva: UN, 1966.

UNITED NATIONS CONFERENCE ON TRADE AND DEVELOPMENT, *Payments Arrangements among the Developing Countries for Trade Expansion*. Report of the Group of Experts. Geneva: UN, 1966.

UNITED NATIONS CONFERENCE ON TRADE AND DEVELOPMENT, *Inter-*

national Monetary Reform and Co-operation for Development. Report of the Group of Experts. New York: UN, 1969.

VEBLEN Thorstein, 'The Socialist Economics of Karl Marx and his Followers', Part I: 'The Theories of Karl Marx', *Quarterly Journal of Economics*, August 1906, pp. 575-95; Part II: 'The later Marxism', *Quarterly Journal of Economics*, February 1907, pp. 299-322.

VICARELLI Fausto, *Keynes: L'instabilità del capitalismo*. Milano: Etas Libri, 1977.

VINER Jacob, 'Mr. Keynes on the Causes of Unemployment. A Review', *Quarterly Journal of Economics*, November 1936, pp. 147-67.

WALTERS Alan A., *Money and Banking. Selected Readings*. Harmondsworth: Penguin Books, 1973.

WARMING Jens, 'International Difficulties Arising out of the Financing of Public Works during Depressions', *Economic Journal*, June 1932, pp. 211-24.

WHITAKER John K., *The Early Economic Writings of Alfred Marshall, 1867-1890*. Two volumes. London: Macmillan for the Royal Economic Society, 1975.

WICKSELL J. G. Knut, *Föreläsningar i Nationalekonomi*. Lund, 1901, 1908. Translation from the Swedish by E. Cassen: *Lectures on Political Economy*. Vol. I, *General Theory*; vol. II, *Money*. With an introduction by Lionel Robbins. London: G. Routledge & Sons, 1934, 1935.

WICKSELL J. G. Knut, *Geldezins und Güterpreise. Eine Studie über die den Tauschwert des Geldes bestimmenden Ursachen*. Jena: Gustav Fischer, 1898. Translation from the German by Richard Kahn: *Interest and Prices. A Study of the Causes regulating the Value of Money*. With an introduction by Bertil Ohlin. Published on behalf of the Royal Economic Society, London: Macmillan, 1936.

WILSON Tom and ANDREWS Philip W. S. (eds.), *Oxford Studies in the Price Mechanism*. Oxford: Clarendon Press, 1951.

WORSWICK George David N. (ed.), *The Concept and Measurement of Involuntary Unemployment*. Papers presented at the conference of the Royal Economic Society held at Durham in March 1974. London: George Allen and Unwin; Boulder, Colorado: Westview Press, 1976.

WRIGHT Quincy (ed.), *Unemployment as a World-Problem*. Chicago, Illinois: University of Chicago Press, 1931.

INDEX

INDEX

Aftalion Albert, 15
algebra, 27-8, 30ff, 45
   simplification, 145, 149, 158-60
American Economic Association, 210, 228
American Statistical Association, 97
analysis, method of, 222-3
Analysis of the Sources of War Finance, 187-8
Andrews Philip W. S., 148
'animal spirits' concept, 162, 166, 211-12, 227, 255-6
Annali di Economia, 4, 23
Aristotle, 20
assets, 33, 45, 140, 148
Associazione Culturale Italiana, 231
Autarky, 231, 254

Balance of payments, 158
Banca Commerciale Italiana, III, XIII, XX, XXI, 218, 219
Bank of England, 14, 50, 55, 82-3
bank rate, 82
banking
   active and inactive deposits, 34, 35-6, 163
   cash holdings, 137-8, 139
   collapse (inter-war), 132-3
   international, 75, 205
   and investment, 72-3, 163-4
   in quantity theory, 77-8, 103
Becattini Giacomo, 11, 205-10, 227, 235-9
benefit, transitional, 87
Beveridge William, 181
Bevin Ernest, 82, 85
bills, Treasury, 35
Bloomsbury, 169, 172
Boffito Carlo, 218
Boffito Domenico, 218
bonds, 139, 140
booms, 151, 205
borrower's risk, 147
Brand Robert H., 82
Bresciani-Turroni Costantino, 52
Bretton Woods Conference, 187-8, 268
Britain's Industrial Future, 77, 78-9
British Academy, 268

Bruni Franco, 212-16, 239-42, 251-2
Budget statements, 79, 81-2
   White Papers, 187
buffer stocks, 242, 263
building societies, 164
Burke Edmund, 187

Cambridge Circus, xxv, 69, 75, 105ff, 109-10, 223-4, 240
Cambridge quantity theory identity, 27-9, 31-3, 48, 53, 57, 58, 206
Cambridge economists, 29, 211, 218, 225-6, 229-30, 241
Cambridge Faculty of Economics, 25, 42, 180
   Italian school, 3-4, 23, 26, 218
Cambridge philosophers, 50
Can Lloyd George do It?, xxiv, 78-9, 79-80, 81, 89, 91ff, 158, 177, 191
Cannan Edwin, 3, 11
capacity restraint, 127
capital
   development, 78, 92
   goods, 71-2, 124, 149, and finance, 162, 165
   marginal efficiency of, 114, 145ff
capitalistic systems, 203, 207, 220, 236-8
Cardani Angelo Marcello, 228-9, 244-6
Casey Francis J. Jr., 8
Cassel Gustav, 239
Cecioni Pier Luigi, 261
Cassen E., 212
Certain Proposals relating to Unemployment, xxiv, 78-9, 81
Chalmers Thomas, 8, 9
Chamberlain-Bradbury Committee, 190-1
Champernowne David, 196
Chicago Conference, 109
Churchill Winston, 79, 81-2
Civil Service, 262-3
Clark Colin, 95-6
classical theory, *see* economic theory
Clower Robert, 203, 214
commercial sector, 63, 164
commodities, 27, 31, 44
   organised produce market, 33, 140

company management
  investment planning, 138, 163, 256
  and shareholders, 162-4
competition, imperfect, 25
confidence, state of, 93, 150, 166
Consequences to the Banks of the Collapse of Money Values, 132-3
Conservative Government (1929), 78
consumption
  goods, 53, 68-70, 107, 124, 165
  propensity, 134-6, 150
corporation tax, 166-7
Courtaulds, 79
Coutts Kenneth, 127
credit, 13, 57, 126
Cripps Stafford, 263-4
crowding-out effect, 164-5
Cunliffe Committee, 190, 191

D'Alauro Orlando, 230-2, 252-4
'Danaid jar' fallacy, 106
Dardi Mario, 261
Davis Ronnie J., 8
debts, fixed, 126
demand, 4ff, 14, 104, 142
  and input-output levels, 99-100
  management policy, 229
  in substitute forms of wealth, 33-4, 148
  and volition, 46
  and money-wage, 126-7
depreciation, 148
devaluation, 86, 87
developing countries, 204-5, 267
Di Pierro Alberto, 227-8, 247-9
disequilibrium theory, 66, 215, 229
distribution theory, 67-9
Dobb Maurice H., 5
Douglas Clifford H., 102
Duesenberry James S., 134
Durnford Hugh, 173

Eatwell John, 25
Economic Advisory Council, Committee of Economists, xxv
  Keynes and, 77, 86, 89, 95-7, 177
  Pigou and, 194
'Economic Analysis of Unemployment', 109
Economic Commission for Europe, 265-6
Economic Consequences of Mr Churchill, 129-30, 191

Economic Consequences of the Peace, 21, 51-2, 171
Economic Journal, 138, 162-4, 191, 195-6
economic policy, 78ff, 88
'Economic Possibilities for our Grandchildren', 238
economic theory
  American, 203-4
  classical, 3ff, 120, 122-3, 160, 177-8, 216, 219, 222
economics
  future of Keynesian, 230, 257
  and human problems, 191, 207-10, 220, 237-9
  language of, 198-9, 177-8, 221-57
economy
  market, 207ff, closed, 75, 231-2, 253-4
  short-period, 68, 122ff, 136, 170, 194, 261
Edgeworth Francis Ysidro, 142
employment, 13, 65, 134
  and export trades, 98ff
  primary and secondary, 91ff
  theory, 203-5, 225
  and falling wages, 126, 129-31
  see also multiplier
End of Laissez-Faire, 238
entrepreneurs, 67, 68, 93, 107, 166-7
  debt burden, 135
  and finance, 162, 164
  and investment-goods, 70
  risk and uncertainty, 147, 149
equilibrium theory, 203-4
equipment utilisation, 123, 244-6
equities, 57, 71
  and real investment, 33, 138, 150ff, 165ff, 251
  elasticity of substitution of money and, 140
Eshag Éprime, xx
Essays in Persuasion, 90, 220, 239
Evening Standard, 81, 87
Exchequer funds, 79, 82, 93-4
expectations, 92, 126, 162, 230
  long-term, 150ff
  and risk, 142-4, 159
  and falling wages, 131-3
export subsidies, 87

Fabians, 264
Fawcett Henry, 205, 206, 207

Federal Reserve Bank, 151
Fetter Frank Whitson, 52
finance concept, 139, 142, 148, 162ff, 251
  defined, 138
Fisher Irving, 28, 32, 48, 53, 146, 147, 207, 227, 228
  quantity theory, 44-6
fluctuations, 15-17, 20, 107, 142, 157, 215
Flux Alfred W., 95
Food and Agriculture Organisation, 263
free trade, 87
Friedman Milton, 204, 226
fundamental equations, 56-7, 65, 68ff, 75
fundamental relation, 98-9
funds, availability of, 162-4, 164

Gasparini Innocenzo, IX-XIII
Gayer Arthur D., 140
General Election (May 1929), 88
General Theory of Employment, Interest and Money
  achievement of, 122ff, 158
  algebraic simplification and, 145, 148-9
  exposition of 'general', 120-1
  effect of IS-LM on, 159-61
  long process of writing, 77, 89, 112-13, 114ff, 177-8
  limitations of, 158ff
  prefaces, 119-21
  preparation, 112-15, 115-18
  involvement of
    'Circus', 223
    Kahn, 222ff
    Modigliani, 222
    Pigou, 11, 195, 198-9
    Ramsey, 247
    Robertson, 185-8
  Chapter discussed, 123
    eleven, 145ff, 256
    twelve, 150, 241
    thirteen, 137-40
    fourteen, 161
    fifteen, 137-40
    sixteen, 135-6
    nineteen, 135-6
German mark, and quantity theory, 52

Gesell Silvio, 102
Godley Wynne, 127
Gold Standard, 85
Goschen George J., 53
Graham Benjamin, 242
Graham Frank, 242
Grandi Piercarlo, 229-30, 243-4, 257
Gregory Theodore, 82, 86
Guillebaud Claude W., 14, 237

Hansen Alvin H., 69
Harris Foundation, 109
  Lectures, 110-11
Harrison Ross, 30
Harrod Roy F., 50, 69, 118, 122, 161, 169, 172, 173, 186, 213, 219
  Towards a Dynamic Economics, 4
Hawtrey Ralph G., 108, 113, 115, 117, 118, 162
Hayek Friedrich von, 181-2, 183, 216
Hemming Francis, 96
Henderson Hubert D., XXIV, 77, 78-9, 92, 94, 148, 172, 186
Hicks John R., 128, 159, 160, 161, 186, 187, 188, 213, 226, 248
  IS-LM, 180-1
hoarding, 35, 44, 54, 62
Hobson John A., 10, 11, 205
Hopkins Richard V. N., 81, 82, 86, 188
  cross-examined by Keynes, 83-5
House of Lords, 184
How to Pay for the War, 186
Howson Susan, 87, 88, 96, 179, 180, 242
Hume David, XVII, 38

Income
  distribution, causation of, 266-7
  redistribution of, and living standards, 31, 34, 67-8, 134
  and money-wage, 127-8
  see also wealth
index numbers, 31-2, 45
Indian Finance and Currency, 50
industrial location, regional control, 264
industries
  nationalisation of, 264
  sheltered/unsheltered, 129
inflation, 103, 214, 231
  and multiplier, 96-7
  wage-, 128, 131, 241-4, 265

input-output levels, 99-100
institutions as shareholders, 166-7
interest rates, 10, 72, 104, 113, 230, 251-2
    causal links and, 249-50
    liquidity preference, 137-41
    money-, by country, 271-2
    natural/market, 74, 161, 214
    risk-free, 142, 146ff, 162
    theory, 225-7
International Monetary Fund, 187
    'Link', 266-7
international monetary institution, Keynes' concept of, 187, 266-8
International Sugar Council, 263
investment
    aggregates, 31-2
    'animal spirits', 156, 162, 211-12, 227, 254-6
    disequilibrium, 66
    finance, 162-4, 164-8
    goods, prices, 70-1
    inducement, 137, 142-4, 145ff, 159, 166ff
    marginal efficiency of, 215
    rates, 67, 104, 107, 110
    real and equities, 33, 137-9, 150ff
    risk, 146-9
    saving and, 73, 99, 101, 164
    see also banking; public expenditure and stability
IS-LM formula, ix, 159-61, 211-12, 214, 226, 248-9
Italy, 3, 216, 218, 254

Johannsen Nicholas A. L. J., 102
Johnson William E., 50

Kahn Richard, x, xi, 3, 74, 96, 105, 107, 113, 138, 205ff, 221ff, 235ff, 261ff
    association with Keynes, 117, 118, 169-72, 174-6, 177-8, 195, 196, 240, 262, 267-8
    in 'Circus', 223, 240
    Civil Service, 262-3
    on international organisations, 265-8
    at King's College, Cambridge, 174, 261-2, 264-5
    life Peerage, 268
    quantity theory, 170-1
    training in logic, 219

'Relation of Home Investment to Unemployment', 91ff, 98, 218, 224
Selected Essays on Unemployment and Growth, 265
Kaldor Nicholas, 196, 264
Kalecki Michal, 204
Keynes Florence A., 75-6, 112
Keynes Geoffrey, 262
Keynes John Maynard,
    career
        at Bretton Woods, 187-8, 268
        at Savannah, 268
        in Chicago, 109
        Committee of Economists, 89, 95-7, 177
        editorship of Economic Journal, 176
        India Office, 50, 189
        at King's College, Cambridge, 170-2 173, 189, 196, 197, 262
        Macmillan Committee, 82ff, 175
        at Treasury, 186-7, 262-3
        Versailles Peace Conference, 21
    on classical economists, 118, 120-1, 159
    farming and country interests, 175
    and human problems, 190
    on the inducement to invest, 165-8
    investment interest, 150ff, 170, 174
    language and style, 77, 169-70, 239
    as a lecturer, 50, 113, 169-70
    effect of marriage, 169, 240
    magnanimity, 106, 171-3, 197-9, 240
    publishing on own account, 171-2
    and rare books, 171, 183
    training, and economics, 50, 189, 219
    work load, 111, 114-15, and health, 196, 268
    correspondence with
        F. and B. Graham, 242
        Harrod, 122
        Hawtrey, 113, 117
        Kahn, 117, 118
        his mother, 75-6, 112
        Robertson, 58, 61, 62, 103-4, 115-16, 125, 177, 185ff, 193
        Joan Robinson, 113
    Obituary of Alfred Marshall, 34-5, 41, 43, 45, 48
    see also Bloomsbury; Tilton

Keynes Lydia, XXIV, 64, 169, 172, 175, 240, 262
Keynes Milo, 172
Keynes Richard, 262
'Keynes Club', 172
Keynes Seminar, 267-8
King's College, 173
Klein Lawrence R., 228, 244

Labour
  skills, 165, 245
  supply, 123
Labour Government (1929), 82, 88
Laidler David, 214
laissez-faire, 6, 203, 208, 238
Lassalle Ferdinand, 207, 209, 235-6, 237
Leigh Arthur H., 37
Leijonhufvud Axel, 203, 214, 215, 216, 229
Leith J. Clark, XIX, 105, 112, 172
lender's risk, 148
Lenin, 52
Lerner Abba, 182-3
Liberal Industrial Enquiry, 77
Liberal Party, 77, 78ff, 88
  We Can Conquer Unemployment, XXIV, 78, 79, 90ff
Lindhal Erik, 75, 216
'Link', 266-7
liquidity preference theory, 33-4, 57, 70, 138ff, 159, 215, 250-1
  basic concept, 137-41
Lloyd-George David, 77, 80
Locke John, XVII, 37
logic, 219
London School of Economics, 179-84, 179-80, 183-4, 186
Lopokova Lydia, *see* Keynes Lydia

McCulloch John Ramsay, 39
McKenna Reginald, 82, 86, 174
Macdonald Ramsay, 77, 87, 89
Macmillan Committee, XXIV-XXV, 86-7, 129, 130
  Keynes on, 79, 82ff, 85ff, 177
  membership of, 82, 194
  Addenda, 86-7, 130
Macmillan & Co., 171
macroeconomics, 211, 213ff

Malthus Thomas Robert, XVII, 4ff, 9, 10
Manchester Guardian Reconstruction Supplements, 3, 4
Manes Pietro, 221-2, 257
market economy, *see* economy
Marris Robin, 265
Marshall Alfred, XVII, XXIII-XXIV, 3, 23-4, 39, 40, 137, 197, 205ff, 223, 227, 235, 236, 261
  and Keynes, 50, 189
  and Lassalle, 207, 209, 235-7
  and quantity theory, 28, 29, 34-5, 41-3, 44, 48, 53
  on Say's Law, 11ff
  on trade cycles, 15, 16, 21
  Money Credit and Commerce, 13-14, 34, 42, 237
  Pure Theory of Domestic Values, 12
  Obituary of, 34-5, 41, 43, 45, 48
Marshall Alfred and Mary Paley, XXIII, 190
  Economics of Industry, 11ff, 21, 207-8, 235-6, 237
Marshall Library, 42
Marshall Society, 181-2
Martin Kingsley, 172
Marx Karl, 102, 207, 209, 226-7 *passim*
mathematics, 219-20
Mattioli Raffaele, X, XII, 3, 218, 219
  Foundation, XVII, XX, XXI, 235
  Lectures, X, XVII, XVIII, XX, 2, 3, 210, 222, 249
  Lectures (Scientific Committee), X, XII
  Library, XII
Meade James, 105, 183, 224
Means to Prosperity, 90, 98, 103, 110
Middle East Supply Centre, 263
Midland Bank, 82, 174
Milgate Murray, 118
Mill James, 9, 39
Mill John Stuart, XVII, 3, 205-7 *passim*
  and quantity theory, 39, 40, 44
  on Say's Law, 7-10, 13
Mises Richard von, 73
Modigliani Franco, 210, 222, 226, 249
Moggridge Donald E., 105, 107, 108, 110, 113, 114, 190, 191, 195, 242
'monetarism', 204, 210, 217-22, 230, 243-4, 249, 254, 257

money
  alternative forms of, 31ff, 42-3, 44-5, 48, 251
  holding, motives for, 138-9
  homogeneous, 34-5
  market elasticity of, 140, 214
  quantity of, 32, 57, 104, 122, 128, 136, 150ff
  supply, 103-4
  transactions, 28, 48, 136-7, 40, 44
  see also hoarding; quantity theory
Moore George E., 50
Morris Robin, 79
Mosley Oswald, 88, 89-90
multiplier, 90, 97-8, 124, 217-18, 225
  defined, 94-5
  UK/US compared, 98-9
  writings on, 101-2, by Kahn, 95-6, 102-4
Mummery Albert F., 10, 11, 205
Myrdal Gunnar K., 216

Nardozzi Giangiacomo, 210-12, 248-9, 254-6
Nation, 77, 78, 172
Nation and Athenaeum (The), 77, 78, 89
National Coal Board, 266
national debt, 135
nationalisation of industries, 264
Neisser Hans, 73
Neo-Classical Synthesis, 204
New Statesman and Nation, 77, 87, 172
Nordhaus William, 127
Norman Montagu, 82-3
Notes on Mercantilism, 158

Obsolescence, 148
OECD, see Organization for Economic Cooperation and Development
Ohlin Bertil, xix, 75, 162, 213
oil balances, 217, 243
'Orange Book', see Liberal Party, We Can Conquer Unemployment
Organization for Economic Cooperation and Development, 254, 266-8
output, 31, 65, 67
  capacity restraint, 127
  causation, 246-7
  and employment theory, 203-5, 225
  and price-levels, 69-70, 100
overproduction, 205-6

Paley Mary see Marshall Alfred and Mary Paley
Pasinetti Luigi, 222-5, 240-1, 249
Patinkin Don, xix, 7, 8, 71, 74, 102-2, 105, 112, 135, 172
Pigou Arthur C., xxiii-xxv, 11, 15, 17, 19, 21, 23, 89, 96, 125, 126, 142, 161, 179, 190, 191, 193, 194-5, 198-9 208, 223, 261
  and quantity theory, 28-9, 31, 44-6
  relations with Keynes, 189ff, 197-9
  Economics of Welfare, 17, 24, 25, 191, 192
  Industrial Fluctuations, 193
  'Real and Money Wage Rates [. . .]', 195-7
  Socialism versus Capitalism, 194-5
  Unemployment, 17-19, 193
  Obituary of, 197, 199
placement, 150
plant and equipment, 124, 244-6
political economy, 219-20
Poor Law Commission, 20
Porta Angelo, xv-xvi
portfolio analysis, 33, 139-40, 151
price hypothesis, normal, 127
price-levels, 27, 38, 40, 51, 53, 66, 68, 140
  capital-goods, 72
  consumption-goods, 68-70, 107
  cost ratio, 244
  disequilibrium, 66
  investment-goods, 57, 71-3
  and output, 69-70, 100
  and wages, 124, 126ff, 194
  and wealth, 31-7
price theory, relative, 206
probability, 143, 189, 229, 241
products, investment, 165
profits, 10, 13, 149
  abnormal, 65-7, 70, 72, 101, 107
  definitions of, 146
  internal rate of return, 146-7, 165-8
property, 34, 48, 53
protection, 179
public expenditure and stability, 79, 85-6, 103-4, 158-9, 243, 257
public sector, see Exchequer funds
public works, and multiplier, 96-7

Quantity theory of money, 27ff, 32, 34, 35-6, 37-8, 39-40, 40-6, 47-9, 50-5, 56-7, 58-9, 74-5

causation according to the, 33, 45, 54, 56-7
Keynes and, 37, 50ff, 58-9
    changing attitude to, 53, 64, 69-70, 78, 128-9, 170
    modern form, 39ff, 44ff, 104
    see also Cambridge, *and* Yale quantity theory identities

Radcliffe Committee, 264
Ramsey Frank P., 64, 227, 228, 247, 248
Ranchetti Fabio, 218-21, 239
raw materials supplies, 263
real balance effect, 135
'repercussion', doctrine of, 58
resources, total, 29
returns, *see* profits
Review of Economic Studies, 182-3
Ricardo David, xvii, 26, 39, 250
    on Say's Law, 5-7, 10
risk and uncertainty, 146-7, 149ff, 159, 241
Rivista Bancaria, 218
Rivista Mensile, 218
roads and bridges, employment, 90-1
Robbins Lionel, 52, 97, 179ff
    appreciation, by, 183-4
Robertson Dennis H., xvii, xxiii-xxv, 3, 14, 15, 23, 25, 67, 73, 125-6, 162, 193, 197, 208, 224, 252, 255, 261
    at Bretton Woods, 187-8
    friendship and correspondence with Keynes, 58, 61, 62, 103-4, 115-16, 125, 177, 185ff, 193
    and quantity theory, 47-9, 51
    on trade cycles, 15ff
    Banking Policy and the Price Level, 61-3, 171, 175, 185-6
    Money, 21-26
    Study of Industrial Fluctuation, 15-17, 19-20, 185, 255
    Obituary of, 188
Robinson Austin, xviii, 105, 106, 113, 172, 183, 195, 240
    biography of Keynes, 161
    Obituary of Pigou, 197, 199
Robinson Joan, xviii, xx, 4, 52, 105, 150, 157, 160, 182-3, 203ff, 210, 211, 216, 220, 227, 229, 240, 243, 248, 256

and 'animal spirits' concept, 211, 227, 256
correspondence with Keynes, 111, 113, 117
'Parable on Saving and Investment', 111-12
Roncaglia Alessandro, 25
Royal Commission on the Poor Laws, 17
Royal Economic Society, xviii, 213, 240
Russell Bertrand, 50

Saltmarsh John, 198
Samuel Herbert, 77
Samuelson Paul, 204
Sauvy Alfred, 231
Savannah Conference, 268
saving, 3-4, 18, 54, 62-3, 70ff
    aggregate, 30-1
    disequilibrium, 66
    and income, 31, 34, 66-70, 134
    and investment, 73, 101, 102, 104, 164
    marginal propensity, 227, 247
    and public expenditure, 103-4
Savona Paolo, 216-18, 242-3, 244 *passim*, 250-1
Say's Law, 3ff, 7ff, 11ff, 205
    and trade cycles, 15-16
Schumpeter Joseph A., 39, 73, 170, 178, 223, 224, 240
securities
    fixed-interest, 33, 57, 138, 140ff, 150
sequence analysis, 31, 108
share prices, 167
Shove Gerald F., 25, 26, 170, 196, 261, 264
Sismondi Jean Charles Leonard Simon de, 8, 9
Simon John, 77
Skidelsky Robert, 88
slump, 31, 78, 192-4, 204
Smith Adam, xvii, 3-5, 7, 8, 11
Snowden Philip, 82
socialist systems, 206-7
'Speeches of the Bank Chairmen', 191-2
Sraffa Angelo, 3
Sraffa Piero, 5, 105, 170, 171, 218, 222, 225, 246-7, 261
    influence on Cambridge economics, 3-4, 23-4, 25-6, 246-7
Stamp Josiah, 96
statisticians, 95-6

sterling parity, 86-7, 129, 190-1
Stock Exchange, 150, 154, 166, 167
Sunday Express, 88
supply, 4ff, 13, 14, 100, 108
    policy, 228-9, 244-6
Swedish economists, 212ff
    see also Ohlin Bertil; Wicksell Knut
'Symposium on Increasing Returns',
    25
systems science, 229, 257

Take-over bids, 167
Targetti Ferdinando, 225-7, 246-7, 248,
    249-50, 251, 254-5, 256-7
tariffs, 87, 179
Tarshis Lorie, 172
taxation, 94, 135, 166-7
technical innovations, 165
third world countries, 204-5
Thirlwall Antony P., 267
Thomas 'Jimmy', 88
Tilton, Sussex, 63, 114, 262
    life at, 172, 175-6, 177
time-lags, 102-3, 125, 126, 226
time preference rate, 227
Times (The), 88, 89, 90
Tinbergen Jan, rule, 229
Tract on Monetary Reform, 34, 45, 50, 171,
    190
Trade, Board of, Working Parties, 263-4
trade cycles, *see* fluctuations
Transvaal Indigency Commission, 18,
    19
Treasury
    Keynes at, 187-8, 262-3
    'Treasury view', 79, 81-2, 83, 86, 88,
        89, 164
Treasury bills, 35, 138
Treatise on Money, 33, 61ff, 82, 137, 150,
    151, 185
    impact of, 25, 75-6
    involvement of
        'Circus', 74, 105, 106, 107, 108,
            109, 111
        Kahn, 99-100, 174-5
        Robertson, 61-3, 67
        Wicksell, 73-5
    preface, 72, 114
    transition to General Theory, 63-5,
        70-1, 78, 107ff, 112ff, 223
Treatise on Probability, 189, 241

Tugan-Baranowsky Michail Ivanovich,
    15

Uncertainty and risk, 143-4, 147ff, 157,
    241
UNCTAD *see* United Nations Conference
    on Trade and Development
unemployment, 9, 17, 19, 78-80
    and balance of payments, 158
    and inflation, 242-3
    involuntary, 192-3, 265
    and state action, 88ff, 98, 193-4
    see also wages
Unemployment Fund, 94
Union de Banques Suisses, 231
United Nations Conference on Trade
    and Development, 266-7, 268
United States, economic theory in,
    203-4

Valuation ratio, 265
value theory, 225
Veblen Thorstein, 227
velocity of circulation, 28, 35-6, 39, 43
Vicarelli Fausto, 215
Victorian social morality, 208-10
Viner Jacob, 120, 142, 148, 241, 257

Wages
    fund theory, 7ff
    money-, 86, 124, 127ff, 136, 252-3
    negotiated, 241, 243, 266-7
    theorem, 129
    and unemployment, 91, 129 ff, 194,
        195-9, 214, 251
Walras Léon
    theory of *general equilibrium*, 203, 204,
        220
Walters Alan A., 38
war expenditure, 17, 19
Warming Jens, 100-1, 224
wealth
    alternative forms of, 31ff, 42-3, 44-5,
        58, 251
    and consumption, 53, 135
    national, 31ff, 66, 67
Wilkinson Patrick, 198
Whitaker John K., 34, 42, 43, 207,
    236
Whitman Walt, 20, 255

Wicksell Knut, xix, 226, 252
   and Keynes, 212ff, 239
   Interest and Prices, 74-5, 212, 239
'widow's cruse' fallacy, 106, 107, 111
Wilson Thomas, 148
Winch Donald, 87, 88, 95, 96, 179, 180

Wittgenstein Ludwig Joseph, 50, 220
Worswick George David N., 120, 192, 265
Wright Quincy, 109

Yale quantity theory identity, 28-9, 32, 33, 44-6, 48, 58, 59, 66

RAFFAELE MATTIOLI
LECTURES

Scientific Committee
(June 1978)
Innocenzo Gasparini, Chairman
Paolo Baffi, Innocenzo Monti, Adalberto Predetti,
Gaetano Stammati, Sergio Steve, Franco Venturi.
Enrico Resti, Secretary.

Raffaele Mattioli Foundation
Fondazione Raffaele Mattioli
per la storia del pensiero economico

Volumes due to be published

Franco Modigliani
The Evolution of Monetary Theory

Charles P. Kindleberger
Economic Laws and Economic History

Peter Mathias
The Industrial Revolution in England

Erik F. Lundberg
The Development
of Swedish and Keynesian Macroeconomic Theory
and its Impact on Economic Policy.

Organization
Banca Commerciale Italiana-Università Commerciale L. Bocconi
Milano

Administration
Banca Commerciale Italiana
Milano

Publisher
Cambridge University Press
Cambridge

DESIGN, MONOTYPE COMPOSITION AND PRINTING
BY STAMPERIA VALDONEGA, VERONA
FEBRUARY MCMLXXXIV